PENGUIN BOOKS
GHALIB: THE MAN, THE TIMES

Pavan K. Varma was born in 1953 in Nagpur. He graduated with honours in History from St Stephen's College, Delhi and then took a degree in Law from Delhi University. While at University he was president of his college debating society and also won the Sir C.P. Ramaswamy Aiyar Memorial English Essay Prize in 1973.

Pavan K. Varma is with the Indian Foreign Service and has been sent on diplomatic assignments to Bulgaria, Romania and New York, where he was with the Indian Mission to the United Nations.

He is married, with two daughters and a son, and lives at present in New Delhi.

D1330066

GHALIB

The Man, the Times

PAVAN K. VARMA

PENGUIN BOOKS

PENGUIN BOOKS
Published by the Penguin Group
Penguin Books India Pvt. Ltd, 11 Community Centre, Panchsheel Park,
New Delhi 110017, India
Penguin Group (USA) Inc., 375 Hudson Street, New York, New York 10014,
USA
Penguin Group (Canada), 90 Eglinton Avenue East, Suite 700, Toronto,
Ontario, M4P 2Y3, Canada (a division of Pearson Penguin Canada Inc.)
Penguin Books Ltd, 80 Strand, London WC2R 0RL, England
Penguin Ireland, 25 St Stephen's Green, Dublin 2, Ireland (a division of
Penguin Books Ltd)
Penguin Group (Australia), 250 Camberwell Road, Camberwell, Victoria
3124, Australia (a division of Pearson Australia Group Pty Ltd)
Penguin Group (NZ), 67 Apollo Drive, Rosedale, North Shore 0632, New
Zealand (a division of Pearson New Zealand Ltd)
Penguin Group (South Africa) (Pty) Ltd, 24 Sturdee Avenue, Rosebank,
Johannesburg 2196, South Africa

Penguin Books Ltd, Registered Offices: 80 Strand, London WC2R 0RL,
England

First published as *Ghalib: The Man, the Times* in Viking by Penguin
Books India 1989
Published in Penguin Books 2000
This edition published by Penguin Books India 2008

Copyright © Pavan K. Varma 1989, 2008

10 9 8 7 6 5 4 3 2

ISBN 9780143064817

Typeset in Sabon by InoSoft Systems, Noida
Printed at Deunique Printers, Noida

In memory of my father who would have been the happiest
To my mother
And for Chutka Bhaiya

Contents

Preface

Some years ago, I went to a well-known bookshop in Delhi and asked for a book on Ghalib. I was told they had none. A search in some other bookshops yielded a few extended booklets, mostly translations into English of some verses of his Urdu *Diwan*. I found this situation very strange. It was like going to a bookshop in London and being told that they had no books on Yeats or Eliot, given that in northern India especially Ghalib is a household name; his Urdu verses tend to crop up in everyday conversation and stories of his humour and *hazir jawabi* are part of familial anecdotage in most homes.

But the example of the bookshop that did not stock Ghalib is only one indication of the cultural malaise that stalks our times. I find it interesting that Ghalib, or for that matter, so much else of what constitutes our cultural heritage, has survived today *in spite* of the post-1947 generation. Most of the people of my age in India—and I am no exception—have grown up as cultural orphans: they have learnt neither Sanskrit nor Urdu and so remain (sometimes sheepishly) incurious about a cultural heritage that may soon dry up due to the indifference of their response. This book, therefore, is not just an act of homage to a great man. It is, on a deeply personal level, an act of penance and a pilgrimage, an effort to overcome in my own life the sense of inadequacy many of my age have felt growing up in such culturally nondescript times.

There is another aspect to the book that I would like to explain. To most of us, history remains merely an account of the remote past. The history of more recent periods, even if it manifests itself in our everyday existence, is ignored in the overwhelming crush of municipal concerns and the struggle for daily survival. Most citizens of Delhi may know in broad, generic terms of the Mughal period as it pertains to Delhi, but have almost no knowledge of what Delhi was like as recently as in the last century. In this context, it is significant that Ghalib, apart from being one of our greatest poets, was through his letters (of which he was a prolific writer) a chronicler par excellence of his times. He lived in Delhi through a fascinating period. Mughal power was slowly but surely fading away. The British had ensconced themselves as the *de facto* rulers. Ghalib, who prided himself on belonging to the feudal nobility, was caught between his loyalty to the Mughal king and his need to cultivate the new rulers, from whom, in the form of his hereditary pension, he received his only source of income. The period of Mughal political decline coincided, ironically enough, with a phase of unprecedented literary efflorescence. Urdu, hitherto the plebeian cousin of Persian, came into its own and acquired a new sophistication, self-assurance, maturity and authenticity that manifested itself in myriad ways, not the least of which was the increasing sway of the eclectic Sufi *tariqah* and secularism over Delhi's way of life. Ghalib's writing and life illumined and mirrored the different facets of Delhi—its problems, diversions, pettiness, achievements, despairs—in a manner rarely seen.

The Revolt of 1857 and its aftermath put an abrupt and traumatic end to Ghalib's Delhi. It signalled the beginning of a new era and the end of the old. Ghalib was perhaps the only great poet in Delhi (Zauq and Momin had died earlier) who lived to see 1857, and its fallout. His role in this event and the manner in which he and others of his class were affected by it is of tremendous interest, both from the point of view of an assessment of Ghalib the man and from the historical perspective.

To turn from the genesis to the making of it. I have greatly enjoyed writing it. Indeed the very writing of it was its greatest reward. After a day of peddling files in office, to sit quietly in my study and work on the manuscript was something that never failed to provide solace. I do not claim to be an Urdu scholar, or even a scholar of Ghalib's poetry. Although I graduated in history I do not claim to have the qualifications of a historian. This book is, therefore, not a literary treatise on Ghalib's poetry, nor a historical dissertation. It is merely an attempt to paint a portrait of Ghalib the man, and through him, of the Delhi in which he lived. If it succeeds in arousing the interest of even a few, it would have, from my point of view, served its purpose.

I would like to record my gratitude to Dr Ravindra Kumar, Director, Nehru Memorial Museum, New Delhi, and to Professor Philip Oldenberg of Columbia University, New York, both of whom read portions of the manuscript and offered encouragement and advice. My gratitude also to Dr Narayani Gupta, who willingly gave guidance whenever I asked; special thanks to H.K. Kaul, the able historian of the India International Centre, New Delhi, and to Sushma Zutshi and Namita Ganguly who work with him. For making my visits to the National Archives of India worthwhile, I would like to thank J.P. Balani, the Assistant Archivist.

A word of appreciation is also due to the very efficient staff at the India Office Library in London and at the New York Public Library. I am indebted to my dear friend Urmila Dongre for her assistance in putting together the photographic section of this book, and to Zoheen Naqvi of the Ghalib Academy for his gracious, old world courtesies. To Khushwant Singh, ever willing to help a first-time author, a very special word of thanks. For assistance without demur, I have no words to express my gratitude to Arturo Lozano, my good friend in New York, who wordprocessed the manuscript. A salute of appreciation to Zamir Ansari; also special thanks to Sudha Sadhanand and Bindu Badshah for their infinite politeness in maintaining that they were enjoying the task of making the manuscript readable. And lastly, and perhaps mostly, my heartfelt gratitude to David Davidar, for his unique ability to allow the professional detachment of an editor to express itself in terms of such genuine warmth and personal interest.

For permission to reproduce photographs or documents in their possession, I am grateful to the India Office Library in London (plates 12 to 16), to the National Archives of India, New Delhi, (plates 6 to 8), to the Ghalib Academy, New Delhi (plates 1, 3, 4, 9 and 11) and to the Librarian, India International

Centre (for access to the India collection) (plates 2 and 10).

One final word. This book would not have been possible but for Renuka, my wife, who in spite of a most trying husband managed to preserve effectively and embellish that sociologically threatened entity called the home. If I have been able to write anything at all, it is because her unique presence created the ambience for me to do so. My two daughters, Manvi, now ten, and Rajasvi, seven, and my son Vedanta, five, provided a many-splendoured distraction, but for which I would certainly have finished this book earlier.

ONE

An Empire in Decline

Mirza Muhammad Asadullah Khan Ghalib was essentially an apolitical person. Both his Persian verse and Urdu *Diwan* are almost entirely devoid of explicit political verse. Though after the Revolt of 1857, his letters make references to political happenings, that has more to do with the fact that the upheaval had such sharp political overtones that comment on it could not entirely be apolitical. The pre-1857 period saw considerable change and flux. As a member of the feudal aristocracy, and as the greatest poet of his time, Ghalib could not but be both an observer and a participant. Left to himself, he may not necessarily have wished to relate to political events. As a poet and philosopher he may have shifted his gaze to other horizons, other imperatives and infinitely more absorbing distractions characteristic of the human predicament. But his destiny was so etched, as to make him the quintessential witness to a tumultuous era. The times were such as to make it impossible for him to insulate himself from the setting of his age.

Even if he did not acknowledge it to himself, many of his reactions were moulded by the political milieu, and an analysis of several behavioural stances shows how deeply he internalized it. His relationship with the political backdrop reveals not only Ghalib the man, but also the reactions of an entire feudal class caught in the vortex of change that swept Delhi and Hindustan, in the last century.

By 1797, the year Ghalib was born, the Mughal empire was in decline. Aurangzeb's extensive empire had, in the course of a century, shrunk to Delhi and a few square miles around it. In 1788, the Mughal emperor Shah Alam had been blinded and imprisoned by Ghulam Qadir, a Rohilla military adventurer who had temporarily seized Delhi. When Ghulam Qadir withdrew, the Marathas occupied the city and excelled the Rohillas in publicly humiliating the royal family. In 1803, the British—the nascent imperial power on the horizon—defeated the Marathas at Patparganj, a village near Delhi. It is said that Shah Alam followed the progress of the battle from a balcony of the Red Fort. Lord Lake, the British commander, was granted an audience by Shah Alam on 16 September 1803. Very quickly the infrastructure of British control was established. The Mughal king was made a British pensioner and his personal allowance fixed at Rs 11.5 lakh a year. On the outskirts of Kashmiri Gate a British Resident settled down to oversee British control. *De facto* political power passed to the British while the king was permitted the illusion of *de jure* sovereignty.

This was the political penumbra in which Ghalib

was born. By legal interpretation, the Mughal emperor *was* the sovereign. The British, after their victory at Buxar, had merely succeeded in obtaining the grant of the *deewani* of Bengal from the Mughal emperor in 1765. This agreement itself demonstrated that the Mughal king did have the political suzerainty to grant and bestow favours. Legally, this suzerain status continued unchanged in the absence of any intervening agreement after 1765. Theoretically, therefore, the British were subordinate vassals within the imperial Mughal framework. But it was the avowed policy of Lord Wellesley to ensure that any lip service paid to nominal Mughal sovereignty did not deflect the British from the serious business of establishing complete political control. Here, he and his successors had to contend with the Mughal policy (of which Shah Alam was chief architect) of clinging tenaciously to every institutional attribute by which *de jure* sovereignty could be perpetuated. Shah Alam, and to a lesser extent his successors, fought tooth and nail against any attempt to question British acceptance of nominal Mughal sovereignty. While the British considered themselves the representatives of a conquering race that deserved to rule, the Mughal kings, not unaware of their pensionary status, continued to consider audacious any attempt by the British to infringe upon the established etiquettes of behaviour expected from a vassal power.

The Mughal dynasty still had a compelling aura which only a truly imperial line, with an unbroken rule of centuries, could possess. The Jats, Rohillas, Marathas and even the British needed the Mughal emperor's name to give political legitimacy to their *de facto* power. To the common man, the emperor, even with his diminished powers, still remained *Hazrat Zill-e-Subhani, Sahib Qiram-e-Sani, Khuld Allah, Mulkahoo-va-Sultanahoo Jahan Panah* (His Majesty, the Shadow of God, the Fortunate, the Refuge of the World). Within the walls of the Red Fort his writ reigned supreme. He and members of the imperial family enjoyed diplomatic immunity and court etiquette continued as before. The British Resident entered the Emperor's durbar like any other courtier: dismounting at the Naqaar Khana and walking the remaining distance. Farhatullah Baig, in his authentic reconstruction of a *mushairah* in the reign of the last Mughal king, Bahadur Shah Zafar, recounts how Karimuddin, the scholar at whose residence the *mushairah* was held, broke into 'a nervous sweat' when required to step into the imperial presence. 'How could I imagine that I would be summoned into the presence of His Majesty, the Refuge of the World . . . The command of the King is as peremptory as the call of death.' Showing Karimuddin in, the *chobdar* cried out, 'Proceed reverently. You are now face to face with the presence of His Majesty, the Refuge of the World. May he live long and prosper. Enter with due respect and courtesy and offer your salutations.'[1] And Karimuddin, who in preparation for the meeting had familiarized himself with court decorum, bent low and offered the customary seven salutations.' Bereft of power, the last of the Mughals retained the demeanour of regality. An Englishman, present in 1828 when Emperor Akbar II received Lord Combermere, the British Commander-in-Chief, made this entry in his journal: 'The old monarch, mindful of his dignity, scarcely deigned to notice, even by a look, the Commander-in-Chief as he approached to present his *nazr* . . . He did not even condescend to raise his eyes towards the rest of the party, as we advanced one by one, salaamed and offered our three gold *mohurs* . . .'[2]

Undoubtedly, the grandeur of the past was missing. The *nazrs* were smaller, the *khillats* bestowed by the king cheap, and the royal processions more a *tamasha* than a demonstration of imperial might. But the king was still the pivot of the socio-political fabric. On ceremonial occasions he was still weighed against seven kinds of grain, coral and silver, even if financial constraints had made it difficult to continue the earlier practice of weighing him against gold and precious stones. On Bakr-i-Id he was still called upon to ceremoniously sacrifice a camel at the Idgah or Diwan-i-Am; his birthday was still an occasion of state celebration, and if he was to fall ill his recovery was still joyously welcomed at the function of ceremonial ablutions—the Ghusal-i-Sehat. As in the past, a court bulletin was still issued every day to inform the people of his activities. Princes still bore the titles conferred by him. For the Delhiwallah, the Jahanpanah still ruled, even if it was from a throne with a fading lustre. His temporal powers had declined, but he remained the 'Pir-o-Murshid', the spiritual monitor and guide. His claim to rule remained unquestioned even though it could be conceded that he had fallen on bad days. This perception persisted beyond the walls of Delhi. Applications, for confirmation of successors to the chieftainship of petty states, were still made to the Mughal emperor. The coins of the Holkars, Maratha chiefs who had long ceased to be vassals, continued to bear the name of Shah Alam II as late as the reign of Tukoji Rao II (1844–86). Similarly, the coins of another erstwhile vassal state, the Scindias of Gwalior, bore the legend of Akbar II till 1886, over two decades after the Mughal dynasty had been wound up by the British.

For Ghalib, who claimed to belong to the feudal aristocracy and the same Turkish stock that had helped establish Mughal rule, the apparent continuation of Mughal rule was a reaffirmation, at the apex level, of the relevance and legitimacy of the monarchic-feudal way of life. Such a reaffirmation filled a crucial psychological need in the face of changes that were fast eroding the politico-economic foundations of feudalism. Like other citizens of Delhi, Ghalib took as axiomatic the legitimacy of Mughal rule. He hankered for access to the Mughal court and if this was denied resented the influence of others. He considered the Mughal capital his true setting, claiming it, with no real basis in fact, to be 'the original abode of my ancestors'. His links with the court were tangible. On Ibrahim Zauq's death in 1854 he was officially appointed the king's *ustad* in poetry. At that time he was already the *ustad* of the heir apparent. Four years earlier Bahadur Shah had commissioned him to write a history of the Mughal dynasty in Persian prose. In his role as Poet Laureate and otherwise, he had written innumerable lavish panegyrics in honour of the Mughal sovereign. In spite of his differences in poetry with

Bahadur Shah, he never wrote anything that could be
construed as irreverent of the monarchy or the king
himself. Even *Dastanbuy,* Ghalib's emphatic and
deliberate pro-British diary of the 1857 Revolt, does
not make any derogatory reference to the king. The
Mughal emperor, in the ultimate analysis, was
the guarantor of a societal order from which Ghalib
drew sustenance. The manifest continuance of the
monarchy sustained Ghalib's own place as a member
of the aristocracy in the ordained scheme of things.
And the strength that he derived from this nexus was
a key element in conditioning his attitude and approach
towards the *de facto* wielders of power—the British.

The British, of course, were never really in doubt
about the irrevocability of the transformation that
had taken place. William Knighton, a British journalist
who visited Delhi during Bahadur Shah Zafar's reign,
recorded with cold clarity: 'In solemn mockery of
royal splendour, the surviving descendant, an emperor
in form, and a slave in fact, maintains the empty state
of sovereignty. He has his throne and his sceptre, his
palace and his servants, his ministers and his grand
officers—the English have his kingdom. He receives
like a King his foreign visitors, and decorates them
with a valueless collar of tawdry tinsel; he wears
jewels and royal robes and has about him all the
paraphernalia of majesty; but the substance has
fled, the shadow only has been retained.'[3] For the
British, the Mughal king was there on sufferance; his
royal pretensions could be indulged up to a point, but
only because it was useful to maintain the fiction of
nominal sovereignty. Within this framework, early

British Residents such as Ochterlony and Seton were less cavalier in their handling of the Qila-i-Mualla's susceptibilities and more punctilious in abiding with prescribed court decorum. Soon, however, this circumspect politeness began to give way to a new spirit of 'firmness'—a euphemism for an increasingly undisguised impatience with the whole charade of propping up the myth of Mughal sovereignty. This change in attitude started creeping in during the Residency of Thomas Metcalfe and Colebrooke, and more obviously during the tenure of Hawkins. The new powers of India, reflecting the Utilitarian doctrines sweeping Britain at the time, were imbued with a resurgent and reforming chauvinism that held British rule to be morally right, English civilization to be inherently superior, and Christianity to be man's only saviour. To genuflect before a native monarch presiding over a heathen backward society, especially when both were powerless to resist, was becoming tiresome, even morally unbecoming. A contemporary British officer visiting Delhi around this time wrote indignantly: 'One of these "kings" (an obvious reference to one of the Mughal princes) who has no more than ten shillings a month to subsist himself and family upon will, in writing to the Representative of the British Government, address him as *Fidwee Khass,* our particular slave; and be addressed in reply with "Your Majesty's command (has) been received by your slave."'[4] The writing was clear on the wall. Time was running out for the Mughals, and for the 'pretensions' of the old feudal aristocracy as a whole.

As a member of the nobility, and as the leading

poet of the city, Ghalib was known to several British Residents, and was even on somewhat friendly terms with some of their subordinates. However, in parallel with the evolution of Mughal–British relations, his own relationship with the British came into sharp focus during his long struggle for justice in his pension case. Ghalib was hardly four when his father Abdullah Beg Khan, died in a skirmish at Alwar, where he was employed by its ruler. His father's younger brother, Nasrullah Beg Khan, served with the Marathas, and rose to command the Agra Fort under General Perron, a mercenary Frenchman, employed by the Maharaja of Gwalior. When Lord Lake took Agra in 1803, Nasrullah shrewdly surrendered the Fort, for which he was suitably rewarded by the British. He was made a commander of four hundred horses, with a salary of Rs 1,700 per month, and bestowed the districts of Sonk and Sirsa, near Bharatpur, for life. Unfortunately, soon after, Nasrullah fell off an elephant and died. Ghalib was then nine. Since Nasrullah had died issueless, his *jageer,* first resumed by the British, was later merged with that of his father-in-law, Nawab Ahmad Baksh Khan. The condition was that he must provide for Nasrullah Beg Khan's dependants, namely, his nephew Ghalib, Ghalib's younger brother, Nasrullah's mother (i.e., Ghalib's grandmother), and Nasrullah's three sisters (Ghalib's aunts). This arrangement was incorporated in a *perwanah* issued by Lord Lake on 4 May 1806, and approved by the Governor-General in Council at Calcutta. The *perwanah* held that Nawab Ahmad Baksh Khan would receive a remission of Rs 10,000 from the *quit* rent (revenue payable to the British) of Rs 25,000 of his newly expanded estate, to enable him to provide for Nasrullah's dependants. A dispute arose because Ahmad Baksh Khan claimed that Lord Lake had given him another *perwanah,* in June 1806, that specifically fixed the amount for Nasrullah's dependants at Rs 5,000 only. Ghalib contested the second *perwanah* as forgery, or as one obtained fraudulently by Ahmad Baksh Khan, particularly since one of the beneficiaries, Khwaja Hajee, had no claim to be listed as a dependant at all. Strangely enough, there was no report of this second document at Fort William—particularly since headquarters were required to endorse all decisions taken by commanders in the field.

Ghalib's case was well founded, and he fought to win it with tremendous tenacity, even undertaking an arduous journey to Calcutta in 1828, to personally press his case with the British authorities. For the next two decades he kept up a ceaseless clamour of reminders, memorials and petitions. He fought at every level: that of the Resident of Delhi, the Lieutenant Governor at Agra, the Governor-General in Council at Calcutta, the Court of Directors of the East India Company at London and finally Queen Victoria herself. But all to no avail. It was not that he had no patrons among the British. Simon Fraser, the officiating Secretary to the Governor-General, and Andrew Sterling, previously Assistant Resident at Delhi and later Persian Secretary to the Governor-General, were both writers and Persian scholars. At the individual level they were not unfavourably disposed to Ghalib. In fact, George Swinton, Chief

Secretary to Government, wrote a remarkable note
highly favourable to Ghalib. But Ghalib lost in spite
of his individual benefactors, because at the macro
level a new indifference to the sensitivities of the old
feudal aristocratic class had set in which was all part
of the growing impatience with Mughal imperialism
itself. It was not that Ahmad Baksh Khan, or later, his
son, Shamsuddin, had better relations with the British,
or tried harder. Judgement went against Ghalib because
of the basic British impatience with individuals who
had no monetary and increasingly little political value.
The attitude was to deal firmly with the claims of
this 'parasite' class, and give even shorter shrift to
their pretensions of social superiority. The merits of
the case were not important. Swinton's detailed and
analytical note was perhaps the sole attempt to
seriously examine the case on merit. The rest were
short, cursory jottings, symptomatic of the policy to
waste as little time as possible on a matter completely
peripheral to the British interest.

It is important to note that throughout Ghalib
took as axiomatic his right to receive a pension as a
reward for services rendered by his ancestors to the
British. This was entirely in keeping with the feudal
concept of the nexus between service and reward. But
a new generation of British officials had begun to
question the very utility of this nexus-in-perpetuity,
and the pension case is ultimately important for the
insight it provides of Ghalib's attempts to deal with
the situation. Being hopelessly in debt, Ghalib
desperately needed the increase in pension; but he
sought to get his *due with dignity, without eroding his*

*place in the social scale and without demeaning his standing
as a member of the nobility.* He was happy when Simon
Fraser received him in Calcutta with courtesy, offering
him *attar* and *paan* and escorting him to the gate at
the time of departure. He was equally happy when
Fraser immediately acceded to his request for a place
of honour in the Governor-General's durbar. Ghalib
was placed number ten in the order of precedence,
sitting next to such eminent persons as Nawab Ali
Akbar Khan, and only just below such notables as the
Vakil of the King of Delhi, the Vakil of the King of
Oudh, and the Vakil of the Raja of Nepal. But not all
British officials were so civilized. Francis Hawkins,
who was the officiating Resident at Delhi in 1829,
was particularly offensive. He was quintessentially
the new Company official, aggressive about the real
power he wielded, and resentful of having to
circumscribe it to suit local sentiment. He refused to
receive *shuqas* from anyone but the king himself,
refused to stand in the queen's presence, dismissed a
bouquet of flowers from the heir apparent because
they were brought by a 'menial gardener', and
considered the presentation of the customary *nazr* to
the king as degrading and humiliating. Not surprisingly,
his approach to the Indian gentry was more
peremptory, and from the very beginning he was ill-
disposed to Ghalib's presumptive questioning of a
document that apparently had the sanctity of Lord
Lake's signature and seal. It did not take him long to
send a report to Calcutta that, 'the complainant had
no right to more than what was expressly provided
by Lord Lake'[5] and of course Calcutta concurred with

his decision. Ghalib appealed the decision and wrote to Swinton alleging that Hawkins was biased in favour of Nawab Shamsuddin. Swinton, who was perhaps the only British officer to have read Ghalib's memorial seriously, concluded that there was merit in the case, and asked Hawkins to send Lord Lake's second *perwanah* for examination. The reopening of the case did not please Hawkins. He failed to see why Calcutta was wasting so much time and energy on this petty matter; and in forwarding the *perwanah,* he left no one in doubt about his own views. 'The Nawab (Shamsuddin)' he wrote, 'has just sent the letter required written in Persian, bearing the Great Seal and Signature of Lord Lake, and in submitting it herewith I trust Government will, on inspecting it, be as fully convinced of its genuineness as I was when, last May, I reported on Assudoola Khan's claim and will not suffer the false assertion of that person which has given so much trouble to you, and to me, and so much offence to the Nawab to pass unpunished.'[6]

As long as Francis Hawkins expressed his views in despatches, there was no ground for Ghalib to take umbrage at a personal level. But, a little later, Hawkins was discourteous to Ghalib, when the latter called on him in connection with his case. This was intolerable. Ghalib perceived himself a petitioner seeking justice, not a common supplicant whose self-respect was negotiable. Hawkins had the right to hold his own views on the merits of the case, but he did not have the right to transgress the norms of decorum and correct behaviour in dealing with a member of the Indian nobility. Ghalib protested in no uncertain terms.

In a letter to the Chief Secretary to Government, at Calcutta, he wrote:

> As my case is under the consideration of the Honourable the Vice-President in Council and as it is likely that my claims will shortly be referred to the Resident at Dehlee for deliberation and examination, I have the honour to solicit that you will have the kindness to submit my Prayer for the consideration of Government that I may be brought to the notice of Mr. Martin, the Resident at Dehlee in such a manner as will ensure to me as the descendant of the late Nassooroolla Beg Khan, Jageerdar of Sonk Sirsa in the district of Agra, the same degree of complaisance with which I was honoured by the Right Honourable the Governor General at the Public Darbars during my stay in Calcutta.
>
> I am under the necessity of making this unusual request in consequence of *my first* visit to the Residency during the administration of Mr. Hawkins, on my return from Calcutta, *being received in a manner totally unsuited to my Rank and Standing in the Scale of Asiatic Society and extremely ungratifying to my Feelings,* when contrasted with the urbanity and civility with which I was distinguished by the Right Honourable the Governor General in Council.[7] (Emphasis mine)

The letter is remarkable for the light it sheds on the historical process under way. In praising the British for behaviour that was becoming and urbane, and complaining against that which was not, Ghalib was in reality voicing the concern of many among the feudal class, who were seeking to preserve their traditional status in the face of deliberate British policy to demean it. In this sense, the pointed mention of his 'Rank and Standing in the Scale of Asiatic Society' could not have been more blunt. The British, of course, were not in a mood to be educated. There is nothing on record to show that 'instructions' as Ghalib had sought them, were sent to Martin, or that, unlike his other petitions and letters, this letter was even acknowledged. Meanwhile, there was bad news on the pension case. In order to verify its authenticity, the disputed *perwanah* had been sent to Sir John Malcolm, Governor of Bombay, who, in 1806, had been attached to Lord Lake. The conclusion was foregone. There was no reason for Sir John to go into the detailed and extremely well-argued petition that Ghalib had sent separately to Governor-General Bentinck and which Swinton had thoughtfully enclosed with the *perwanah*. Like Hawkins, Malcolm must have seen little merit in encouraging a member of the native class—whatever status he may claim in society—to question a document that apparently did have Lord Lake's seal and signature, especially when there was little the British had to gain in the process. To encourage such a claim would instigate other useless descendants to reopen hereditary claims on the largesse of the British. In a one-para minute,[8] remarkable for its dismissive, cursory and irrelevant appraisal of the entire case, Malcolm upheld the validity of the document. It was 30 November

1830. Ghalib had lost his case.

The loss of the case naturally had an adverse impact on Ghalib's precarious financial situation. But in the feudal milieu of which he was a part, the loss was equally an affront to his prestige. As a nobleman whose ancestors had been powerful and wealthy, and had enjoyed the due consideration of the British, it cast a shadow on his standing in society. To his peers it meant less that his case had been found weak on legal grounds and more that he did not carry enough weight with the *feringhees.* Thus the matter could not be given up so easily. In December 1831, during the durbar in Delhi, Ghalib presented a fresh petition, in person, to the Governor-General, and also forwarded an *arzi* through Secretary Prinsep. In April 1832 he wrote to remind the Governor-General to re-examine his case. A year later he wrote to Swinton, the Chief Secretary:

> It must be known to you that my father the late Abdoolah Beg Khan departed this life previous to the establishment of the British authority over Hindoostan, at which time I was nine years old, and my Uncle Nusseroolah Beg Khan was then ruler of Agra on the part of the late General Perron, and continued in obedience to the rulers of the British Government, and with a party of 400 horsemen, he attended on the late Lord Lake and rendered great services to the Honourable Company, in return for which the Pergunnas of Sonk and Sirsa were granted to him in Jageer by the British Government the particulars of which are entered in the Government records. I humbly hope that

you will be pleased to ascertain the character and dignity of the late Nusseroolah Beg Khan from the records of Government and favour me with a certificate to that effect so that through the means thereof I may wait upon the British Gentleman, who will listen to my case *and treat me with respect.*[9] (Emphasis mine)

The very fact that Ghalib needed a certificate to prove his status, indicates the increasing brittleness of British relations with the Indian gentry. In the early years of their rule, British officials had personal knowledge of, and often more than a nodding acquaintance with, members of the 'native elite'. Now locally available knowledge of status, obvious signs of breeding and education, and verbal introductions were not enough. A certificate in writing from British headquarters at Calcutta was necessary to persuade senior Delhi officials to be civil in their dealings. Hawkins was no longer the exception. To complain against one case of bad behaviour was not the answer; endorsements of lineage were needed from the rulers themselves.

Again, there is nothing on record to show that Ghalib got the certificate he sought. A little later in the year he wrote another letter to the Chief Secretary, this time enclosing a *qasida* addressed to the Governor-General.

God be praised that the Ruler of the time being is entirely disposed to do justice, and is the discerner of merits, but I regret to say that in this happy time my affair has been left unsettled and my merits not appreciated.

I have composed a *Ghazal* (ode) in your praise and a *qasida* in that of the Honourable the Governor-General. In the Stanza I have expressed my wishes, and I humbly hope that at a propitious moment it may be read in a praise-worthy manner in the Government House on Christmas Day.

I trust that his Honour will be graciously pleased to favour me with a *perwanah* under his Signature in reply to this, and if his Honour will direct the Ode, and Stanza alluded to, to be published in a Persian Newspaper, it will afford me a satisfactory proof of his approval of the same, and encourage me to cherish greater hopes of his favour and kindness.[10]

The letter is very interesting for two reasons: first, Ghalib sought a *perwanah with the Chief Secretary's signature* as a reply; secondly, he wanted the Chief Secretary to have the ode and stanza published *in a Persian newspaper*. Since an explicit certificate was not forthcoming, other means had to be employed to achieve the same purpose. If the Chief Secretary complied with the request, it would hopefully have the desired impact on those British officials with whom Ghalib had to deal with in connection with his case. It would also provide proof of his continued influence and status to his own peer group. Some of the British were boors; but as an entity they were powerful, thus their publicly perceived favour was important. A *qasida,* addressed to the Governor-General, and acknowledged by the Chief Secretary through a *perwanah* bearing his signature, would be testimony of his favour. An ode, which the Chief Secretary himself had published in a Persian newspaper (the few that were published were read widely by the Indian literati and nobility) would serve the same purpose. The central concern remained the same: to preserve the traditional status in an established societal scale—the balance of which was being relentlessly tampered with by the British and socio-economic shifts. The most desirable evidence of retaining this status would, of course, be a favourable decision in the pension case; but since the matter was taking time to be decided, there was no option but to resort to other means, in the short term.

The dilemma, of course, was how to obtain from the British without losing self-respect. To ask was unavoidable; but to do so abjectly, as any common favour seeker, would negate the very reason for doing so. Ghalib was more than conscious of this and took care to maintain a careful balance. It was not Ghalib but 'Asadullah Khan, the nephew of the late Nasrullah Beg Khan, Jageerdar of Sonk, Sirsa in the district of Agra' who wrote to the British. The letters were never unduly fawning. Customary compliments in the preamble were brief, and often—as in the letter quoted earlier—embarrassingly so. Sometimes they were missing altogether. When British officials were not sufficiently polite—as in the case of Hawkins—Ghalib complained; when this had no effect he still sought to extract more civilized behaviour by seeking endorsements of his status from Fort William. He did not consider it out of place to write directly to the

Governor-General. In composing odes of praise, he somehow managed to convey that he was doing the Governor-General a favour by making him the object of his poetic labours. He did not think he was overreaching himself by wanting his *qasida* to be acknowledged by a personally signed *perwanah* from the Chief Secretary to Government; nor did he doubt that the *qasida* was important enough to be read in Government House on Christmas Day. In an encomium written for Lord Hardinge, in 1846, he compared him to Afrasiyab, the great Persian general, but also called himself—*Shah-e-Kalam-Rau-e-Naziman*—King of the Kingdom of poetry.[11] On occasion he could adopt a tone that was hardly indicative of his supplicatory status. In 1832, on his request that his case be re-examined, the Governor-General—with typical bureaucratic sleight of hand—had decided that the case should first be dealt with by the Lieutenant Governor at Agra. Ghalib remained in correspondence with the Lieutenant Governor, submitting a list of seven queries that he wanted answered. The Lieutenant Governor provided no answers and decreed against Ghalib on 18 June 1836. By now Ghalib had appealed directly to the Governor-General. But the Lieutenant Governor's decision was endorsed by the Governor-General in Council, and communicated to Ghalib through the Agent at Delhi on 17 October 1836. Within a month, Ghalib wrote again to Lord Auckland, who had succeeded Bentinck as Governor-General. The letter, just falling short of being rude, but stark in its accusatory tone, is so pertinent to this analysis that it deserves to be reproduced here in full:

Most Respectfully Sheweth,

1) That your Lordship's petitioner has received through the Agent at Delhi, Mr. Secretary Macnaughton's Letter of the 17th Ultimo, signifying 'that your Lordship in Council sees no sufficient ground for a reconsideration of your petitioner's claim which appeared to have been finally disposed off by the order of the Lieutenant Governor of the North Western Provinces past on the 18 of June last.'

2) That your petitioner begs respectfully to state that having suffered manifold injustice from the Lieutenant Governor of Agra appealed against the decision of that Authority to your Lordship in Council; and afterwards submitted an illustrative statement of his case under date the 14 of July last, and ventured to offer seven points or queries to which he implored that replies may be obtained from the Lieutenant Governor of Agra, and that your Lordship bestowing due consideration upon the queries and His Honour the Lieutenant Governor of Agra's replies thereto, should decide your petitioner's case; and this procedure your petitioner, begs most respectfully to observe, was worthy of Your Lordship's consideration.

3) That your petitioner begs humbly to state that if your Lord-had obtained replies from the Lieutenant Governor of Agra to the seven points, and had admitted them, your petitioner begs permission humbly to state, that he should have been favoured with a copy of them, and made acquainted with the grounds on which your Lordship was pleased to admit them. But if your Lordship did not demand replies from the Lieutenant Governor of Agra, to the seven queries, your petitioner begs leave with every deference to state that your Lordship ought to have satisfied your petitioner in respect to them.

4) That your petitioner has the honour to solicit now, that your Lordship will be pleased to transfer his case with all the papers therewith connected (which your petitioner had had the honour of submitting, from time to time, since your Lordship's ingress into India) to the Sudder Dewanee Adawlat, in Calcutta, with injunctions that your petitioner's case be investigated in that Court by a regular procedure and, should your petitioner's claims prove valid in the decisions of that Court, the Authorities presiding as Judges over that Court will make new intimation to your Lordship, that your Lordship may grant your petitioner his just and lawful due; but should they consider the orders of the Lieutenant Governor of Agra, in your petitioner's case, just and equitable, they should explain to your petitioner, the grounds on which they may confirm the orders of the Lieutenant Governor of Agra, through a regular Roobakary.

5) That your petitioner begs humbly to state, that should your Lordship deny compliance with the above supplication (i.e. of transferring his case for decision to the Sudder Dewanee Adawlat in Calcutta), he must be under the necessity of entreating most humbly that your Lordship will

be graciously pleased to forward his case, with all the papers therewith connected, to England, in order that it should be tried before King in Council. And your Lordship's petitioner will, as in duty bound, ever pray for your Lordship's long life and prosperity.[12]

This letter, crisp and to the point, barely conceals the cold anger of its author. In it Ghalib gave notice that he was not asking for compassion but redress, not pleading for favours but asking for his rightful due, through procedures open to him as per the British laws themselves. It was an expression of no confidence in the Governor-General's ability to dispense justice— and the drafting of the letter leaves no doubt on this score. His Lordship is admonished for his omissions; he is told how to proceed in the future; and he is informed that, should he not do so, the petitioner has every intention to appeal to the king in England. Not everyone in the Indian nobility could presume to write directly to the Governor-General. But to write a petition so transparently indignant in tone, and shorn of the customary, long-winded preamble, conclusion of praise and good wishes, required courage. This letter convincingly demonstrates that Ghalib may have been a petitioner and a pensioner of the British, but not a sycophant.

It is probable the British were more amused than annoyed by the letter. As per normal procedure, the petition of appeal was referred to the Court of Directors of the East India Company in London. While awaiting the decision, Ghalib sent a set of Persian verses to Maddock, the Chief Secretary to Government in December 1836. In the verses he said, 'I have composed an Eulogy on the eminent qualifications of His Lordship (the Governor-General).' Of course, the eulogy was accompanied by a memorial 'on the subject of my claims touching my allowance'.[13] Neither the memorial nor the eulogy was acknowledged. In April 1837 he reminded the British that he was awaiting a reply. A polite but curt reply was sent to him stating that 'His Lordship in Council has been pleased to express his gratification at the mark of attention which you have shown in sending him a copy of your Persian verses'.[14] In February 1842, six years after the matter was referred to them, the Court of Directors expressed their judgement in a one-sentence ruling: 'This claim has been negatived and on good grounds previously to the sequestration* of the *jageer*.'[15] Undeterred, Ghalib then preferred an appeal to Queen Victoria herself. 'The petitioner,' he wrote to Governor-General Lord Ellenborough, 'feeling dissatisfied with the order passed in his case, has the honour of appeal to the August Throne of Her Most Gracious Majesty. He therefore begs leave to supplicate most humbly, that your Lordship will have the kindness to take compassion on him and forward the Enclosed Memorial for the most liberal and humane consideration of Her Most Gracious Majesty.'[16]

---

*In 1835 Shamsuddin, Nawab of Ferozepur and Jhirka, had been hanged for complicity in the murder of William Fraser, the British Resident in Delhi. His estate had then been sequestered by the British and Ghalib's pension was thenceforth paid directly from the British Treasury.

The British must have wondered whether they would ever shake off this persistent petitioner. By acting on several petitions of his appeal they had been less concerned about extending Ghalib a courtesy than about upholding the 'enlightened' infrastructure of British justice for 'native' benefit. But this petitioner was never satisfied. The more perfunctory their replies, the more he sought to hoist them on the petard of their own institutions and procedures.

Now he had presumed to appeal directly to the queen. Ghalib, of course, did not think he was being audacious at all. As a member of the aristocracy, and a leading poet, he had direct access to, and a place of honour in, the court of His Majesty, the Shadow of God, the Mughal emperor. He did not see why it should be different in the case of Her Most Gracious Majesty Queen Victoria. In his culture, mighty potentates indulged renowned poets. He expected the queen to do the same. In the polity he knew, a citizen had the right to appeal directly to the sovereign. He therefore considered himself entitled to write directly to the queen, over the heads of an indifferent British officialdom. It was a classic dichotomy of perspectives. The British, not knowing what to do with the appeal, and with no intention of bringing it to the notice of the queen, transmitted it again to the Court of Directors, 'to be dealt with as the Honourable Court may think fit'.[17] Ghalib, on his part, thought that his reasoning had been vindicated. 'I feel most sincerely grateful,' he wrote to Chief Secretary Maddock on 15 August 1842, 'and beg to offer my most unfeigned acknowledgements to the Right Honourable the

Governor-General of India, and to you. May God Almighty pour down his choicest blessings upon His Lordship and your Honour and all your endeavours be attended with success.'[18]

Queen Victoria never read Ghalib's memorial. When Ghalib persisted with his reminders, he was informed that 'Her Majesty has not been pleased to make any communication to us on this subject'.[19] There was no further movement in his case. The memorial gathered dust in some pigeon-hole in the East India Company office in London. The matter was decided by the simple expedient—mastered by all bureaucracies—inaction. Ghalib kept writing his petitions. They mostly remained unacknowledged. A year before the Revolt of 1857, he was still soliciting intimation on his case from Governor-General Canning. The only answer the British had was that his papers had been forwarded to England. In the aftermath of 1857, Ghalib's principal concern was the resumption of his pension. The question of its increase, for which he had fought relentlessly for almost three decades, was buried forever.

Ghalib had fought for what he considered his due. It had not been his intention to question the *legitimacy* of British power. Nationalism in the anti-colonial context had yet to germinate. In the unsettled conditions of nineteenth-century India, loyalties were routinely clipped to accept the *de facto* wielders of power—be they Afghan, Maratha, Jat or British. Ghalib's family background meshed well with this scenario. His father, in the best traditions of a mercenary warrior, had served the Mughal emperor

Shah Alam, Nawab Asafuddoula of Oudh, Nizam Ali Khan of Hyderabad and Raja Bakhtawar Singh of Alwar. His uncle had shifted allegiance with ease from the Marathas to the British. Delhi, Lucknow, Hyderabad, Alwar or Agra, the family shifted allegiance to as many masters. It was a time when survival was conditioned by a political agility that could keep loyalty mobile. For Ghalib, acceptance of him who usurped *de facto* power had the sanctity of normalcy. Besides, Ghalib was hardly six when the British established themselves at Delhi. He grew up taking their presence for granted. In the early years of British rule, he genuinely looked upon some British officials—like William Fraser—as friends and benefactors. He would have been happy to subsume this foreign presence within the familiar continuum of his own milieu. At a different level, for pointedly political reasons, the Mughal kings were seeking to do exactly the same. Lord Lake may have looked upon himself as the harbinger of definitive British control over the Timurids; but Shah Alam, with imperious if shrewd magnanimity, sought to pre-empt such a presumption by conferring on Lake the familiar title of *Khan Dauran, Khan Bahadur Sipah-i-Salar* (Commander-in-Chief). In a similar vein, Ghalib once described Francis Hawkins (before his rift with him) as *Nazim-al-Mulk* Francis *Bahadur Haibat Jang*. As beneficiaries of the industrial revolution, the British were ushering in new developments in both the scientific and industrial fields. Unlike many of his contemporaries, Ghalib appreciated these. In a letter, from Calcutta, he once wrote, 'May it not remain concealed that the steamer is one of the inventions of these people. It moves faster and many a time steamers have covered the distance between Calcutta and Allahabad in two weeks.'[20] He was equally appreciative of the wireless and postal services the British had introduced. Ghalib was, therefore, quite prepared to accept British power; but definitely not at the cost of negating his own *locus standi* as a hereditary nobleman. He was not inclined to question their legitimacy; but he was keen to assert his own, in his acceptance of theirs. From the beginning he maintained the premise that if the British had the power to be the final arbiters in his case, he would approach them for redressal on its merits, but, always, in conformity with his 'Rank and Standing in the Scale of Asiatic Society'. It was for this reason that he was a petitioner and not a sycophant. Of course he wrote panegyrics in their praise. That was a poet's training and probably the only way for him to earn his keep. A *qasida* was an investment in the powerful in return for patronage and monetary benefit; and it represented both sanction and respectability under prevailing norms. In fact, the rulers *expected* this from poets, and if the British were not so inclined, Ghalib knew of no other way to approach them. To write a *qasida* did not connote slavish genuflection; it did not necessarily indicate servility; it was more an instrument of introduction, a customary *peshkash,* meant to prepare the ground for an appropriate and respectful relationship between benefactor and beneficiary. Undoubtedly, the praise in a *qasida* was hyperbolic, but it was not meant to be taken seriously or literally. Ghalib wrote such panegyrics routinely, with little effort, and often joked about them. He once wrote one in praise of Amjad Ali Shah, the deposed king of Oudh. Amjad Ali died before it could be presented, so Ghalib put the son's name, Wajid Ali Shah, in place of the father's. 'After all,' he quipped, 'God himself did the same.' There was the highest precedent to justify this kind of flippancy. Ghalib maintained that the great Persian poet Anwari routinely rotated the same ode for presentation.

Ghalib lost his case because the British never had any intention of judging it on its merits. Their business was to consolidate political control, and they considered 'undue' indulgence of the Indian pensionary nobility not particularly conducive to that goal. It was an ideological impatience which, in time, was translated into definitive policy. Ghalib sought to clothe his dependency under notions of service and reward. The British wanted to get down to harsh basics: is it necessary? how much? and for how long? Such an approach, so contrary to the feudal ethos, was galling to Ghalib. 'As a member of a declining aristocracy what he came to resent was British inability to give gracefully, for that inability inhibited his ability to receive gracefully, as a gentleman should.'[21] A robe of honour, an appropriate acknowledgement to a *qasida,* or the rightful place in a public durbar were important not only in terms of personal vanity but also as indicative that the British accepted this gentlemanly status, and therefore the socio-political order, in which, alone, such a status had meaning. At the pinnacle of that order, was the Mughal emperor. He too was fighting for his rightful place under the sun. And, like Ghalib, his weapons were the same: representations, memorials, petitions, appeals. In 1805, Lord Wellesley had promised to pay Akbar Shah II an annual stipend of Rs 15 lakh. Later the British refused to increase it beyond Rs 12 lakh. Akbar Shah protested against this breach of faith and, when that proved ineffective, sent Raja Ram Mohan Roy as his envoy to England, to complain directly to the Court of Directors. A similar appeal, this time to the king in England, was made when the British insisted on curtailing the Mughal prerogative to nominate any son as successor. A protracted battle was also fought on the presentation of *nazrs*. Legally the British were vassals of the Mughals, and during an audience or ceremonial occasion, presented *nazrs* to the Jahanpanah in acknowledgement of this status. When the practice of paying such *nazrs* was sought to be stopped, Bahadur Shah protested vehemently. Once again the matter went up to the Court of Directors, who seemed inclined not to bring matters to a head so bluntly. Bahadur Shah was aware that a communication to this effect had come to Fort William from London. In a style very similar to Ghalib's many memorials and petitions, he wrote to the Governor-General: 'I hope from your Lordship's high and pre-eminent character for justice and liberality that you will have the kindness to cause search to be made among the records of Government in Calcutta and on finding that such instructions were received from Europe, be so gracious as to pass the necessary orders in the Agent's name for the payment and presentation of the amount of *nazrs* for the past two years, and that the custom be regularly observed for the future. By doing this I will be gratified, and it will add to your fame.[22] But to no avail; the practice of presenting *nazrs* was formally abolished in 1851; the annual stipend was never increased; and the question of choosing a successor was taken firmly out of Mughal hands.

What Ghalib fought for and lost at his level, Bahadur Shah fought for and lost at his. In the absence of any other means to enforce their rights, both fought spiritedly to obtain *legal* redressal. Both their cases were legitimate on legal grounds. Both attempted to appeal over the heads of British officials in Delhi to the Court of Directors in London. When this proved futile, both appealed directly to the British sovereign. While appealing to the British sense of justice and fair play, both were neither abject nor fawning, preserving a public demeanour in conformity with the status they claimed. Beneath the polite language of petitions and memorials, Bahadur Shah knew he was fighting a political battle for survival. Ghalib was fighting for recognition in British eyes of his rightful place within the Mughal framework. The fates and destinies of Bahadur Shah and Ghalib were inextricably linked. Recognition by the British of nominal Mughal sovereignty meant, by implication, the recognition of the feudal order over which he presided. Ghalib approached the British with full regard of his own status precisely on the strength of this recognition. But the Mughal emperor and Ghalib were victims of the same process. They sought legal redressal from a power which, consciously, sought to erode their legal rights. It was not a legal battle at all; it was a political battle, in which the Mughal emperor was obviously losing. And Ghalib's ultimate tragedy is that he could not but have been aware of this.

The paraphernalia of royalty, still retained by the Mughal king within the Red Fort, may, perhaps, have lulled the common man into believing that the Mughal show was still on. But, because he was a poet, extraordinarily sensitive and with a razor-sharp intelligence, it is almost certain that Ghalib, without understanding the real forces at work, was aware of the eroded foundations of the Mughal edifice and its concomitant institutions. As in the case of other citizens, the imminence of change eluded him; but unlike the common man he had both the perception and the opportunity to understand that change *was* taking place and that the political order, as he knew it, was disintegrating.

That Mughal authority had already been unprecedentedly humiliated must have been known to him. The vicissitudes of the Mughal king, in the eighteenth century, at the hands of the Jats, Marathas, Afghans and Nadir Shah, were part of anecdote and legend. Being a regular visitor to the Fort, and later the king's *ustad* in poetry, Ghalib must have been privy to Bahadur Shah's unavailing and humiliating attempts to move the British. He must have also noticed the extent to which the Qila-i-Mualla had physically declined from its bygone splendour. Like a plant that shrivels for lack of water, the palace had withered, once the galvanizing impulses of political power had begun to dry. Its ruinous condition was not due to Nadir Shah's carrying away the peacock throne; nor was the damage caused by the plundering of the Jats and Ghulam Qadir irreparable. The squalor of the Lal Qila was because the Mughals themselves had ceased to be imperial rulers. Their power was less than that of a petty provincial satrap; their finances worse than those of a medium-sized *mansabdar* of Akbar's days. Bishop Heber, who visited the palace in 1824, recorded that the once magnificent Diwan-i-Am was 'full of lumber of all descriptions, broken palanquins and empty boxes, and the throne so covered with pigeon dung that its ornaments were hardly discernible'. The jewel-like Moti Masjid was 'in the same state of neglect and dilapidation, with *peepuls* allowed to spring from its walls'.[23] At about the same time another visitor noticed that the precious stones in the Diwan-i-Khas had been replaced by artificial ones which created an illusion of shine but lacked the lustre.

A difference that symbolically summed up the real transformation of the Mughal kings. For Ghalib, the ruin and decay was there to see, not because he could compare it to more prosperous days, but because he had grown up on stories extolling the imperial riches and grandeur of the Mughals. The diamonds and emeralds, rubies and sapphires; the exquisite inlay work of lapis-lazuli, jade, rose-quartz, turquoise and many others, with tracery in pure gold, the curtains of the richest silks, the lavish carpets and the peacock throne had been in existence until too recently to have been forgotten. Ghalib, even as he bowed low in salutation to his sovereign, could not but have dwelt on the desuetude of the surroundings and seen the growing shadow of the British Resident dwarfing the king.

As a poet Ghalib was not unusual in having a heightened sensitivity to the travails of the time. The three great poets of the preceding century—Sauda, Mir and Mir Taqi Mir—had a similar receptivity to events of their age. In several of his writings Sauda lamented the prevailing chaos and anarchy, and the helplessness of the Mughal king. Mir, a contemporary of Sauda, gave voice to a similar anguish.

The blinding of Shah Alam II by the Afghan Ghulam Qadir in 1788 stunned every Delhi citizen, but it was Mir Taqi Mir who immortalized the tragedy in verse.

In Ghalib's time, upheaval and trauma had been driven underground. The chaos and anarchy of the preceding century had been replaced by the frozen inequity of 'British peace'. Adventurous marauders and treacherous *dewans* had been subdued by the enforced stability of British rule. The British did not come to Delhi like Ghulam Qadir or Nadir Shah on a quick hit–plunder–run operation. Colonial rule demanded the establishment of law and order and an end to political uncertainty. The British had the physical force to back their political control, and used both to set up an administrative infrastructure calculated to convey that theirs was a power to stay. Efficient revenue collection could be pursued only when the instability of political opposition was firmly obliterated, and the giver sufficiently convinced that he who received was firmly in the saddle. It was this colonial process that restored a semblance of normalcy

to the beleaguered citizens of Delhi. But, beneath this
deceptive calm, Ghalib sensed a deep foreboding that
some fundamental change was taking place, and
institutions, anchorages and signposts—as he knew
them—were irrevocably altering. In a Persian verse
he wrote:

> The wind is contrary, the night pitch dark,
> And the sea is lashed by storms;
> The anchor is broken
> And the ship's master is asleep.[24]

The coincidence between the consolidation and
expansion of British power and the decline of Mughal
sovereignty was too obvious to escape notice. It is
understandable that Ghalib could not correlate the
two in terms of an exploitative colonial force
overcoming a decadent feudal order. He was prepared
to accept the British presence because—in his eyes—
this was not a 'moral' question at all. Bowing before
the Jahanpanah, and presenting salaams to the *angrez*
Resident did not, in the context of his times, imply
a contradiction or dichotomy. The weight of precedent
and the pressures of uncertainty had synthesized both
in a harmonious application of the God and Caeser
formula: give unto both what is due unto each, to one
the reverence due unto *de jure* sovereignty, to the
other the cognizance due unto *de facto* power. But in
course of time—and with his own experience in the
pension case—he probably did come to grasp that the
British were both non-assimilable in, and antithetical
to, the established order. This never took the form of

a wholly rationalized resentment, it was more a glimmer of comprehension, an embryonic, even hazy, realization of what the colonial process really implied. There is nothing explicit in his writings—at least in the pre-1857 period—in evidence of this realization, but the scathing sarcasm in the following couplets, in spite of the deliberately ambivalent imagery, points the finger quite clearly:

> Were I not robbed in broad daylight
> How could I sleep so well at night?
> No fear of theft remains now
> I give blessings to the dacoit.[25]
> How unfair for us to claim the return of past glory
> What has been stolen was but a debt due—'tis not
>   robbery.'[26]

On occasion the imagery could be dangerously explicit:

> Misfortune came, and having come
> made no signs to leave
> A checkmate somehow was deflected
> and the king got reprieve.[27]

The word *rehzan* or robber recurs frequently

> Thou hast set over us
> The sky for our destruction;
> Whatever the robber has from us snatched
> Does not reach thy treasury.[28]

In the face of this *rehzan* who would not go, there was a sense of helplessness and resignation, a feeling that all levers were beyond one's reach and whatever one might do, the result would be the same:

> Ghalib there's nought to gain
> From the efforts I deploy
> Lightning will burn the crop
> Else the locusts will destroy.[29]

Another couplet expresses the same sentiments but with remarkably relevant imagery:

> My struggle is the same
> As do captive birds engage
> Collecting twigs to build a nest
> Even in their cage.[30]

In great measure, this feeling of helplessness stemmed from the perceived weakness of the Jahanpanah himself. In one of his Persian couplets Ghalib links his own situation with the leader of the caravanserai:

> Everyone who sees the way
> That I am sleeping, knows
> That in the caravanserai
> The leader of the caravan is fast asleep.[31]

Sometimes he could even be flippant about the situation:

> This naïveté will be the death of me, O God
> He fights, and in his hand not even a sword.[32]

But there is no doubt that, as the quintessential product of the feudal–monarchic order, he keenly felt the absence of a strong imperial focus to identify with:

> How long must I cry behind the flappings of his tent
> It was not fate that I could have a solid wall to lament. [33]

Or again,

> Ghalib, there is no doubt
> About the piquancy of this hemistich;
> 'Hind is a paradise
> That has no Adam in it.' [34]

At one level this absence of imperial focus was internalized as a political abstraction, at another, it had very concrete implications. In the medieval tradition, a professional poet's principal source of livelihood was royal patronage. If the poet lived in a period of imperial munificence, his royal patron's indulgence could be excessive. Ghalib's expectations were nurtured by this tradition, and came into head-on collision with the political realities of the time. The tawdriness of the Mughal court was there to see. Bahadur Shah Zafar was himself a poet and a patron of poetry but political conditions had only left the Mughals with the sensitivity to appreciate poetry, but not much wherewithal to financially indulge those who wrote it. Ibrahim Zauq was the royal tutor in poetry, and did receive financial remuneration for his services. The frayed edges of Mughal largesse could display one court *ratna* with difficulty; it could not afford to sustain nine in the grand splendour Akbar the Great did, with such effortless ease. At a personal level, Ghalib resented Zafar's choice of Zauq as the Poet Laureate. In the ultimate analysis, however, the king could be forgiven for his taste, but not so the times, which had constricted imperial generosity to an extreme where a poet of Ghalib's renown had little to own except renown.

Glimpses of Ghalib's lurking resentment are evident from his writings. In the preamble to *Mihr-i-Nimroz* (the first part of an intended history of the Mughal dynasty) he reminds Zafar of the days of Shah Jahan when the poet Kalim was frequently weighed against silver, gold, pearls and rubies; the accusation acquired sting when he went on to insinuate that Kalim's verse would pale in comparison to his own. If the Mughals were unable to live up to Ghalib's expectations, the British were unwilling to do so. In an ode in honour of Queen Victoria, Ghalib pointedly indicated what his expectations were by mentioning that the emperors of Persia, and other conquering kings, had customarily granted great wealth to their poets, giving them villages and showering them with pearls and gold.

This vision of the past stood in sharp contrast to Ghalib's penury in the present. Not surprisingly, he preferred to invoke the past in protest against the present, and it is possible that his emphatic and publicly stated preference for Persian over Urdu, had its origins precisely in this syndrome. Urdu was the popular living language of his time having the effervescence and energy of a young language that had come into its own, in literary terms. But Urdu was tainted. It was the product of a period of political chaos and decline. It was not the language of a powerful and renowned court like that of Akbar or Shah Jahan. It was more the compensation of a weakened and increasingly impoverished nobility. It could be indicative of a new literary efflorescence but it was not the *lingua franca* of a strong feudal–monarchic order as Persian was. Viewed from the detachment of a historian there was an undeniable piquancy in the situation: a literary renaissance, in a modern language, was taking place within a decaying and stultified feudal framework. Though this created the foundations for the literary growth of Urdu in later times, it also left those who laid these foundations largely without avenues for material reward or benefit. For Ghalib to accept Urdu would have meant giving legitimacy to this situation. To reject it would symbolize his sense of deprivation, unfulfilment, and his feeling of being born at the wrong time in the wrong place. Hali, a contemporary of Ghalib, his biographer, and a poet of no mean talent, noted that Ghalib did not consider writing in Urdu an accomplishment. Indeed, he considered it below his dignity to write in it at all.

Persian had ceased to be a living language, for historical reasons linked to the creation of a composite Indian culture by the Mughals themselves; but for Ghalib the fact that there were few left to understand and appreciate it was vindication enough of the bastardization of his times. One of his frequent laments was that while there were admirers enough of his

Urdu *ghazals,* there were none to appreciate his Persian odes. He publicly deprecated his Urdu verse—and, in a famous *nazr* written for the king, even stated that he made no claims to be an Urdu poet at all. Of course, he wrote exquisitely in Urdu; and later adopted it as the medium for all his prose, including his letters. His public non-acceptance of it was, probably, more a peg to hang his unrationalized alienation from a historical period of which this language had become a singularly striking symbol. As he said:

> Ghalib was a nightingale
> In the garden of 'Ajam':
> In my ignorance
> I named him the parrot of Hindustan.[35]

To cling to the past, to squeeze comfort from any aspect of the present which assures the continuity of the past, is not an unusual reaction for those caught in the mire of a collapsing feudal system. Ghalib's oft-repeated and exaggerated assertion of his aristocratic ancestry is traceable to this reaction, and is certainly more understandable when seen in this light. His ancestors were mercenaries who had prospered enough to allow him to legitimately claim the status of nobility. Convincing the British of this was a matter of prestige and of tactic. But there is evidence that Ghalib had persuaded himself to actually believe his frequent hyperbole on his exalted lineage. It was an age when, under the umbrella of *de facto* British power, an impotent king and a castrated nobility were left to colour their evenings with little more than memories of their warrior past. The more remote their pensionary lives became to the days of their ancestors—when empires were built and fortunes made—the more they spent their idle hours extolling their aristocratic and martial lineage. This preoccupation was tangible enough for even a casual visitor to notice. 'It is not only the desire for office that makes the educated Mohammedans cherish the recollections of the old regimes in Hindoostan; they say "We pray every night for the Emperor and his family, because our forefathers ate of the salt of his forefathers'—that is, our ancestors were in the service of his ancestors; and consequently were of the *aristocracy* of the country." Whether they really were so matters not; they persuaded themselves or their children that they were.'[36]

The British occupation of Delhi sterilized any political ambitions that may have lurked in the feudal aristocracy. Simultaneously, and not coincidentally, this class was also burdened with financial stress. As we have seen earlier, through inheritance, reinforced by temperament, Ghalib was feudal in outlook. He resented the erosion of the patrician domain, the trampling, by the hoi polloi, on the intricate aristocratic fabric that had always enwrapped Mughal power. His reaction was in keeping with the times: an attempt to glorify his past and assert its continued relevance in order to escape the unpalatability of the present. Thus, living in penury, under the shadow of an emasculated king bent double under British tutelage, Ghalib asserts, more than once, to being a descendant of the exalted House of Timur, son of Faridun (a legendary king of ancient Persia), and of his high connections with the great Turkish rulers such as Pashang, Sahjar and others:

> Ghalib, we are from the sacred dust of Turan,
> Doubtless, we are glorious in dynastic origin;
> We are *aibaks,* from amongst the class of Turks,
> In fulness, we are ten times superior to the moon.[37]

Or again,

> O *Saki,* as I belong to the line of Pashang and
>   Afrasiyab,
> You know that my origin is from the House of
>   Jamshid;
> Give me now the wine which is the legacy of
>   Jamshid
> And then will pass to me Paradise, which is the
>   legacy of Adam.[38]

Such references to the origins and lineage of his family are frequent occurrences in Ghalib's writings. It is a refrain articulated strongly enough for his contemporaries—such as Hali—to have specifically noticed and commented upon it; it is also the reason he preferred to be in debt rather than renounce a life-style expected from his own image of his aristocrat-warrior past.

Indeed with British forces massed on the ridge overlooking Delhi, it is understandable that Ghalib preferred to look past them to the times when his own ancestors came as successful conquerors to India.

For if he returned to the present, the fact of the matter was that British occupation had decisively sanitized feudal aspirations in the political sphere. Somewhere, subconsciously perhaps, a gnawing regret remained on this score. In his collection of Persian verse, while pointing his finger squarely at the British, he speaks of other compensations:

They have plucked the pearls
From the banners of the kings of Ajam,
And in place have given me
A treasure-scattering pen

They have carried away the crown
From the head of the Turks, descended from
    Afrasiyab;
They have given me speech which has the bearing
Of the splendour of the Kayanian kings.[39]

In a more candid passage, in one of his letters, he laments, 'Alas for my fate; born to be struck down by misfortune and to see my granaries reduced to ashes. I had not the means to ride to war like my ancestors . . .'[40]

Embedded in this lament is the psychological genesis of Ghalib's glorification of the past, a glorification which drove him, in a famous poem, to proclaim that his ancestors had been soldiers for centuries; and he did not seek recognition on account of his poetry.

Fact and myth blend more easily in twilight periods of history. The Mughal Empire was dying, but was not yet dead. The British were the new rulers but had

yet to proclaim it openly. In this penumbra, institutions
of the past persisted, lifestyles remained the same,
but new developments were chipping away at both. It
was a period of transition, of diffused and overlapping
constituencies, of a deep and complex interplay of
shadow and reality. The objective forces and agents of
change were present but had yet to become manifestly
discernible. Political consciousness stood mesmerized
by the momentum and weight of the past. The final
dip in the descending gradient had begun, but for
those part of it, there was no light at the end of the
journey. 'This world of mediatized sovereignty, of
Weimar-like elegance against a backcloth of squalor
and despair, a Mughal sunset glow, might have faded
imperceptibly into the night of oblivion.'[41] But the
British were impatient to force the pace. In 1854,
they decided that after Bahadur Shah's death the royal
family was to be removed from the Red Fort and
shifted to premises outside the city, near the Qutab
Minar. It was further decided that Bahadur Shah's
successor was to have the title not of 'king' but of
'prince' and that the allowance given to him by the
British was to be reduced. Mirza Muhammad Asadullah Khan Ghalib, Mughal courtier, British petitioner,
indigent aristocrat, proud nobleman and Delhi citizen,
was quick to sense the approaching denouement. In
1854, he wrote to his friend, the poet Junun, 'Inside
the Fort a few princes get together and recite their
verses. Once in a while I attend these gatherings.
Contemporary society is about to vanish. Who knows
when the poets would meet next or meet again at
all.'[42] Three years later, the court, along with an

entire way of life that Ghalib knew and could identify with, came crashing down amidst unprecedented upheaval and violence. The Mughal dynasty was wound up and Bahadur Shah was sent into exile. But even as Pax Britannica was proclaimed with pomp and fanfare, Ghalib the prescient poet-observer could stand aside and pronounce the eternal verity:

The world is contingent—boast not of greatness
This zenith one day defeat will depress.[43]

TWO

The City of Good Living

'At about one o'clock in the morning I looked out of my palanquin, and saw in the glorious moonlight the minarets of the Jama Masjid, the great Mohammedan mosque that is one of the chief beauties of Delhi and of Northern India. As we got nearer I could see the wonderful red walls that surrounded the city . . . It was the most marvellous moonlight I have ever seen, and as we crossed the river, the view in both directions with this magnificent city lying before us, was quite wonderful, so many exquisite minarets towering up into the sky belonging to the Mohammedan temples . . .'[1] The year was 1848, the day 20 January. The writer was Emily Bayley, daughter of the British Resident at Delhi, Sir Thomas Metcalfe. The sight which she so rapturously described was the profile of Ghalib's Delhi as she approached it over the bridge of boats across the river Jamuna. On reaching the British Resident's imposing mansion outside the Kashmiri Gate, Emily, on her father's gentle urging, overcame her excitement and caught some sleep. But had she waited a little longer, she may have witnessed the dawn break over the city, and watched the rays of the rising sun pick out its main landmarks: the red sandstone pre-eminence of the Red Fort, known as the Qila-i-Mualla or the Fort of Exalted Dignity, hugging the Jamuna to the east; the city before it to the west, in the shape of an arc, hemmed in on all sides by a masonry wall (6664 yards long, four yards wide and nine yards high); the many gates in this wall, Kashmiri Gate in the north, Mori, Kabul, Lahori and Ajmeri on the western face, and Turkman and Delhi gates on the south; the two main streets running through the city—Chandni Chowk and Faiz Bazaar—intersecting at right angles; the imposing loftiness of the Jama Masjid, its spatial grandeur and soaring minarets, facing with equality the magnificence of the Red Fort to its   north-east; and beyond the city, the Ridge, its wooded heights separated from the city walls by a flat and short interregnum of trees, bushes, orchards and dilapidated ruins.

The central figure, the accepted presiding deity, of the composite culture of the city was the Mughal king. Although Akbar Shah II was the Mughal emperor in the younger days of Ghalib, it was his successor Bahadur Shah, more than he, who truly encapsulated the ethos of the city. He was the touchstone of correct etiquette, the symbol of the dominant themes of his age, its achievements, its weaknesses, its distractions. He was a fine marksman and a good horseman. He was an accomplished poet, adopting the *takhallus* 'Zafar' as his *nom de plume*. He was a scholar who authored a learned commentary on Saadi's *Gulistan*. He composed *khayals* and *thumris* under the pen-name 'Shauq Rang'. He was an accomplished calligraphist, and a patron of painting; it was largely court interest which kept the Delhi school of painting alive, nurturing artists such as Raja Jivan Ram and Hussain Nazir. Notwithstanding his empty coffers, he found the means to somehow express the Mughal love for gardens, laying out one in Shahdara and one below the palace wall. He played chess and cards, enjoyed kite-flying, and liked bird fights. His own *bulbul—Bulbul-e-hazar dastaan—*was greatly admired by the public. He liked good food—mangoes, in particular, became the fruit célébre of the city thanks to the royal weakness for them—and beautiful women. He was poor but dignified, politically impotent but still the Jahanpanah. The culture of Delhi had acquired a certain authenticity. Over a period of time, varying elements had synthesized to produce a composite life-style for its inhabitants—not laboured, not grafted— but effortlessly woven into the city's own personality. Its socio-cultural ethos, distinctive enough to give even the witticisms of the city an unmistakable Delhi flavour, was what prompted Zauq to say: *'Kaun jaye par ab Dilhi ki galiyan chod kar'* (Who then can leave the streets of Delhi). Bahadur Shah Zafar, no longer the suzerain of a mighty empire, was the acknowledged symbol of this zeitgeist.

The king was a devout Muslim, but the milieu was strikingly non-sectarian. The court celebrated Hindu festivals such as Raksha Bandhan, Dussehra, Holi, Diwali, Shivratri and Basant Panchami with enthusiasm. This was not a calculated stance of secularism; it was more the natural unfolding of a genuine synthesis starting from the days of Akbar the Great when the assimilation of Hindu elements into the Mughal ambience became noticeable. Akbar married Rajput princesses and appointed Hindus to prominent positions in the state. For the populace he was both Jahanpanah and Mahabali. Shah Jahan's son, Dara Shikoh, had the *Yoga-Vasistha,* the *Gita* and the *Upanishads* translated into Persian. He himself wrote a book, *Majmua-ul-Baharain,* a comparative study of Hinduism and Islam. Aurangzeb could only arrest, not stem this process. By Zafar's time this composite culture had become an inherited lifestyle, which the king could strengthen perhaps, but not question.

When the conditions for strengthening a tradition exist, minor incidents that can bolster it further are unconsciously exalted to the level of institutions. Thus perhaps the celebration of Raksha Bandhan was institutionalized by the king. According to lore, a Brahmin lady, Ramjani Gaur, returning at dawn from the river Jamuna after her bath, spotted the murdered corpse of Emperor Alamgir II. Unquestioningly she kept watch over it until the king's men found and retrieved it. Alamgir II's son and successor, Shah Alam, thought it fit to reward the lady for this act. Every year, on Raksha Bandhan, Ramjani would go to the Fort on a richly caparisoned palanquin and tie a *rakhi* on her grateful Shah *bhai.* The emperor would, in return, load her with presents. The ceremony became an annual celebration, followed by Shah Alam's successors, Akbar Shah II and Bahadur Shah, and the ladies of Ramjani's house.

Every year, the rainy season saw all communities of Delhi enthusiastically celebrating the festival of flowers—Phoolwalon ki Sair—which became an annual event in the reign of Zafar. The festival had an interesting origin. Zafar was the prince chosen by the British to succeed Akbar Shah II. But Akbar Shah, instigated by his favourite queen, Mumtaz Mahal, sought to have the decision changed in favour of her son—Mirza Jahangir. The British were not agreeable. Mirza Jahangir was a spirited lad and, emboldened by his indulgent parents, gave vent to his resentment by taking a shot at the British Resident, Seton. The attempt merely knocked Seton's hat off. But the British were sufficiently annoyed to have Mirza Jahangir exiled to Allahabad. His grieving mother took a vow that, if her son was allowed to return to Delhi, she would make an offering of a four-poster flower bed to the holy shrine of Khwaja Bakhtayar Kaki at Mehrauli. After some time the British agreed to his return, but only after the king guaranteed his good behaviour and agreed not to question Zafar's status as heir apparent. Mirza Jahangir's return to Delhi was celebrated with great fanfare. Mumtaz Mahal commenced elaborate preparations for fulfilling her vow. A beautiful flower canopy was created to which the *phoolwale* or flower sellers added an elaborate flower *pankah,* at their own cost. Both these were then ceremoniously carried in a large procession to the saint's shrine.

Mirza Jahangir did not change his ways. He was exiled again, and ultimately died in Allahabad at the age of thirty-one. He was apparently suffering from cirrhosis of the liver caused by the excessive intake of cherry brandy. But the pilgrimage of the court and the people of Delhi to Mehrauli became an annual institution.

A few days before the festival, the king, the queen and all the ladies and noblemen of the court, would leave Delhi by palanquins or *hawadars,* with the princes riding escort on their prancing steeds. After visiting Humayun's tomb, Nizamuddin and Safdar Jung (where they tarried for lunch) the royal procession reached Mehrauli to be accorded a befitting reception. The Jungli Mahal near the Durgah of Khwaja Bakhtayar Kaki, now in ruins but standing in all the glory of a royal palace in those days, was richly decorated with carpets and chandeliers. The king would go to the *Jharna* the next day—where in the seclusion of *kanats* and curtains, ladies of the court could be at leisure. More often than not there would be a light drizzle and the royal party would move to the *Amarian,* a mango grove to the east of the *Jharna* and a beautiful picnic spot. Here, the delicacies of the season would be prepared by the royal ladies themselves and there would be fun for all with singing and dancing.

On the first day of the festival, the procession of fans and flowers would start from the *Jharna,* with musicians, athletes demonstrating sports and fencing, and soldiers in their colourful uniforms, and pass through the richly decorated and brilliantly lit Bazaar of Mehrauli to the Jog Maya Mandir. The next day another elaborate procession would go to the tomb of Khwaja Bakhtayar Kaki.[2]

What began as a Muslim woman's obeisance in gratitude at the shrine of a Muslim saint, became an occasion of pilgrimage and celebration for the entire city—transcending barriers of community and class. The king went both to the tomb of Khwaja Bakhtayar and to the Jog Maya Mandir. Those who followed him in the procession were Hindus and Muslims alike. Ghalib makes a reference, in one of his letters, to the mass involvement and secular nature of the event: 'In this city there is a festival called the Flower-men's festival. It takes place in the month of *Bhadon* (August–September), and everyone in the city, from the nobles to the artisans, goes off to the Qutab (Minar). There they stay for two to three weeks. All the shops in the city of Muslims and Hindus alike—stay closed throughout this time.'[3]

There were no communal riots in Ghalib's Delhi. In 1854, there was some tension when on the occasion of Bakr-i-Id cow slaughter was permitted by the British Resident, Thomas Metcalfe. The Mughal kings, sensitive to the sentiments of the Hindus, traditionally sacrificed a camel on Id and had prohibited cow slaughter. The British insensitively lifted this prohibition. But although the Hindus protested, there was no communal violence. Ghalib mentions the incident in a letter of the same year: 'I'll tell you what happened here at (Bakr) Id. But let me tell you first what they're saying here about what happened in Aligarh. God save us! Wherever people met they were saying that there had been a great civil war in Aligarh. Hindus and Muslims had drawn their swords on each other, and ten to twenty on both sides had been killed.

I was intending to write to you about it, when in the meanwhile your letter came and I learned the true situation. I expect the same sort of reports have been current there about Delhi—that swords were drawn and so on. Well, my good sir, swords were not drawn and there was no fighting. For two days the Hindu shop-keepers kept their shops closed, whereupon the British Magistrate and the Chief of Police toured the whole city. Persuading and cajoling and insisting and threatening, they got the shops opened, and both goats and cows were sacrificed.'[4]

Ghalib's description of the episode has a sense of genuine incredulity that Hindus and Muslims could come to violence. When given the true picture, his sense of relief is obvious and he is quick to dispel the exaggerated rumours about what happened in Delhi. It is true that communal conflicts in north India were not entirely unknown even in the pre-colonial era. But in Ghalib's Delhi, on the few occasions when we do have evidence of communal tension, the context was not necessarily Hindu versus Muslim. In 1816 and 1834 it was tension between the Hindus and Jains over a Jain *rathyatra,* which almost (if the then Resident Charles Metcalfe is to be believed) led to a riot. On other occasions the tension was between Shias and Sunnis. The British did keep troops in readiness to diffuse tension during the celebration of Id and Ram Lila. But there is no record that they were used. On the contrary, there is evidence that participation in the celebration of these events transcended community limitations. 'The popular religions were highly eclectic in their beliefs and practices . . . Hindus and Muslims shared common saints and *pirs, mazaars, dargahs* and other holy places, and even popular gods and goddesses.'[5] Zafar himself ordered that the route of the Ram Lila procession be modified to pass in front of the palace, so that he could also enjoy seeing it. He is also reported to have been 'very much pleased' by the presentation to him of the Bible in Arabic.

Munshi Zakaullah, one of the oldest and most respected citizens and scholars of Delhi, met C.F. Andrews in Delhi in 1904. A close friendship ensued, and, Zakaullah, who was one of the very few people still alive who had actually lived through Ghalib's Delhi, spent hours talking to Andrews about the city, its people and their lifestyle during the last days of Mughal rule. The noted historian Percival Spear has advised caution in accepting, fully, the slightly euphoric conclusion drawn by Andrews (as a result of his talks with Zakaullah) on the state of communal relations prevailing then. But, quite obviously, Zakaullah and others must have spoken with considerable conviction for Andrews to be so unequivocal and categorical on this point:

> The intimate residence together side by side in the same city of Mussalmans and Hindus had brought about a noticeable amalgamation of customs and usages among the common people . . . *I have had more convincing and corroborative evidence about this especially friendly relationship between Hindus and Mussalmans in old Delhi than I have had concerning any other factor.* The information has come to me from both sides, and has been practically the same.

It was evidently a feature of the city of which the inhabitants themselves were proud. These older residents whom I approached, whether Hindu or Mussalman, spoke of this fact with enthusiasm, and contrasted it with the bitterness of modern times. . . The art of living peacefully with neighbours of a different religion had reached (during Bahadur Shah's reign) a very high level.[6]

The age did have its proponents of traditionalist Islamic orthodoxy, but their hold was greatly weakened by men like Shah Waliullah, who was regarded the founder of the powerful reform movement within Islam, in India. The 'Protestant' movement which Waliullah initiated, at the end of the eighteenth century, encouraged a freedom of debate on religion, hitherto unknown. There were the so-called Wahabis guided by the writings of Syed Ahmad Barelavi and Shah Ismail; and there were the traditionalists staunchly opposing the Wahabis. Delhi became an important centre of theological research and enquiry, with religious beliefs not merely the preserve of the *mullahs,* but a topic of discussion for all educated Muslims. What is significant is that religious issues, and doctrines, even when argued with fervour, did not succeed in arousing passions prompting any violence or implacable hostilities. Ghalib was himself asked by one of his closest friends, Maulana Fazl-i-Haq, a leading traditionalist, to write a *masnavi* refuting Wahabi doctrines. Ghalib did, but his verse hardly mirrored Fazl-i-Haq's doctrinaire views on the question. Haq was not fully satisfied at Ghalib's effort, but, in character with the times, continued to remain a close friend.

The dominant theme of the age was the Sufi tradition, which, gaining in strength from the twelfth century onwards, had in Ghalib's time become an accepted way for Muslims to follow. The Sufi *tariqah,* with its emphasis on personalized spiritual experience, enabling direct communion with a pantheist, approachable, personal and immanent God, was naturally impatient with religious externalia. Ghalib made no secret of his deep contempt of ritualistic religion, and the *maulvis* who advocated it. In a letter of 1862, he angrily tears to shreds a *maulvi* who had conveyed a message to him to abstain from drinking, which remained a passion with Ghalib throughout:

'You see how he vouchsafes me drink? To make a name as a *maulvi* by teaching the banias and brats of Dariba, and to wallow in the problems (in Islamic observances) of menstruation and post-natal bleeding is one thing: and to study the works of the mystics and take into one's heart the essential truth of God's reality and His expression in all things, is another.'[7] Indeed the *maulvi* became the target of more than one diatribe and much literary satire. As it was a period of non-sectarianism, with Hindus and Muslims merging with ease, there was an extraordinary degree of casualness, even flippancy, towards the requirements of formal religion.

Ghalib was at his delightful best poking fun at the hypocrisy of the self-righteous *vayiz:*

The tavern door and the preacher
Are truly poles apart
All I know is I saw him enter
As I left to depart.[8]

Or, in a similar vein there is this couplet in Persian:

The devout one is not concerned
About the houri of paradise,
Except that his lustful desire might ravish her
Yet leave her virginity intact.[9]

At a more substantive level, his opposition was to use piety as a bargaining chip with the Almighty:

How can I believe
The devout in their austerity:
Not hypocritical—just too greedy
To get the fruits of their piety.[10]

There is a similar thought in his Persian collection:

For the devout one the exercise of prostration
Is, alas, his pretentious claim to a pious existence
Unless the devil robs him on the highway
He has no wish for an escort of angels.[11]

It was his conviction that man has direct access to a truly religious experience, by the very nature of his being, and through the unbounding compassion of the Supreme Being. To the spiritually evolved, the *form* of reverence was not important in the search for direct communion:

When affinity is strong, O Ghalib,
Be not punctilious for reverence;
Has thou not seen that the arch of the altar
Has its back towards the Kaaba.[12]

He believed that a preoccupation with religious externalia deadened sensitivity, bred bigotry, and stunted spiritual growth:

One who is drunk with the desire for recompense
Has to contend with paradise and hell
But he who craves only His munificent grace
Does not distinguish between the flame and the
    rose.[13]

And he left no one in doubt that it was the guardians of orthodoxy who were the main targets of his criticism:

Proud of what special precepts
Are the claimants of wisdom?
Too shackled they are
By daily ritual and custom.[14]

For himself, he proclaimed without fear the iconoclast's freedom:

I know the virtues of worship and devotion
But for such matters I have no inclination;
To Kaaba Ghalib with what face you will go
No trace of remorse if you ever show.[15]

Although it was known that Ghalib was born a Sunni, his pronouncements and lifestyle led to much speculation as to what exactly his religious standing was. In the circles of the court and the nobility he was suspected by some to be a Shia and by others to be a *Tafzili.** Ghalib himself revelled in this ambivalence. His ridicule of the demands of formal religion was a subject of much amusement. Not only did he not keep the Ramzan fast, but he could joke about it with others who devoutly did—including the king. He openly declared that since he drank wine he was but half a Muslim claiming that, where matters of religious convention were concerned, he had freed himself of any concern about what others might have to say about his behaviour.

Underlying this overt contempt for religious rituals was a profound eclecticism, a deep-seated conviction in the brotherhood of the human race, holding all men in the ontological sense to be symbols of the divinity and love of the one Almighty.

The philosophical counterpart of this vision was the doctrine of *Wahdah-al-wujud*—the Unity of Existence. For Ghalib it was a matter of genuine intellectual conviction:

> God is one, that is our faith;
> All rituals we abjure.
> 'Tis only when the symbols vanish
> That belief is pure.[16]

---

* One who, though not a Shia, acknowledges the pre-eminence of Ali.

In one of his letters he militantly announced that he regarded every man—Muslim, Hindu or Christian—to be his brother, adding for good measure that he did not care if others subscribed to such an approach or not. In another of his couplets he asserts:

> Steadfast devotion
> Is the foundation of all faith;
> If the Brahmin dies in the temple
> Bury him in the Kaaba.[17]

Or again,

> In the rosary or the sacred thread
> No special grasp is threaded;
> It is the devotion of the Sheikh and Brahmin
> That are to be tested.[18]

But perhaps the most lyrical example of his catholicity is his beautiful Persian poem—*Chirag-i-Dair*—extolling the glory of the temple city of Banaras!

> May heaven keep
> the grandeur of Banaras, arbour of this, meadow of
>   joy
> For oft returning souls
> Their journeys end.
> In this weary Temple-land of the world,
> safe from the whirlwind of Time,
> Banaras is forever spring,
> Where autumn turns
> Into the touch of sandal on fair foreheads,

Springtide wears the sacred thread of flower waves,
And the splash of twilight
Is the crimson mark of Kashi's dust on heaven's
    brow
The Kaaba of Hind, this conch-blowers dell;
Its icons and idols
Are made of the Light
That once flashed on Mount Sinai
These radiant, idolations naiads
Set the pious Brahmins afire
When their faces glow
Like moving lamps
On Ganga's banks.
Morning and moon-rise
My Lady Kashi
Picks up the Ganga-mirror
To see her gracious beauty
glimmer and shine.
Said I one night to a pristine seer
(who knew the secrets of whirling Time)
'Sir, you well perceive,
That goodness and faith,
Fidelity and love
Have all departed from the sorry land.
Father and son are at each other's throat;
Brother fights brother. Unity
And Federation are undermined.
Despite these ominous signs
Why has not doomsday come?
Why does not the Last Trumpet sound?
Who holds the reins of the final catastrophe?'
The hoary old man of lucent ken

Pointed towards Kashi and gently smiled.
'The Architect,' he said, 'is fond of this edifice
Because of which there is colour in life; He
would not like it to perish and fall.'
Hearing this, the pride of Banaras
Soared to an eminence
Untouched by the wings of thought.[19]

It is typical of Ghalib that he actually contemplated
settling down in Banaras. In a letter to his friend he
wrote, 'I wished I had renounced the faith, taken a
rosary in my hand, put a sectarian mark on my
forehead, tied a sacred thread round my waist and
seated myself on the bank of the Ganges so that I
could wash the contamination of existence away
from myself and like a drop be one with the river.'[20]
The synthesis is total; we see here the spiritual
pursuit totally liberated from the constraints and
narrowness of organized religion. The divisive walls
of religion have been levelled by the simple assertion
of their irrelevance. Symbols of differentiation have
been subsumed in a vision of humanity that transcends
labels of Hindu or Mussalman. In this secularism,
there is a conviction and an intellectual integrity that
alone could make it possible for Ghalib to proclaim:

In the Kaaba I will play the conch-shell*
In the temple I have draped the 'ahram'.[21]**

---

* Played by Hindus at the time of worship in a temple.
** Clothes worn by Muslims when on the Haj pilgrimage.

It can, of course, be argued that Ghalib's radical secularism was not fully mirrored by the man on the street. Undoubtedly, Ghalib did symbolize the most eclectic fringe, even within the Sufi spectrum. But it would not have been possible for him to openly declare his views and practise them, or achieve such a tremendous following as a poet, except in an age somewhat in tune with his beliefs. In times of fundamental discordance with his views it may have been impossible, for instance, for a Hindu, Munshi Hargopal Tufta, to become Ghalib's foremost *shagird* and closest friend. Nor would it have been possible for Ghalib to declare another Hindu—Shivji Ram Brahman—to be like a son to him; or for Bahadur Shah Zafar to appoint a Hindu convert to Christianity—Dr Chaman Lal—as his personal physician. In fact, it is said that when some people angrily complained to Bahadur Shah about Dr Chaman Lal's conversion, he retorted that there was nothing wrong with it.

This eclectic mood played a catalytic role in the development of the Urdu language. The Mughals had made Persian their court language, using it for administrative purposes as well. Persian was also the language of Islamic orthodoxy. But Persian never became the language of the common man and was not even spoken at home by the elite. The evolution of a language gaining from Persian, but drawing real substance from the idiom and vocabulary of the everyday language of the people, had been a continuous process. The Sufis had always preferred to use the spoken language of the masses to propagate their ideas.

In literature, the Deccan poet Wali (1668–1744), who is called the father of Urdu poetry, became the first to discard Persian in preference to Urdu. Other poets such as Hatim (b. 1669), Mir Dard (d. 1788), Mazhar (1700–81), Sauda(1730–80), Mir (1722–1810), Insha (d. 1817) and Nasikh (d. 1838) followed. The contribution of Mir and Sauda was particularly noteworthy. The brilliance of Sauda's satires and the pathos and imagery of Mir's love poems, showed the immense literary potential of Urdu for the first time. Mir took deliberate pride in asserting the validity and distinctiveness of Urdu as it had evolved into a spoken language in Delhi. It is said that once when approached in Lucknow to recite his poems, he refused saying that Lucknavis would not understand his poetry. When pressed, he retorted that only a knowledge of Urdu, as it was spoken on the steps of Jama Masjid at Delhi—a knowledge Lucknavis could never have—would enable them to understand what he wrote. This notwithstanding, the Nawabs of Oudh did extend valuable patronage, not only to the Urdu poets of Lucknow, but also to those like Mir of Delhi, who migrated there. In 1803, the Koran was translated, for the first time, from Persian into Urdu, a landmark event not only from the religious point of view but also for the impact it had on the acceptance of Urdu prose. Thus, at the beginning of the nineteenth century, Urdu had acquired both strength and credibility as a language. This development, coinciding with the social acceptance of the Sufi *tariqah* and the loosening hold of the Islamic orthodoxy, created the appropriate intellectual milieu for it to replace Persian as the *de jure lingua franca* of the Mughal court.

Undoubtedly, the psychological legacy of Persian
was still strong. Ghalib, for instance, continued to
stubbornly look upon Urdu as a plebeian trespasser
on the language of true Mughal tradition—Persian.
However, as the forces leading to the development of
Urdu had come to fruition in his time he ultimately
adopted it and became its most outstanding craftsman:

> To he who asks incredulously
> Can Urdu be envied by Persian?
> Recite to him once Ghalib's verse
> And say that yes, certainly.[22]

It would appear that by the 1850s Urdu had almost
wholly replaced Persian as the popular literary
medium. Farhatullah Baig, in his immortal classic—
Dilli ki Akhri Shama—(The Last *Mushairah* of Delhi),
which authentically reconstructs a *mushairah* at about
this time, comments on the audience's reaction to
Sehbai, the sole poet who recited a composition in
Persian: 'It (Sehbai's *ghazal*) received lavish praises
too but to be honest, the audience did not much relish
the Persian . . . those unfortunates who did not
understand Persian merely looked on. The fact is that
to force Persian poetry at an Urdu *mushairah* was not
a good idea at all.'[23]

Ghalib's contemporaries included such literary
luminaries as Zauq, Alawi, Azurda, Nayyir, Aish,
Momin, Shefta, Jauhar, Sehbai, Nazir Akbarabadi and
Tufta. Bahadur Shah writing under the *nom de plume*
of 'Zafar', was himself a poet of repute. In his younger
years his *ustad* was the famous poet Naseer; later he

is said to have consulted the poet Beqarar, until finally he turned to Ibrahim Zauq. After Zauq's death Ghalib was appointed the royal tutor in poetry. Under Zafar, the Mughal court became the pivot, guiding the efflorescence in Urdu writing. Regular poetic symposiums, *mushairahs,* were held at the palace twice a month, on the fifteenth and the twenty-ninth, when His Majesty prescribed the *zamin* for Persian and one for Urdu. Several princes were good poets, and special mention must be made of Mirza Fakhru, the second son of Zafar. Weekly *mushairahs* were also held at the Ghaziuddin *madrasa,* near Ajmeri Gate where Delhi College was located. The poet Mamnun's residence was also a regular rendezvous of poets.

Each established poet had his own devoted band of disciples or *shagirds.* Indeed, the *ustad–shagird* relationship had become an institution in itself. Prominent among Ghalib's *shagirds* were the poets Alai and Hargopal Tufta; Momin's disciples included Shefta, Tamkeen, Raqam and Haya; Veeran was Zauq's most devoted and abrasive student, forever ready to attack anyone who criticized his *ustad.* The writing and appreciation of Urdu poetry became essential learning for any aspirant to the cultured life. Not surprisingly, the *ustads* were inundated by verses for correction and comment. The correct writing of Urdu was a matter of intensive study and often bitter controversy. The rivalry between Ghalib—the Poet Laureate of the city—and Zauq, the king's *ustad,* was followed with lively interest by the entire city.

Elaborate protocol surrounded the commencing of *mushairahs,* with special attention paid to *nashist, nishast.*

A point of acrimony was who would begin and who would end the *mushairah*. The prescribing of the *tarah*—the meter or base line for a *mushairah*—was also the cause of controversy and dispute. In fact, these disputes became so virulent that Bahadur Shah had to discontinue his fortnightly *mushairahs*. There is no doubt that if one were to isolate a single symbol that could vividly represent Ghalib's era, it would be the all-pervasive ambience of Urdu *shairi*. And the fact that verses of leading poets were sung by bards and musicians in the streets is one indication that this *shairi* did not remain the passion of the cultured elite alone, but was enjoyed and comprehended by the common man. As Zakaullah informed C.F. Andrews—'be it the king or the beggar, everyone was a victim of the poetic muse'.

Farhatullah Baig's description of the preparations at the *haveli* of Mubarak-un-nissa—the venue of the last *mushairah* under Zafar—deserves to be quoted in full:

The entire house had been whitewashed with a mixture of lime and mica which caused the walls to glimmer. The low-lying courtyard had been so filled up as to raise it to the level of the plinth of the house. The platform was then laid out with wooden planks on which were spread cotton rugs. These in turn were covered with *chandni*. On all four sides of this platform was a border of expensive woollen carpets and rows of long upholstered cushions for seating the guests. There was such a profusion of chandeliers, candelabra, wall lamps, hanging lamps, Chinese lanterns and other lights that the house was converted into a veritable dome of light. Everything was elegant, in good taste and in its appointed place. In the dead centre of the middle row stood a small embroidered canopy of green velvet, supported on gold and silver-coloured posts fastened with green silk tent cords. In this pavilion was placed the green velvet embroidered seat with embroidered green cushions. On each of the four tent-posts was hung eight small silver lanterns. These lotus-shaped lights with glass globes were poised on the golden crests of green poles from which streamed garlands of *motiya,* which resembled a *sehra.* The middle strands of these flower curtains were gathered up and tied with gold cord tipped with brocaded gold tassels, in such a way as to form archways of flowers around the pavilion. Flower wreaths were hung on the walls on pegs and nails driven into the wall for the purpose. A white cloth, with embroidered green borders on all sides, was stretched across from one end to the other to make a white and green awning. From the centre of the roof were hung rows upon rows of jasmine garlands and streamers and these were fastened all round the walls of the canopy and created an umbrella of flowers. In one of the small courtyards there was provision for drinking water in new earthenware vessels and in pewter goblets cooled in saltpetre or rock salt. In another courtyard people were preparing *paan.* Neatly laid out in the kitchen were *huqqahs* and accessories. Everywhere servants in clean smart livery were standing respectfully and expectantly with folded hands, ready to serve the guests. The whole house was fragrant with musk, amber and aloes. Arranged in a row, at short intervals along the carpet, were *huqqahs*. The *huqqahs* were so burnished and brightly polished that it seemed they had just been bought from the market. In the space between the *huqqahs* were placed small tripods on which napkins made of *lalqand*, with alternating layers of flowers in between. Placed against each *khasdan* was a small boat-shaped dish with the traditional cardamom, betel-nut and roasted coriander seeds. In front of the chief throne-like seat (for the presiding poet) were set two silver candle-holders with camphor-scented candles and pale green shades made in the form of the lotus flower. Each candle-holder was placed in a small water basin perfumed with *kiyora* . . .[24]

Linguistic activity enlarged its base and area of impact with the introduction of a press for Persian and Urdu lithography in Delhi. Ghalib's Urdu *Diwan* was published in 1841 and his Persian *Diwan* in 1845. The fact that his Urdu *Diwan* went into a second edition in 1847 is proof not only of the popularity of his Urdu verse but also of the widening circle of literary appreciation. Some of India's earliest newspapers also appeared now. According to C.F. Andrews, the first Urdu newspaper was edited by one Maulvi Mohammed Baqir. Two others—the *Fawaid-ul-Nazarin* and the *Kiran-us-Sadai*, were edited by the noted scholar Master Ramchandra, who with Dr Chaman Lal, was one of the prominent Hindus to have converted to Christianity. The first paper in English was the *Delhi Gazette*. There is evidence that by the 1830s people had the choice of subscribing to more than one paper, and had begun to discriminate between a good and a bad one. A friend of Ghalib's wrote to him for help in enlisting subscribers, in Delhi, to a newspaper, *Aina-i-Sikandar,* to which Ghalib replied:

My friend, the sight of *Aina-i-Sikandar* brought lustre to my eyes, and its pure style threaded pearls upon the string of my gaze. Its reports are well written, its news succinct: the points it makes are pleasing to the mind, and the eye rejoices to read all that it writes. With all my heart and soul I obey your command, and intend to make every effort to secure the circulation of its pages. The people of the city feel strong dissatisfaction at the inaccuracy of the news that appears in *Jam-i-Jahan-numa*. It happens but rarely that the news which the editor of *Jam-i-Jahan-nuna* publishes this week is not declared false next week by this very same editor. One week he threads upon the string of writing this pearl, that before winter comes (the British) will declare war upon the ruler of Lahore; and two weeks later he writes that this news proved to be false. One week he gives the news that the mosque in Agra Fort and the Taj Mahal mausoleum have been sold for such-and-such a sum. Again two weeks later he writes that the authorities of the Council have declared this sale invalid.[25]

The failings of the *Jam-i-Jahan-numa* could not, however, insulate Ghalib from an increasingly contagious 'newspaper culture'. Newspapers began to be increasingly sought out for confirmation of rumours or speculation and in his letters Ghalib mentions his own proclivity to do this.

By mid-century, newspapers appear to have had the strength to incorporate newsworthy events from towns other than their own. Thus, *Ahsan-ul-Akhbaar* an Urdu newspaper of Bombay, published lengthy details of Ghalib's arrest in 1847 on charges of gambling. In Delhi itself, a contemporary newspaper expressed editorial indignation. *Sirajul Akhbaar,* a weekly newspaper, was published from the printing press in the palace, in the nature of a court bulletin. But it also carried reports from 'correspondents' as far away as Kabul and Dera Ghazi Khan, or commentaries on such relatively remote matters as the struggle between the French and the English in Cyprus. The reports were not always accurate but indicate the increasing ambit of news coverage by newspapers, and the widening scope of interest of Delhi citizens in events outside their immediate focus.

It is claimed that the establishment of 'British Peace' aided the resurgence of Urdu in Delhi, by preventing the siphoning of poetic talent to Lucknow and other cities. There is empirical evidence that the population of Delhi did increase after 1803, but the British impact on the intellectual milieu of the city can be identified in much more definitive ways. From their earliest days in India, the British had devoted their attention to setting up educational institutions, motivated primarily by a desire to enable British officers to learn the native language and culture, in order to consolidate colonial rule. These institutions would also facilitate the cultural colonization of the ruled, particularly its elite. Thus Warren Hastings established the famous *madrasa* at Calcutta in 1781, Sir Duncan founded the Hindu Sanskrit College at Banaras in 1791 and Lord Wellesley set up the Fort William College at Calcutta in 1800. By 1803, Dr John Gilchrist of the Fort William College had—with the use of Roman characters—already translated a selection of English stories into Hindustani, Persian, Arabic, Braj Bhasha, Bengali and Sanskrit. The Agra College was founded in 1823, and later universities were started in each of the Presidency provinces of Bombay, Bengal and Madras. In Delhi, a school functioning at Ghaziuddin *madrasa* since 1792 was refurbished, through special funds allotted by the British Committee of Public Instruction, to found the Delhi College.

From 1824 to 1857, Delhi College became a nodal point for the introduction of, what C.F. Andrews has called, the 'new learning'. Inevitably, the most obvious focus was linguistic. English classes were introduced in 1827, with a syllabus that included Goldsmith's *Traveller and Deserted Village,* Pope's *Essay on Man,* Milton's *Paradise Lost* and—in the highest grades—Shakespeare's plays, Bacon's *Advancement of Learning* and Burke's *Essays and Speeches.* The College also had a separate 'Oriental' section for Urdu, Arabic and Persian literature, which, by 1848, equalled the English section in the scope of its courses—and was extremely popular. Andrews observes: '. . . the Oriental Department . . . became very popular indeed. The classes, taught through the medium of Urdu, were not deserted for the new English studies. The standard reached in Persian and Arabic was often high.'[26] Indeed, some of the most outstanding literary names are associated with the Oriental section: Altaf Hussain Hali, the renowned Urdu poet; Nazir Ahmad, master of Urdu and Persian prose; Maulvi Ziyauddin, eminent Arabic scholar; Maulvi Zakaullah, historian and author of innumerable translations; and Muhammad Hussain Azad, author of *Khumbhan-e-Javed,* a work of literary criticism.

For several reasons, the educational renaissance associated with Delhi College was noteworthy more for the excitement it generated and the avenues it opened for scientific learning rather than literary activity. This is what distinguishes it from the 'Calcutta Renaissance' where the emphasis was more on literary studies. The first educational institutions in Calcutta, established with the primary aim of teaching 'native languages' to officers of the East India Company, had kindled a new interest in English poets and novelists, and the more scientific study of vernacular Bengali literature, Persian, Arabic and Urdu. This led to a literary efflorescence that went far beyond the limited Utilitarian concerns of British officials, to become the dominant cultural theme of the Bengali elite. In Delhi, however, the introduction of English classes was met with a reluctance, linked to the fear of Christian proselytization; this was only partially neutralized by the rich endowment, made for Delhi College, in 1829, by a leading nobleman of Lucknow, Nawab Itimadud-

Daulah. More importantly, the real resurgence of literary activity, culminating in the unprecedented popularity of Urdu, had *preceded* the founding of Delhi College. The College could only supplement an ongoing process, not initiate it. Also, the Mughal court, under Bahadur Shah Zafar, provided an institutional focus for literary pursuits that diluted the exclusive role the College could have played in a place such as Calcutta, where similar royal patronage was absent. Thus Delhi College really caught the imagination of the people for the windows it opened to western advances in scientific learning. English books on science were laboriously, but enthusiastically, translated page by page into Urdu—and copies circulated. Eager students commenced the publication of a monthly magazine printed at fourpence and exclusively devoted to the sciences. The literary confidence already gained by Urdu facilitated its transformation to a medium for the imparting of technical knowledge. First exposure to experiments in physics and chemistry, or to the application of mathematics, appears to have created an electric spark of excitement. C.F. Andrews records: 'By far the most popular side of the education offered in the old Delhi College was that which dealt with science . . . Munshi Zakaullah, in his old age, used to tell me with kindling eyes how eagerly these scientific lectures were followed, and how, after each lecture, the notes used to be studied, over and over again, and copied out by many hands. It was like entering into a wholly undiscovered hemisphere of the human mind . . .'[27]

Some of the Colleges' students distinguished

themselves later for their contribution to science. Master Ramchandra, a notable alumnus of Delhi College who had completed his education by winning scholarships and prizes, went on to become a Professor of Mathematics, with his work on differential calculus attracting attention in Europe. One of the first doctors in northern India, Dr Mukund Lal, widely respected for his knowledge of Western medicine, was an alumnus of the College. Another distinguished product was Sir Syed Ahmad Khan, who was equally at home in mathematics or archaeology, and later founded the Muslim Anglo-Oriental College at Aligarh in 1877. Students seemed to have had a genuine respect for faculty members and they, in turn, appear to have been greatly involved in the progress of their eager students. There is evidence that, Taylor, the Principal of the College, specially inspired his pupils. Others such as the Frenchman Boutrous and the German Sprenger, were also looked up to with affection. About Sprenger, Emily Bayley, recalled in her memoirs: '. . . a very curious German, Dr. Sprenger, was the Principal (of Delhi College). His wife, also a worthy, but common, German whom I knew, told me she was obliged to hide her husband's trousers to prevent his going out of an evening and leaving her alone.'[28]

Certainly, Western scientific beliefs were not without detractors in the city. This was inevitable since the 'new learning' could not remain quarantined within the College premises. Excited students often gathered at home to continue their scientific discussions; or to perform new experiments in the presence of parents quite at sea about what was going on. Master Ramchandra wrote in his memoirs: 'The doctrines of ancient philosophy taught through the medium of Arabic were thus cast in the shade of the more reasonable and experimental theories of modern science. The old dogma, for instance, that the earth is the fixed centre of the universe, was generally laughed at by the higher students of the Oriental, as well as those of the English Department of the Delhi College. But the learned men, who lived in the city, did not like this innovation on their much-loved theories of the ancient Greek Philosophy which had been cultivated among them for many centuries past.'[29] The fears— if not the dogmas—of the orthodox and the elderly were not entirely without basis. There was, at this time, a connection made between the new ideas introduced by the British, and Christian proselytization. The Baptist Missionary Society had opened business in 1818, and when the 'Society for the Propagation of the Gospel' was founded in 1852 fewer attempts were made to conceal its real intention. Even the eclectic Ghalib took note of the growing influence of the missionaries when he wrote about their activities:

If faith holds me back
Disbelief tugs at me;
The Kaaba is behind me
The church ahead of me.[30]

The orthodox thus had reason to look upon the 'new learning' as a devious means to destabilize established beliefs, with the aim of winning converts. The fact that Master Ramchandra—one of the most well-known and brilliant votaries of 'new learning'—had converted to Christianity, seemed to vindicate their fears. Not surprisingly, they tended to look askance at the gullibility of some of their younger brethren. A contemporary Britisher has recorded, perhaps in deliberately caricatured terms that dramatize 'native' ignorance and superstition, how a Nawab from Moradabad reacted to the mention of Copernicus.

And do you suppose, sir, that I would put the evidence of one of your *Doorbeens* (telescopes) in opposition to that of the holy prophet? No, sir, depend upon it that there is much fallacy in a telescope—it is not to be relied upon. I have conversed with many excellent European gentlemen; and their great fault appears to me to lie in the implicit faith they put in these telescopes—they hold their evidence above that of the prophets, Moses, Abraham, and Elijah! It is dreadful to think how much mischief these telescopes may do! No sir, let us hold fast by the prophets; what they tell us is the truth, and the only truth that we can entirely rely upon in this life. I would not hold the evidence of all the telescopes in the world as anything against one word uttered by the humblest of the prophets named in the Old or New Testament, or the Holy Koran. The prophets, sir, keep to the prophets, and throw aside your telescopes—there is no truth in them: some of them turn people upside down and make them walk upon their heads; and yet you put this evidence against that of the prophets.[31]

As we've seen earlier it was fear of Christian proselytization that made orthodox reaction more vehement, deliberately ostrich-like; otherwise, the same ethos which had allowed Urdu to supersede Persian, or led religious eclecticism to hold such unprecedented sway, would also have worked in favour of the new science. In fact there is evidence that notwithstanding orthodox reservations, the impact of Western scientific learning was widespread, even if some of those so influenced were not as demonstrably effusive about it as Master Ramchandra or Munshi Zakaullah. In the early 1850s Syed Ahmad Khan was bringing out an edited version of the *Ain-i-Akbari*—Abul Fazl's classic on Mughal administration in Akbar's time. Ghalib, along with other prominent men in the city, was approached to contribute an introduction. But Ghalib considered the expending of energy on the *Ain-i-Akbari* a futile wallowing in the past. Hence he told Sir Syed: 'Look at the Sahibs of England . . . They have gone far ahead of our oriental forebears. Wind and wave they have rendered useless. They are sailing their ships under fire and steam. They are creating music without the help of the *mizrab* (plucker). With their magic, words fly through the air like birds. Air has been set on fire . . . Cities are being lighted without oil lamps. This new law makes all other laws obsolete. Why must you pick up straws out of old, time-swept barns while a treasure-trove of pearls lies at your feet?'[32] In times when an exaltation of the past was instinctive, Ghalib's response had certainly something to do with the influence of Western

knowledge and science, and the contempt for all things
antiquarian which its votaries advocated.

***

Purely in physical terms, the British presence in Delhi
was sparse. The British Resident lived outside the city
walls and administered the city with a handful of
British civilian officers. British army officers and the
troops they commanded were very discreetly
quartered, out of sight, on the Ridge. This certainly
enabled those who wanted to believe that nothing had
changed, to continue believing it. But, in actuality,
the British impact on the psyche of the city was
palpable and (with power backing it) difficult to ignore.
When the British Resident Thomas Metcalfe 'Sahib'
died (1853), Ghalib could not but note in a letter that
one lakh people attended his funeral. The official
residence of the British Assistant Resident was over
the principal gateway of the Red Fort, a vantage
point whose symbolic significance could not but be
noticed by the Delhiwallah. The British Resident
himself lived outside the Kashmiri Gate, in a splendid
mansion—'Metcalfe House', whose extensive grounds
bordered the Jamuna. The judge, the doctor, the
chaplain, a few army officers and a handful of British
officials, assisting the Resident in administration,
constituted the cream of British society. Below this
charmed circle were the merchants, bankers and
subordinate staff at the administrative level. In a class
by themselves were adventurers such as the famous
Colonel James Skinner—born of a Scottish father and

a Rajput mother—whose flamboyance, and loyalty to the British cause, invested him with social standing—notwithstanding his mixed parentage. Members of Colonel Skinner's irregular cavalry—'Skinner's Horse' conspicuous in their yellow caftans, red turbans and *cummerbunds*—about whom Bishop Heber exclaimed 'the most showy and picturesque cavaliers I have seen since I was in the South of Russia'—were a familiar sight in Ghalib's Delhi. Colonel Skinner built the St James' Church at Kashmiri Gate, which became the most important church of the Christian community in Delhi. But for all this, British social acceptance of Skinner was peripheral and not without a discernible trace of condescension. Emily Bayley records in her memoirs: 'Colonel Skinner was a man of dark blood, and his wife was a native lady, and their children were all, of course, very dark in complexion, and spoke English with an extraordinary accent, and the whole family was a marvellous revelation to anyone fresh from England . . . although they looked upon themselves as English people and held a prominent position in Delhi society, they had very little education and were more native than English in their ways.'[33] This derisive condescension was apparently directed towards all Anglo-Indians, who remained perpetual but unsure aspirants for British social acceptance. The Reverend David Thompson, although held in 'great esteem' by Thomas Metcalfe, was noticed by Emily to be 'very dark, having a great deal of native blood' in his veins, which accounted for him and his family being in 'utter ignorance of English customs as regards dress'.[34]

Another important member of this community, Mrs Forster, the wife of a celebrated officer, Colonel Forster, and her sister, Mrs Fuller, although 'excellent old ladies' were observed as 'being half-castes'. . . 'dark in complexion, (speaking) English with a very curious accent' and having a tendency to wear dresses 'made very like bed-gowns'.[35]

Some of the peripheral British members lived in Daryaganj, but the main British-Christian enclave came up to the north of the city, in the vicinity of Kashmiri Gate. The house of the Resident Commissioner occupied justifiable pride of place. Other imposing buildings such as Ludlow Castle, built by the surgeon Dr Ludlow, or St James', Church, built by Skinner were also noticeable. An arsenal and a post office were built behind the church. Some British officials also rented houses just inside the walled city, in the Kashmiri Gate area. The British thus 'developed a miniature metropolitan life of their own, with the Resident (later Commissioner and Agent) as its centre, Ludlow Castle as its Buckingham Palace, Metcalfe House as its Windsor, the Dilkusha at Mehrauli (Thomas Metcalfe's country retreat near the Qutab) as its Sandringham, and St. James' Church in Kashmiri Gate for its cathedral'.[36]

The British attempted to duplicate, in Delhi, the norms of social intercourse then prevailing in England. Every year, on Queen Victoria's birthday, there was a ball held at the 'Assembly Rooms'; every month the Resident hosted a sit-down dinner for twelve or sixteen, with service in Derby or Worcester china; formal social visits were exchanged at a fixed time before lunch, and there were rigorous conventions as regards dress, which, more often than not, confused the 'half-castes'——Emily's phrase for the Anglo-Indians. To these were added certain inevitable elements of British colonial life, such as the congregation in the cantonment to hear the military band play. On these occasions, gentlemen in formal attire would move from one carriage to another making social conversation with the ladies.

But although the cultural umbilical cord with 'home' was sought to be assiduously preserved, the 'nativizing' influence was obvious. Sir Thomas Metcalfe's clothes may have been sent out regularly every year from Pulford in St James' Street, or he may have got out a box of books from England twice a year, but every morning after breakfast, his *hookah* with a stand of solid silver, was brought in and placed behind his chair. Much later his daughter would still recall its musical gurgling vividly. Keeping in mind Indian weather conditions, his house had a *taikhana,* and a *chabootra* on which he sat in the evenings amusing himself with the pranks of his pigeons, of which he had quite a number. Like many among the Indian nobility, he too built a country house outside the city, and gave it, significantly enough, a name in Urdu— Dilkusha. Thomas Metcalfe's elder brother, Charles, who was twice Resident of Delhi, had his country retreat at Shalimar Bagh, where he is said to have built a house for his Indian family to live in. Colonel Skinner's town house at Kashmiri Gate for all its Anglican pretensions, had *hamam ghars* in the Mughal fashion and a *zenana* unmistakably 'native' in style.

The institution of the harem was easily borrowed; the two Metcalfe brothers—whose Victorian morality was a trifle more inflexible—were more restrained; but their other peers were nothing less than flamboyant in this regard. The French traveller Jacquemont, who visited Delhi at this time, has recorded that William Fraser, British Resident in the 1830s, and a friend of Ghalib's: 'has six or seven legitimate wives, but they all live together, some fifty leagues from Delhi and do as they like. He must have as many children as the king of Persia, but they are all Moslems or Hindus according to the religion and caste of their mammas . . .'[37] Sir David Ochterlony, twice Resident of Delhi, had thirteen wives, and Delhi residents looked on with scarcely concealed amusement—when all thirteen came out on a procession of elephants for an outing—a spectacle Ghalib may well have seen.

Each British *burra sahib* had a horde of servants—peons, *hurkaras, chobdars, huqqabardars, khansamas,* head bearer, *jamadar, malis, dhobis, chowkidars,* etc., prompting a newly arrived British merchant to comment that English residents in India, 'have servants to put on their stockings. I am only surprised that they do not keep men to masticate their food for them.'[38] An assumption of nawabi mannerisms was thus not surprising, particularly in an alien milieu where the very physical distance from 'home' helped erode inhibitions against behavioural deviations. A knowledge of the local language, customs and lifestyle was also good colonial policy—and certainly much of the 'nativization' was rationalized by the British on this score. But there was an additional factor: in the initial stages at least the British looked up with genuine respect to the authentic culture of the city and civilization they ruled. Colonel Sleeman, a British official, who visited Delhi in 1836, wrote:

On the faculties and operations of the human mind, on man's passions and affections, and his duties in all relations of life, the works of Imam Mahomed Ghuzallee and Nirseerooddeen Jansee, hardly yield to those of Plato and Aristotle, or to those of any other authors who have ever written on the same subjects in any country. These works . . . with the didactic poems of Sadee, are the great 'Persian spring' of moral instruction, from which the Mahomedan delights to 'drink deep' from infancy to old age, and a better spring it would be difficult to find in the works of any other three men.'[39]

Reading Persian classics was, for Charles Metcalfe, a relaxation. When transferred from the Residentship of Delhi to that of Hyderabad, he recalled with nostalgia; 'the ruins of grandeur that extend for miles on every side . . . The palaces crumbling into dust, the vast mausoleums of Delhi', and confessed 'that these things cannot be looked at with indifference'.[40] William Fraser knew Urdu and Persian like a native and had an excellent library of Persian and Arabic books. Many among the British composed Persian and Urdu couplets; some even adopted *takhalluses* of their own such as General Joseph Bensley 'Fana', George Puech 'Shor', and Alexander Heatherley 'Azad'. Others, such as Dr Howard and Dr Hoey, continued the work of Dr John Gilchrist—the original British pioneer of Urdu learning—and became noted Urdu scholars.

It is significant that the Indian elite did not seek to imitate British lifestyles. There was, of course, the odd exception, such as Prince Mirza Babur, a younger brother of Zafar. He wore European clothes, built a European-style house behind the 'Rang Mahal' in the Red Fort, and provided much material to wits in the city by driving around in an English coach, dressed in top boots and a European uniform with stars on both breasts. As a class the Anglo-Indians, and to a lesser extent the occasional middle-class converts to Christianity, were the others who sought to consciously adopt British mannerisms; but, in general, the life-styles of the Indian elite persisted fairly unchanged along established traditional grooves. 'Ghalib, Momin, and Zauq, to mention only the leading poets of the period . . . lived and moved and had their being in a perfectly insulated medium . . . and should be treated as the last representatives of the aristocratic tradition represented by Mughal civilization'.[41] To the extent that the British presence was unavoidable, it was acknowledged; but it never seriously threatened—at a socio-cultural level—the self-assured, indigenous ethos of the city. Many Indians did learn English at the Delhi College; but this was in addition to a full grounding in all aspects of traditional education, and pursued generally to further their employment prospects.

In these early years, the British were themselves somewhat swept away by the encapsulating ambience, the *tehzib* of an evanescent Urdu culture that seemed to mesh so effortlessly with the lifestyle of the Indian nobility. It is for this reason that, initially, the Indian *umara* and the British interacted with a certain equality, even camaraderie, meeting over dinners or other social engagements, or fraternizing through common membership in institutions such as the Delhi Bank, and the Archaeological Society. Ghalib himself was on familiar terms with many important British officials, and had particularly cordial relations with William Fraser. But the relationship was not entirely smooth. As arbiters in matters of civil disputes, British administrators frequently aroused considerable animosities. The sensational murder, in 1835, of Ghalib's friend and admirer Fraser at the behest of a prominent nobleman Shamsuddin, who was aggrieved at Fraser's espousal of his brother's claims in a property dispute, is a dramatic case in point. The British did absorb the flavour of the Indian cultural milieu, but even the most well disposed among them could but partially synthesize it into a true understanding of the carefully evolved and time-honoured etiquettes and conventions of Indian society. During the great famine of 1837, Thomas Metcalfe refused to force grain dealers to reduce prices as this would be contrary to the Bengal Regulations; but the Delhi citizens believed that a ruler needed to dispense justice, not blindly follow the letter of some legislation. The basic clash of two different value systems remained, even in non-political spheres. Hence Thompson, the Provincial Secretary, could not understand why he should receive Ghalib, as always, at the door, when on this occasion Ghalib was coming to see him as an applicant for a job. Ghalib, on his part, as a member of the nobility, could not fathom Thompson's boorishness in not fulfilling the mandatory courtesies. In the face of this infringement, the job was of little significance. It is said that when Nawab Shamsuddin—sentenced to death for the murder of William Fraser—requested the British that he be allowed to wear personal clothes for his execution the request was refused. The British became the purveyors of a new public morality and ethics, contextual in the British situation, but very often foreign in the Indian context. In many cases the principles underlying these ideas were those of a modern society; but, inspired by the Utilitarian impatience for 'reform', they were applied with an evangelical inflexibility, insensitive to a society having its own well-developed and finely tuned norms of behaviour. In 1847 Ghalib was arrested on charges of gambling and sentenced to a fine of Rs 200 and six months of hard labour. The Indian nobles were perplexed about the exceptionally harsh punishment meted out. Ghalib knew the British Sessions Judge who tried the case quite well; but he was genuinely bewildered when the judge acted as if he didn't know him. The newfound British emphasis on 'correctness' of behaviour was linked to a fundamental change in their attitude to India—that became increasingly pronounced in the years leading to 1857. The foundations of the strong ideological dismissal of everything 'native' had been laid in England by the Evangelists Charles Grant and William Wilberforce, and other members of the Clapham sect.

Their main aim was to prove the need for Christian rule, as a cleaning agent, to rid a degraded and sunken India of its overwhelming 'moral' evil. The Utilitarian credo, espoused by James Mill and his son John— both of whom were employees of the East India Company, provided philosophical reinforcement to such a bias. The earlier relaxed relationship with the Indian elite was now to be frowned upon. Even the more favoured such as Begum Samru, who had converted to Christianity, and had entertained Lord Lake himself at her *kothi* (the present Bhagirath Palace)—and whose parties were popular events with the British—was considered not exactly fit for the British to fraternize with. '. . . it is strange . . . to find an enlightened British community, the victors of the soil, doing homage and seeking favours at her (Begum Samru's) footstool, or even condescending to partake of her hospitality' was the remark of an Englishman at this time,[42] and rather appropriately sums up the new British outlook. In a far cry from the extract of Colonel Sleeman's memoirs, quoted earlier, Lord Macaulay now dismissed Indian culture as consisting of little else than 'medical doctrines that would disgrace an English farrier—Astronomy, which would (be laughed at by) girls at an English boarding school—History, abounding with kings thirty feet high, and reigns thirty thousand years long—and Geography, made up of seas of treacle and butter'.[43]

When Ghalib was still in his teens, Charles Metcalfe, during his first tenure as British Resident, had promulgated the abolishment of *sati* and capital punishment. The latter appears to have been motivated both by humanitarian considerations and policy: capital punishment had to be confirmed by the Mughal king and its abolishment took away one more aspect of authority from him. In general, the British administration did not immediately attempt any radical restructuring of existing institutions; but some of the 'innovations' they brought in did create ripples in the ebb and flow of the city's life. One such ripple was the introduction of income tax in the 1850s. Ghalib refers to this in a letter of 1853:

> . . . An epidemic is raging in the city. That is, the (East India) Company's agent has examined the papers of past years to see who owes dues to the government, and has presented a demand for them. In fact, 'demand' is too mild a word. He is fully determined to exact them. Among others, he found that I too owed dues—five hundred rupees and eight annas—and demanded this sum on pain of imprisonment. I'd be hard put to it to raise even the eight annas, where am I to find the five hundred rupees?[44]

Another 'innovation' that made its impact on everyday life was that of the 'post office', particularly so for a person like Ghalib who was a prolific letter-writer. That there were teething problems, before this institution stabilized, is evident from Ghalib's frequent jibes at its working:

> What do you think of the state of the British postal services? I don't know what innovations they've

introduced, but all organization is at an end and you simply can't place any reliance on it . . . Complaints have come from Meerut too, and one hears the same thing in letters from Agra. So far no letter of mine has gone astray, but in a general epidemic who is safe . . .?'[45]

Displaying the same ingenuity that harassed consumers in Delhi today are prone to develop in the face of shoddy services, Ghalib came up with a simple stratagem.

'Am sending this letter unstamped,' he told Tufta, 'so that it reaches you safely. Half an anna is nothing but the *Dak* people treat unstamped letters as urgent and despatch them quickly. Post paid is delayed.'[46]

When in 1854, the British introduced the more impersonal letter-box, an indication that postal traffic had considerably increased, Ghalib's reaction was one of indignation and suspicion:

The post office department has gone all to pieces . . . Now they've put a big box in the post office. It has an open mouth, and anyone who wants to post a letter can go and drop it in the box and come away. No receipt, no stamp, no evidence of posting. God knows whether the letter will be despatched or not . . . And if it doesn't arrive, the sender has nothing in writing to base a claim on— not, that is, unless he pays four annas extra and sends it registered; and we send off letters all over the place practically every day. Where are we going to get eight annas and more a week to register them all? . . . In short, sending off a letter is a headache; it's asking for trouble . . . It's like shooting an arrow in a dark room. If it hits, it hits, and if it misses, it misses.[47]

There was a distinct improvement in law and order. The depredations of the neighbouring Gujar tribes was brought under control. The Assistant Resident was put in charge of the city police, although the Mughal institution of the *kotwal* and his twelve *thanedars* was retained intact, with the sweepers continuing to be the main source of police intelligence. 'We considered ourselves as safe there (Delhi) as if we were in London,' recalled Emily Bayley.[48] Outside the palace, the British assumed judicial powers, setting up separate civil and criminal courts. The British assumption of administrative and judicial control had an inevitable impact on traditional institutions, and while some of them were retained in form, there was a substantive modification or diminution in their actual role or function. A recent study concludes that 'by 1850, the framework of institutions and moral ideas which had been the framework for the ideal Indo-Muslim city was widely in disarray. The *kotwal* had been reduced to an inferior officer of police, the *qazi* was a little more than a glorified registrar, the religious sensibilities of learned Islam no longer bore on the officers of government through the *mufti*.'[49]

The mutilation of the old system for dispensation of justice was particularly noticeable. Justice was removed from the familiar environment of the village panchayats, and depersonalized through an institutionalized system of appeal—where no account could be taken of a litigant's locally known reputation, background and character. The discovery of the truth became less important than how it was proved or disproved. Once this fact dawned on litigants, they realized that witnesses could be found in plenty, who, with a straight face, would testify to anything in court, for a fee. Litigation, especially that relating to land disputes and moneylending, steadily increased, and with it perjury by witnesses. In fact the amoral witness became a distinct social character of the times, so much so that it was considered unbecoming for respectable people to testify in court. Ghalib, brought to court several times for defaulting on credit payments, and once on a gambling charge, must have known this situation well. Given the costs and complexity of the British court system, criminal cases were rarely reported, being decided, as far as possible, locally through the traditional village tribunals or the intervention of the *mukhiya* or village chief. However, an interesting by-product of the populace's interaction with the British administrative and legal system was the incorporation into Arabic and Persian of names of British institutions and legal procedures. Constructions such as *amla-i-konsil* for Staff of Council, *kaghzat-i-stamp* for stamp papers, *daftar-i-residency* for residence office, *report-i-sanawi* for Second Report, *report-i-muqaddama* for Report on Law Suit, etc., came into common usage. These are found in abundance in Ghalib's own petitions and memorials to the British in connection with his pension case.

A fundamental aspect of the British administration in India was revenue collection. It is not my intention here to discuss the British revenue system, except to make the assertion that over assessment, coupled with severity in collection, greatly impoverished the peasantry in Delhi. Several couplets of Ghalib, in both his Persian and Urdu *Diwan,* use imagery that reflects the hardships being faced by the farmer. But essentially Ghalib's concern was with the city; it provided both the social framework and the most appropriate setting for his personality. His cultural conditioning was 'narrow-mindedly, obstinately urban. It regarded the city as an oasis in a wilderness, the city wall as the bulwark of culture against a surrounding barbarism.'[50] The physical features of Delhi buttressed such an approach. The sophisticated urbanity, the effortless cultural fluency drawing confidently from universally recognized norms of social behaviour and conventions, held sway within the protective city walls. Outside, the city culture gave way, dramatically and drastically, to the rustic ethos of the countryside; green fields stretched out from the very edge of Ajmeri Gate and Braj Bhasha and Khari Boli replaced Urdu and Hindustani. Heber speaks of an overpowering feeling of 'desolation' as he approached Delhi from Agra. 'The ruins really extended as far as the eye could reach, and our track wound among them all the way . . . Except ruins and sun-burnt rocks, there is nothing to be seen without the ramparts of Delhi.'[51] Charles Trevelyan, who had worked as Assistant Resident under Metcalfe in 1827, made a similar observation, 'The population of Delhi is crowded within the walls,

around which immense fields of ruins extend . . .'[52]
In the political situation that formed the backdrop to
Ghalib's life, law and order conditions were such that
to venture too far from the city was inviting danger.
Zakaullah recalled that, 'the city gates were shut each
night and opened again every morning . . . (People)
rarely went outside, except either to visit the tomb
of some saint, or to go on a long distance journey.'[53]
The situation improved under the British; very
tentatively a few suburbs came up outside the city
walls, primarily to the north of the city, outside the
Kashmiri Gate, where the British colonial settlement
had been established. The security of the environment
also stabilized and Ghalib, in fact, undertook a journey
up to Calcutta; but travelling conditions were arduous,
and it is not surprising that in references to this
journey Ghalib recalls only the cities—Lucknow,
Banaras and Calcutta.

Before 1857, the British made but fledgling attempts
to introduce municipal administration or inculcate
municipal consciousness in the modern sense. Town
duties were proposed, in 1823, by Governor-General
Amherst, to pay for 'local improvements' but were
soon withdrawn; a Local Roads Committee was
instituted to look to road repair but remained
hamstrung for shortage of funds. In 1857, *Sirajul Akhbar,*
the weekly court bulletin, was still suggesting that a
petition be addressed to the Collector, asking that 7
per cent of the toll collected should be used for upkeep
and maintenance of pucca roads. Often local enthusiasm
outstripped British interest in furthering municipal
projects, as in the case of the construction of a

dispensary, where local subscriptions were almost four times the amount contributed by the British authorities.[54] The occasional repair and cleaning of mosques, or a punitive demolition of shops encroaching on roads, were other examples of British civic concerns. But clearly, the institutionalization of full-fledged municipal activity was not a British priority until after 1857—and then the motivating factor was to make the city 'safe' for British rule. It is interesting that, in spite of his financial penury, Bahadur Shah sought to continue the Mughal tradition of royal initiative in construction and upkeep and maintenance of important buildings in the city. An inscription, in the mosque at Qudsiya Bagh, states that the mosque was repaired by Bahadur Shah in 1833–34. The Sunehri Masjid was repaired by him in 1852. He also designed and constructed Moti Mahal, Hira Mahal and Zafar Manzil in the Hayat Baksh garden, inside the Fort, a *haveli* for his wife Zinat Mahal in the Lal Kuan Bazaar in the city and two gardens—one near the palace and the other in Shahdara. It would appear that in the early years of their rule, the British sought—perhaps unconsciously—to emulate this Mughal tradition. Individual officers built mansions and country-houses and some even spent their own money to plant trees along the Chandni Chowk.

As a city, Delhi symbolized one thing above all—continuity. The original features of the planned city, built by Shah Jahan, were discernible, but heavily covered over by the natural process of acculturation which is the inevitable feature of all historical cities. Shah Jahan built the two principal streets emanating from the palace—Chandni Chowk and Faiz Bazaar—intersecting each other at right angles. He also built the encircling city wall (although this was considerably strengthened subsequently), and provided for an adequate water supply and a functional drainage system. Subsequently, *havelis, katras, kuchas, mohallas,* bazaars, *waras, chowks* and gardens came up at different intervals, not as per any master plan, but in tandem with the city's evolution and growth. For instance, Chawri Bazaar, and the Marathi suffix *waras* denoting quarters of occupational groups (Baidwara, Naiwara, Dhobiwara, etc.) were the contribution of the Marathas, in the brief period when the city was under their control. The Marathas left but the city absorbed their impact, integrating it in a multifaceted but unbroken continuum. The artificial and synthetic features of many modern cities were absent in Ghalib's Delhi. Mir, the great poet of the eighteenth century, rhapsodized in verse that no city could equal the uniqueness of Delhi. Every landmark recalled an authentic association with individuals or events not yet erased from memory or lore: Habash Khan Ka Phatak, Bangash Ki Serai, Haveli Haidar Quli, Qasim Jan Ki Gali, Jarnail Bibi Ki Haveli, Begum Ka Bagh, Kucha Ghasi Ram, Namak Haram Ki Haveli, etc.

In Ghalib's time, the population of the city had decreased, due to migration caused by repeated plunder and invasion, in the preceding century. There are no reliable figures, but estimates vary between 100,000 and 150,000) from 1800 to 1857. The British claimed that after they established control, the population began to increase. Even if this was so, fewer people lived in Delhi in Ghalib's age than they did a century ago, in Emperor Aurangzeb's time. It is instructive to compare Delhi's population with Lucknow, which as per the British census, totalled over 350,000 in the 1850s, more than twice the size of Delhi. It would appear, therefore, that in relative terms, Delhi was not one of the larger cities (Calcutta, Bombay and Madras were even larger than Lucknow)—and this probably contributed, in Ghalib's time, to the particular Delhi ambience of a greater familiarity between the city and its inhabitants. In a letter to his *shagird* Tufta, Ghalib asserted confidently that although he had recently shifted residence, this was not important; to reach him letters need merely be addressed: Asadullah, Delhi.

The city had its problems: Ali Mardan's canal, built during Shah Jahan's rule, and the city's principal source of water, had dried up. Charles Metcalfe repaired and reopened it, and, on 30 May 1820, for the first time in eighty years, the water of the canal once again gurgled its way through the city—from Najafgarh to the Fatehpuri mosque, through Chandni Chowk and on to the Red Fort. The citizens of Delhi greeted the clean water with flowers and *ghee*. Once again the city's many gardens could be irrigated, the fountains could function, and the people were assured a supply of fresh water. But the jubilation was short-lived; the canal was tapped so heavily upstream by farmers, its flow dwindled in the city. The stagnant waters led to silting, which, together with clumsy attempts by the British to repair the Shahjahani drains, distorted the drainage system, preventing the rainwaters from flowing out, thus causing severe flooding in the city. With so much standing water, the incidence of malaria greatly increased. And the problem of water supply remained, since the city wells had been neglected; the situation would become particularly acute (as it does even now) in summer, and then water was brought in goat-skins from the Jamuna and sold in the bazaars.

Bishop Heber, sojourning in Delhi on the eve of the new year of 1825, has remarked in his journal: 'Its (Delhi's) principal streets are really wide, handsome, and for an Asiatic city, remarkably clean . . .'[55] Emily Bayley has also recorded: 'I used to enjoy driving through the streets of Delhi as everything was new and striking; the buildings of marble and red sandstone were so magnificent, the shops were so quaint, the colours of the cotton cloths hanging from the windows and across the streets were so gorgeous, the costumes so picturesque, and the crowds were so extraordinarily thick . . .,'[56] It would be unwise to generalize from these accounts about the condition of the city as a whole. At about this time, another European visiting another historic city in northern India, Lucknow, has commented: 'When visited in detail, the gorgeousness of the picture is obscured by the more than ordinary degree of dirt, filth . . . placed in juxtaposition with its grandest features: the lanes leading from the principal avenues are ankle deep in mud . . .'[57] *Mutatis mutandis,* the remark could as well apply to Delhi. Zakaullah reminisced that, 'inside the city, the ordinary roads and by-lanes were full of holes. They regularly became a mass of mud during each rainy season, and the people used to get along the sides close to the shop fronts on stones which stood out above the mud . . . The dust in the dry weather was more trying than the rain.'[58] Colonel Sleeman, who visited Delhi in the 1840s, lamented that, 'no place in the world is, I suppose, more infested by them (flies) than Delhi at present . . .'[59] In 1854, an epidemic of virulent and recurring fever convulsed Delhi; Ghalib noted that almost every family was down with it and there had been some deaths too. Boils (the Delhi Sore) and malaria were the most prevalent diseases. Arif, Ghalib's nephew whom he had adopted as a son, died in 1852 when still young and so did Arif's wife. Tuberculosis appears to have been the killer in their case. Two years later Ghalib's entire household, including Hussain Ali, Arif's son, fell seriously ill. From Ghalib's description of his wife's symptoms—a fit of shivering with high fever at noon each day—it would appear the malaise was malaria, and apparently in epidemic form. Ghalib himself was afflicted with the Delhi Sore. This was to seriously incapacitate him in his last years, but in 1857 he could speak of it lightly: The two boils on his feet, he quipped, provided a lame excuse to excuse himself from accompanying Zafar for the annual *sair* at the Qutab.

The city had its *hakims*, who followed the *yunani* school of medicine, locally called *tibbia*. The most famous of them lived on the street Ballimaran, off Chandni Chowk, where Ghalib himself lived as a tenant of Hakim Mohammad Khan. Imamuddin Khan appears to have been Ghalib's favoured *hakim* for quite some time; but later he began to consult—and not only for medical purposes—Hakim Ahsanullah Khan, physician to Zafar and an important functionary of the royal court. Purging, dietary regimens, and traditional home remedies were the most popular cures for all ailments. Ghalib was quite knowledgeable in this field. He had carefully studied the various *tibbia* manuals and was fond of prescribing remedies to his friends and relatives, urging them on to try goat whey or the extracts of *neem* leaves or *chappatis* made of gram, seldom hesitating to admonish them when he felt they were not following the regimen properly.

Medical facilities for the British were far from satisfactory. There were no English chemists; medicines procured from England and not always in stock, were distributed by the British, free of cost, to officers and civilians. Emily Bayley was amazed and disgusted on getting a dose of senna in a black bottle, and huge pills sent in a rough wooden box.[60] She also complained that Dr Ross, the British Civil Surgeon, was rather fond of curing pains and aches by sending leeches across. For the Britishers, the biggest enemy was the heat. 'It is so very HOT, I do not know how to spell it large enough,' the loquacious Emily Eden (sister of Governor-General Lord Auckland), wrote soon after her arrival in India, in 1835.[61] *Punkahs* were the traditional answer to counter it. *Tattis*—screens made out of the sweet smelling *khus khus* grass—were also a must. These were fixed on doors and window frames and kept constantly wet by a coolie who sprayed water on them the whole day; when a breeze passed through the wet grass, it cooled both the interior and filled it with a pleasant scent. But the specific British invention—which is the classic prototype of the desert coolers now in use all over India in the cities—were the thermantidotes. *Khus tattis* were used in these, too, with the difference that they were made part of a wooden case in which an artificial breeze could be generated by a wheel with a long iron handle that was vigorously rotated, throughout the day, by the same long-suffering coolie. *Tattis* were used by the more well-to-do Indians as well. Traditional means to beat the heat were basement *taikhanas*—a normal feature of most houses, and *kothris* or small rooms with thick walls which did not get the direct sun. Ghalib himself spent the long summer days confined to just such a darkened hide out in his home.

Ice was much in demand, not only by the British but also the Indian aristocracy. It was laboriously made during the winter months and stored away for use during summer. On the coldest nights of December and January, the specialized community of ice-makers would be at work between the Turkman and Delhi gates, keeping water in shallow earthen receptacles out under the frosty sky; by morning a thin layer of ice would have formed, which was then beaten together and stored in ice-pits deep underground, to be opened only at the beginning of summer. For all the attempts to preserve it, a good deal of the ice did melt in summer, and what remained was both in short supply and expensive. In one of his couplets, Ghalib in his usual tongue-in-cheek style, comments:

The means to sustenance and shelter
from where shall I get?
The many necessities for comfort
from where shall I get?
I do have faith in the Roza fast but yet
A *khus*-cooled room and iced-water
from where shall I get?[62]

The affluent members of the feudal aristocracy had large estates in the city. Recalling those of two such nobles, Ghalib wrote: 'These two men of noble lineage have several houses and halls and palaces, all adjoining one another, and it is certain that if one measured the land on which they stood it would equal the area of a village, if not a town.'[63] Important members of this society were the Nawabs of Jhajjar, Bahadurgarh, Loharu, Farukhnagar, Dujana and Pataudi, and the Raja of Ballabgarh—all rulers of estates under the Delhi Agency. The residential palaces or *havelis* that they and others built often became focal points for the creation of their own *mohallas*. But for every feudal-affluent, there were scores of the impoverished-feudal, left high and dry by the receding ebb of a feudal system in decline, conscious of their noble lineage but without the means to support a matching lifestyle any more. 'There are two Ghalibs,' Ghalib wrote. 'One is the Seljuq Turk who mixes with *badshahs*, the other is poor, in debt, and insulted.'[64] The citizens of Delhi, with their characteristically irreverent wit, had a doggerel to describe the young beau about town, who persisted in his aristocratic mannerisms on an empty pocket:

Dilli ke banke jinki
Jooti mein sou sou tanke.[65]
(The dandies of Delhi whose shoes have a hundred
patches)

There were also those who came into money
suddenly, but, in the prevailing socio-economic milieu,
lost it as quickly. Ghalib writes:

Here in Delhi they have a term 'a new nawab'.
This term can be applied to anyone Hindu or
Muslim. When a man dies—a wealthy man, that
is—and his property comes to his son, bad
characters get together and begin addressing him
as 'Lord of Bounty' and 'Your Exalted Lordship'.
They tell him, 'Such and such a courtesan is
desperately in love with you,' and 'such and such a
lord was praising you to his assembled friends. You
must certainly send for this courtesan and give a
party for this lord. This is what worldly wealth is
for. You cannot take it with you. Did your father
take anything with him? And will you? Anyway, to
date your humble servant has seen three such new
nawabs. One was Khatri Todar Mal. He had a
hundred thousand rupees to his name, and in six to
seven years he lost it all, left Delhi and disappeared
without a trace. The second was a Punjabi boy
named Sa'adat. He lost all he had—some forty to
fifty thousand rupees. The third was named Khan
Muhammad—the son of Sadaullah Khan. He too
had twenty to twenty-five thousand rupees and used
to ride around in a buggy. Now he clip clops around
in down-at-heel shoes. . .'[66]

The merchants of the city—mostly Jains and Khatris—participated in the retail trade in grain and food, and in banking—more a euphemism for money-lending at usurious rates of interest. 'The transfer of urban property into the hands of money-lenders . . . was as striking in the towns as it was in the countryside . . . Much Muslim property in the Chandni Chowk area of Delhi was mortgaged to merchant families before 1857.'[67] Ghalib himself remained in heavy debt to moneylenders throughout his life.

An important avenue of commerce was the manufacture and retail of traditional handicrafts—jewellery, shawls, brassware, gold lace, and shoe-making. Bishop Heber was especially taken by Eliott, the British Agent at the Mughal court, to see a 'shawl manufactory' in the house of a wealthy merchant. The Bishop found the shawls expensive and not 'very beautiful', but he was very taken with the merchant's house. 'The house itself was very pretty and well worth seeing as a specimen of eastern domestic architecture, comprising three small courts surrounded by stone cloisters, two of them planted with flowering shrubs and orange trees, and the third ornamented with a beautiful marble fountain.'[68] What Heber saw was a typical *manzil* or *haveli,* whose style of construction was structurally introverted: a blank wall on the street, opening out inside into rooms built around one or more courtyards, and (sometimes) a garden with fountains—as in the case of this merchant's. Ghalib's house, on the corner of Ballimaran and Gali Qasim Jan, was built on the same pattern, with a high, blank, brick façade facing the street, surmounted by arched corridors on three sides that enclosed an open courtyard. Such a construction was primarily conditioned by the need to ensure privacy, particularly for the *zenana,* and was in contrast to the 'bungalow' format of construction, introduced by the British later and still prevalent today.

Without doubt Chandni Chowk was the most prestigious focal point of the city's trading establishment. Europeans mistakenly thought that its name translated as 'silversmiths' street.' Fruits, textiles, *hookahs,* weapons, birds and animals, and all kinds of costly handicrafts could be purchased there by the connoisseur. One contemporary recorded that it was inhabited only by jewellers and silversmiths—an impression that was probably due to the fact that the jewellery shops were more numerous. 'Of course, they never displayed their wares in public, all valuables being kept in the back-rooms of the houses; the front room being open to the street, without doors, carpeted with a white cloth on which one or two men would be sitting, working at their trade, with some very simple tools and a small crucible alight for their metal work. If a European stopped at a shop he generally sat on the edge of the floor of the shop, which was always raised a few feet above the road, and bargained for any articles he wanted.'[69] But ultimately Chandni Chowk was more than just the city's first commercial street. Its location, as the principal boulevard from the city leading to the palace, and its historical pre-eminence in the city's evolution, gave it pivotal importance. From it radiated the most important *kuchas* and *galis* of the city; and along its tree-shaded canal causeway, rich and poor, traders and noblemen, intellectuals and artisans, scholars and poets, congregated to discuss the concerns of the day. 'You cannot even imagine,' Zakaullah told C.F. Andrews, 'how stately the Chandni Chowk looked in the old days. It was the centre of the city . . .'[70]

Hindus and Muslims were roughly of the same number in the city. Acting as a link between the two religions were the Kayasthas. (Ghalib's chief *shagird*, Hargopal Tufta, was a Kayastha.) Relatively new immigrants to the city were the Khatris, who had come from the Punjab. The poor in the city were from all communities and in substantial numbers. They lived in mud hovels, often washed away by rain or flood. Ghalib wrote in 1855 that many houses in the city had collapsed due to rain. His own house became a veritable sieve during the monsoons and he quipped, in one of his letters, that if it rained for two hours his roof dripped for four. Slums were most in evidence on the periphery of the city—Mori Gate, Farashkana, Ajmeri Gate, Turkman Gate and Delhi Gate. Here lived the potters, butchers, *chamars,* dyers of cloth, the miscellaneous manual labourers, artisans, peasant immigrants and the unemployed. Economic decadence and poverty hung low as a pervasive pall over the entire city. It was strikingly in evidence in the palace itself. One foreign visitor remembered being 'pestered by a fresh swarm of miserable beggars'[71] inside the Fort, when he went for his presentation to the emperor. The *'salatins'* of the palace, distant relations and hangers-on of royalty, lived in conditions of the most stark poverty. 'The *salatin* quarter consists of an immense high wall so that nothing can overlook it. Within this are numerous mat huts in which these wretched objects live. When the gates were opened there was a rush of miserable, half-naked, starved beings who surrounded us,' wrote a British official.[72] Sleeman has also derisively recorded that 'kings and queens of the house of Tymour are to be found lying about in scores, like broods of vermin, without food to eat or clothes to cover their nakedness'.[73]

However, the cost of living, as compared to present times, was incredibly low. A rupee could buy as much as forty seers of wheat or four seers of *ghee*. In a letter in 1853 Ghalib complained that wheat, gram flour and gram were selling in Delhi for forty to forty-five pounds to a rupee. The British defined poverty as a net household income of less than three rupees per month. Not surprisingly, Ghalib, on a largely fixed income of sixty-two rupees and fifty paise a month, could afford to keep and maintain four servants. It is unlikely that (except in famine years) even the poorest lived below starvation levels.

The composite rhythm of the city included all sections in its sweep; the poor, in spite of their deprivations, remained active participants in many of its diversions and entertainments. It was this indefinable allure which probably prompted Mir to lament: The ruins of Jaha-nabad were ten times better than Lucknow; Oh that I had stayed there to die— not come to live distracted here.'[74] A visitor approaching the city could hardly fail to notice kites dotting the horizon, particularly in the rainy season.

The sandy slopes of the Jamuna near Delhi Gate—
Mahabat Khan Ki Reti—was the kite-flyers' arena,
and it is said that *patangbazi* matches were arranged
here, with teams from as far away as Lucknow. Ghalib
writes, half-complainingly, that on the king's insistence
he joined him at Salimgarh (the northern extremity
of the Red Fort) for kite-flying, which was apparently
a daily ritual in the evenings. Pigeon-flying or
kabutarbazi was another popular sport. Bahadur Shah's
state procession through the streets of Delhi always
included one elephant which carried the royal pigeon-
house. Quail-, partridge- and cock-fighting were also
daily pastimes; it was not uncommon to see the
nobility and princes of the Fort go about with their
prized quails and partridges perched on their shoulders.
Once a year, the swimming competition was held—
Tairaki Ka Mela—for which almost the entire city
gathered along the Jamuna. Interested groups
maintained several *akhadas* or wrestling clubs in the
city. Chess and *satta* gambling, and *ganjfa,* were also
popular. On the steps of the Jama Masjid the
storytellers—*dastangos*—always attracted large
crowds. Chandni Chowk was a favourite meeting
place—where peeple congregated, almost without
specific purpose, just to meet and talk or watch the
world go by. In the evenings, there was the attraction
of a stroll along the bridge of boats across the Jamuna,
or the gatherings at the Urdu Bazaar, where the
studious could read and the others were assured a
meal, or a visit to the Gudri Bazaar (in the open
space between Khanam Ka Bazaar and Khas Bazaar)
to sample a *kabab* or two, and be entertained by the

charm and persuasive ingenuity of its salesmen. For those so inclined there were the taverns, open, it would appear, almost the whole night. In addition to the local brew, foreign liquor (mostly French wine and champagne), retailed largely by English merchants, was easily and cheaply available. Ghalib, who drank every evening, claimed that it was his habit to drink only French wine. Not surprisingly, wine, the tavern, the *saki* and the sanctimonious hypocrisy of the *vayiz* were recurrent themes of poetic symbolism. It was only after 1857, due to the politically disturbed conditions, that the British imposed restrictions on distilling—and simultaneously, the price of foreign wine became (temporarily) prohibitive. In the monsoon there was the Phoolwalon Ki Sair, and in winter the entire family could picnic in the many gardens of the city, watching the fountains and buying *chana jor garam* and *pakoras* from eager vendors. The *bhands, bahuroopias* (quick change artists, capable of alternating from one role to another with amazing rapidity), *bhagat baz* (performers of religious epics), *katputhli baz* (puppeteers), acrobats and conjurers, provided readily accessible entertainment to all. These artists saw their heyday in the reign of Muhammad Shah 'Rangila', when royal patronage gave a fillip to the development of their traditional skills. But in Zafar's time, they were forced more than ever before to take their performance to the people in order to earn a living. The frequent royal processions through the city were a special attraction. These were no longer the grand show of wealth and power of Shah Jahan's day. 'A straggle of foot soldiers went in front and behind;

musicians sounded trumpets and rhapsodists sounded the imperial praises . . .'[75] But it was a colourful spectacle, and the long row of richly caparisoned elephants never failed to win spontaneous applause. C.F. Andrews writes that 'among the reminiscences of old Delhi, these elephant processions, on State occasions, occupied a prominent place. Those who related the story to me were themselves young children in those early days, and the gorgeousness of the scene had evidently impressed their young imaginations.'[76] On Friday, there was, as there is now, the usual congregation of the faithful at Jama Masjid. A British contemporary who witnessed this once wondered how the worshippers found their footwear later, 'as the shoes lay side by side from the top to the bottom of the (Jama Masjid's) steps, and were almost all of the same pattern'.[77] Weddings, both Hindu and Muslim, were expected to be occasions of prolonged festivities, and while they added colour to the city's life—they were also a common cause for indebtedness. Daily life was overloaded by the performance of rituals and the observance of omens. It was said that Delhi had more festivals than days in a year. 'One important result of extreme insecurity and economic decline was the loss of hold upon life, reflected in the widespread belief in magic and in the supernatural.'[78] Astrologers were much in demand and quacks prolific. Casteism was an accepted way of life and appears to have affected the Muslim consciousness as well. 'Marriage and other social customs and practices (between Hindus and Muslims) tended to be uniform or at least mutually influenced, in both their good and bad features. Some elements of the caste system, for example, food taboos, pollution and marriage restrictions, had become common to both.'[79] It is said that Nawab Shamsuddin submitted his neck with perfect equanimity for the noose to be adjusted, only to recoil in horror on observing that the executioners were of the sweeper caste.

The rootlessness and alienation, the societal atomism and isolationism, which is the malaise of our cities today, was largely absent. Even relatively new immigrants, such as impoverished peasants from Rajasthan, soon succeeded in carving out a place in the 'jajmani system'. A person had a sense of belonging, of being part of a larger unit—community, caste, locality, or profession. Ultimately, he belonged to the city, a Delhiwallah—'that stereotype who has been attributed certain characteristics—his dislike of innovations, his lack of any sense of deferring to another, his lack of interest in issues outside his narrow ken'[80]—which, while distinguishing him from others, sometimes also fostered a uniformity of outlook and appearance resented by the individualist among its numbers. 'In this uncouth city (Delhi),' Ghalib complained, 'everybody wears a sort of uniform. *Mullahs,* junk-dealers, hookah-keepers, weavers, green-grocers—all of them wear their hair long and grow a beard. The day your humble servant grew a beard, he had his hair shaved . . .'[81] Such homogeneity, Ghalib's exasperation notwithstanding, was probably something much more elusive and intangible than physical. In any case, it did not blur sartorial variations indicative of social background and position. The ordinary man wore homespun cotton cloth; wool was uncommon and expensive, the padded cotton quilt being used instead. The affluent *karkhandar* or artisan was fond of being in spotless white with spangled caps for headgear. The rich wore silk and used richly embroidered shawls. *Pyjamas,* both *chooridar* and open, made of white cloth or brocade and *kurtas* of Dacca muslin were in vogue. The *angarkha,* again of muslin, was popular in summer. It was customary to wear a cloak or long coat—*chogah*—over the *kurta.* Very often this was coloured and intricately embroidered. In winter, the *jubbah*—a long outer robe like a Roman toga— was in use. Headgear was a must. Caps, made of velvet or muslin and embroidered, could be round or four-cornered and sometimes even five-cornered. The *khirkidar* turban, peculiar to the Mughals, and the Mongolian *arkhachin* cap were other styles in use. Ghalib (going by his extant portraits) often wore something resembling a *kullah papakh*—a tall cap tapering upwards, commonly used in Uzbekistan and Turkey. Since men of the nobility spent a considerable portion of the day in the *mardanah,* receiving or entertaining visitors or attending to business, it was quite normal for them to be in full formal dress. Among the elite, considerable attention was paid to details in attire. In one letter Ghalib gives minute instructions about the kind of turban he wants: 'I want a silk turban, the kind they make in Peshawar and Multan, and which distinguished men in those places wear. But it must not be of bright colour or a youthful style; and it must not have a red border. At the same time it should be something distinctive and elegant, and finely finished. I dont want one with silver or gold thread in it. The silks in the material must include the colours black, green, blue, and yellow.'[82] The fashion conscious could be really elaborate and fastidious in their appearance. It is said that Momin, the famous poet and Ghalib's contemporary, was one such. Farhatullah Baig draws this portrait of him: 'He wore a wine-coloured muslin tunic with a long bodice and long sleeves. He wore no *kurta* underneath so that a part of his chest was visible through a slit in the flap of his tunic. Round his neck was a small gold amulet on a black ribbon. A deep purple sash was folded into a girdle, round his waist, with the two ends hanging in front. In his hand he held a small *kharpusht (kharpusht* is a little pet hedgehog. Momin carried one about with him, as some carried quails). His paijamahs, loose at the hips and tight at the ankle, was made of red material called *gulbadan,* and was held at the waist with a fancy scarlet cord. Occasionally he sported the single-width loose paijamah also—whatever the style, the material was always costly silk. The sleeves of his tunic were sometimes cut short. Sometimes he wore them rolled up and sometimes let them hang full-length to the wrist. His cap, capacious enough to fit well down over his head, was made of double bands of cloth called *gulshan* with very very delicate lace at the edge, clearly revealing the parting of his hair and a portion of his forehead . . .'[83]

An important institution was the salon of the courtesan, which provided the setting for much of the symbolism and imagery of the poetic renaissance.

1. Ghalib (clockwise from top left) and some of the notables of his time 2. Bahadur Shah Zafar, the Mughal Emperor, 3. Ibrahim Zauq, (poet Laureate) and 4. Momin Khan, one of the greatest poet of the period.

The house in Agra where Ghalib was born

Ghalib's seal

W. H. Macnaghten Esqr
Secretary to the Government
Fort William

Sir!

I have the honor to request, that you will, with your usual kindness, best obliging, as to lay the enclosed petition with its Enclosures, for the more liberal & impartial consideration & orders, of the Right Honble the Governor General in Council: — I submit three Papers with reference to myself already pending the decision of the Honble the Court of Directors. —

I have the honor to be
Sir
Your most obedient, devoted & Humble Servant
Asud oollah Khan

Delhi
the 9th Augt 1837.

One of Ghalib's letters to the British. His personal seal can be seen at the bottom left hand corner.

آئینهٔ سکندر

نمبر ۲۰۸ تاریخ ۲۳ ماه فروری سنه ۱۸۳۸ عیسوی روز دوشنبه

آئینه سکندر جام جم است بنگر ۞ تابنمودت از احوال ملک دارا ۞

۞ قجزه اهل لجلا قروملی ۞

۞ ماه سما ای کرم محمد سپهر چشم ۞

۞ خسرو دارا اجمر مالک مملکت و حلم ۞

The Aina-i-Sikander, one of Delhi's earliest newspapers

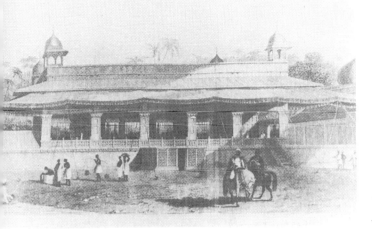

The Diwan-i-Khas, the inner sanctum of the Red Fort

The Kotwali where Ghalib was incarcerated when he was arrested on a gambling charge

The Red Fort and the city before the Revolt of 1857

The city after the Revolt—destroyed and rubble strewn

The Red Fort stands alone after the destruction of the city. The British soldiers now had 'a clear line of fire'

One of Delhi's greatest landmarks—the Jama Masjid before the Revolt of 1857

The Jama Masjid, post 1857, after the houses around it were demolished

The Jama Masjid, one of the last surviving witnesses to the grandeur of an era

In a highly conservative society, where the *purdah* system was at its zenith and the complete segregation of the sexes was a totally accepted social norm, the *kotha* of the courtesan alone provided the most easily accessible forum for men to mix socially, and without inhibition, with women and colour such encounters with all the poetry of romance, yearning, separation and union. In this way the image of the beloved became 'the image of the courtesan, the woman without a family context, without attachments and obligations, who could be transformed for that reason into woman as such, into a purely aesthetic concept'.[84]

The courtesan was an accepted part of society. Ghalib's letters, when they touched on this subject, do not make a moral judgement. The tone is descriptive, matter of fact. When a courtesan dies, with whom a friend Muzaffar Hussain Khan is deeply in love, Ghalib (in one of his most famous letters) gives him advice on how to bear his loss with fortitude; there is no censure of the institution itself. Men were considered to be inherently polygamous. Particularly in the nobility and among the rich, it was socially accepted, even expected of them, to have a dalliance outside the home. Once in a while the experience could be unfortunate. The courtesan could lead a man to financial ruin, siphoning off the family wealth of generations for her own enrichment; or even make a man break off from his family. Ghalib once complained how such a courtesan—whom he preferred to call a whore—had done precisely this to his brother-in-law, much to the dismay of his family. But then this was a risk to be taken. The courtesan herself did not feel an outcast. *Umrao Jaan Ada,* Rusva's authentic novel of Lucknow at this time, brings this out forcefully. In it Umrao Jaan, the accomplished courtesan, 'takes it for granted that there would always be respectable women and courtesans and that there would always be an uneasy rivalry between them . . . she seems to suggest that like people in other walks of life a courtesan too lives by a code of conduct, and she has been true to her code of ethics. When she calls herself a sinner she merely bows to conventional rhetoric, because her matter of fact and objective tone of narration seldom betrays any serious feeling of guilt.'[85] Society gave the courtesan cognizance as a part of the social mainstream; on festive occasions she was engaged to sing and dance at the *urs* or death anniversaries of saints. It is said that after Nawab Shamsuddin was hanged by the British, the courtesans composed a song lamenting his fate, which became very popular. In the eighteenth century, the salon of the courtesan was a school for manners to which sires of well-to-do families were sent—as daughters of the wealthy are sent today to finishing schools; it was a cultural focus, and played an important role in the development of the *khayal, gayaki* and *kathak.* In Ghalib's time, the declining feudal system left less money in the hands of fewer patrons, and courtesans could not but become a little less meticulous about their cultural accomplishments. But even so, society did not equate the courtesan with a prostitute *simpliciter;* such an equation was to await the new morality of the Hindu and Muslim revivalist movements at the turn of the century. Till then the courtesan remained an integral part of a certain way of life, and her existence, as that of her patrons, cannot be understood merely in the context of the moral opprobrium now attached to the *kotha*.

In the ultimate analysis, Ghalib's Delhi will itself be remembered for the richness and grandeur of its assertion——that validated a *tehzib*——an assertion stuck to with refinement——(and sometimes pathetic obstinacy) in the face of the remorseless erosion of the political and economic structure which had nurtured it. The consolidation of the British presence put into temporary abeyance overt political activity; instead the quality of cultural life became the prime focus of elite endeavour——setting standards of emulation which percolated downwards. By the prevalent rules, the polished conduct of social intercourse was an end in itself, and there could be no better or more satisfying expression of one's cultural accomplishments than to use them in achieving this end. The mild-mannered, cultured, poet-king Zafar was both the natural product of such times as also a catalyst for its achievements. His court was a school of manners——whose etiquette and conventions were emulated as far away as the Deccan. 'Long after Delhi had ceased to be the Paris of power it continued to be the Versailles of good manners.'[86] It is said that during *mushairahs,* 'if someone had unwittingly sat down in the wrong place,* then instead of embarrassing this person by making him change his seat (the host or

---

* The seating plan was drawn up keeping in mind the standing of the participating poets, inevitably a controversial exercise.

chief organizer) would himself go and sit down in the place assigned for this gentleman. After a suitable interval, he would make out that he wanted to communicate some particular news and beckon to the said gentleman to join him, and would continue talking to him until a guest, for whom the vacated seat was appropriate, had arrived. He would then invite the newcomer to be seated in the place he himself had occupied. This done, he would find some pretext to move on.'[87] This urbanity, with all its meticulously observed nuances, was played out in apparent obliviousness to the forces that would lead, in but a few years, to the cataclysm of 1857. With 1857, and the exile of Zafar, an entire milieu died. Ghalib's Delhi had its vices—corruption, decadence, obscurantism, sterile intrigues and of course economic exploitation and poverty. But these were part of an authentic socio-cultural framework which gave mooring to individual response and behaviour. The period after 1857 saw the systematic demolition of this framework, and it was Ghalib's fate to live to witness it.

THREE

A Turbulent Genius

Ghalib was born in Agra on 27 December 1797. His links with Agra were, however, not ancestral. His grandfather, Quqan Beg Khan, who Ghalib claimed had come to India from Samarqand, was a military adventurer employed at different times with the Governor of Punjab, the Mughal Emperor Shah Alam, and the Maharaja of Jaipur. Of Quqan Beg's large family we know that two sons, Abdullah Beg Khan and Nasrullah Beg Khan, followed in their father's footsteps, seeking their fortune as mercenaries, a profession for which opportunities were in plenty in the fragmented and troubled politics of the eighteenth century. It was both an uncertain and a dangerous profession. As we have seen, Ghalib was hardly four when his father died. After his death, Nasrullah Beg took his brother's family in his care, consisting of Ghalib, his younger brother and sister. Two years later, in 1806, Nasrullah, who had risen to become the Commander of Agra Fort under the Marathas, and had later been rewarded by the British for surrendering the Fort to them, also died. Thus, by the time he was nine, Ghalib had lost both his father and uncle. But to some extent he was insulated from the tumult of these early years. His father had married into an affluent family of Agra. Given the uncertainties of the life of a soldier-mercenary, he had wisely allowed his wife to live at Agra with her parents. Ghalib was born in the home of his maternal grandparents, and continued to lead a relatively sheltered and comfortable life there, even after his father and uncle died. From the references in his letters later, it would appear that he recalled those early years with considerable clarity. 'We (Nazir Bansi Dhar, a contemporary of the same age) were close friends and used to play chess together; we would often sit together until late into the night. His house was quite near mine and he used to come and see me whenever he liked. There was only Machia the courtesan's house and the two by-lanes between us. I used to spend most of the time in the stone summer-house near the main entrance. I used to fly my kite from the roof of a house in one of the lanes nearby and match it against Raja Balwant Singh's. There was a big house called Ghatia Wali, and beyond that another near Salim Shah's *takiya* and then another adjoining Kala Mahal and beyond that a lane called Kashmiran Wala—that was the lane where the house was.'[1] Not uncommonly, his nostalgia for the carefree days of his childhood increased over the years, more acutely during periods of adversity, of which there were many later in life. Thus, long after he had left Agra, he rhapsodizes in a letter to a friend who is visiting Agra.

Let no man look upon Agra as of slight account,
but as he passes through her roads call on God's
preserving and protecting power to hold her in its
keeping . . . To every grain of dust of that land in
flower my body sends its message of love, and on
every leaf in those fair gardens my soul calls
benedictions to rain down.[2]

This panegyric appears to be based on poetic
euphoria rather than on memory. Time fades out harsh
memories; nostalgia gives a softer hue to
remembrance. Life with his maternal grandparents
may have given Ghalib material comfort, and allowed
him to escape the direct impact of unsettled and
uncertain times. But the trauma of the untimely death
of his father and uncle must have given him a
permanent feeling of deprivation. For a person so
inordinately proud of his ancestry, the fact that he had
no choice but to live with his mother's parents must
have been resented by him. Undoubtedly, his early
years did see considerable mental and emotional stress,
and it is perhaps not coincidental that he began to
write poetry when still very young—possibly in the
same year his uncle died (1806). Fortunately, his early
education was such that it could nurture the growth
of so precocious an intellect. Sheikh Muazzam, one of
the most learned scholars in Agra at the time, taught
him; perhaps he also attended a *madrasa* run by Mir
Azam Ali. His grounding in the traditional sciences
taught then—logic, astronomy, medicine and
metaphysics—was thorough. But his real inclination
was towards linguistics and literature, particularly

the mastery of Persian. It was fortuitous that a noted scholar of both Persian and Arabic—Abdus Samad[3]— visited Agra at this time. Ghalib became his pupil. Samad stayed at Ghalib's house for two years (1811– 12). Ghalib never acknowledged anyone as his *ustad,* but the glowing terms in which he has later referred to Abdus Samad comes closest to such an acknowledgement.[4] It would be fair to conclude that the foundations of Ghalib's vast erudition in Persian were laid in these early years.

Ghalib was writing verse in Persian when not yet nine. Throughout his life he proclaimed Persian to be his first love, but there is evidence that even at this early age he wrote in Urdu as well.[5] Hali has recorded that a gentleman named Kanhayya Lal had preserved a *masnavi* in Urdu written by Ghalib at the age of eight or nine; Ghalib had forgotten its existence, but, much later in life, when it was shown to him, read it with great delight. Obviously, what Ghalib wrote even then was of sufficient merit to attract attention. It is said that Nawab Hussain-ud-Dawlah, a respected nobleman and poet of Agra, once took some of the young poet's couplets to the legendary Mir at Lucknow.[6] Mir was known as much for his poetic genius as for his acerbic temper and contemptuous dismissal of anything but the best in poetry. The very fact that somebody felt that Ghalib's writing could be shown to him, is evidence of the recognition of Ghalib's talent. On reading the *ghazals,* Mir's wry comment was that under the guidance of a good *ustad* the boy could become a great poet; otherwise he would write rubbish. Coming from Mir this was encouraging enough.

On 8 August 1810, a few months short of thirteen years of age, Ghalib was married to Umrao Begum, daughter of Nawab Ilahi Baksh Khan. Shortly after that he shifted his permanent residence from Agra to Delhi. The exact date of this event is not known. In a letter written in 1862, he describes himself as a resident of Delhi for the last fifty-one years. This would mean that he shifted to Delhi as early as 1811. But Ghalib's remembrance of time and dates was not very accurate, particularly towards the later period of his life. The general consensus appears to be that he shifted some time between 1813 and 1815. In any case, Delhi was not a new city for him. By his own admission, he had been visiting it since the age of seven. His father-in-law was an important and influential member of the Delhi aristocracy and, writing under the *takhallus* Maruf, an established poet in his own right. Even otherwise, for an ambitious poet, Delhi, the seat of the Mughal court, was a much more appropriate setting than Agra. The ceaseless political turmoil of the previous century had forced Mir and Sauda to leave their beloved Shahjahanabad. But, at the beginning of the nineteenth century, the British colonial presence had imposed a relative political calm in Delhi, not an unimportant consideration for a new migrant to the city. As Ghalib grew up, and particularly so after his marriage, staying with his mother's family must have been unacceptable to him. It is also probable that, after his maternal grandfather's death, even the material affluence in his mother's house could not be taken for granted.

Several factors combined, therefore, in prompting

Ghalib's move. He came to Delhi determined to take his place in the aristocracy, and get his rightful due as a poet. The untimely death of his father and uncle had deprived him of an assured niche in the Mughal capital. His claim to be a member of the nobility needed assertion. Throughout his life, but much more keenly in the early years when he was seeking to establish himself, Ghalib went out of his way to exalt his lineage. This may seem a ridiculous, even childish, facet of so extraordinarily intelligent and perceptive a poet. But in his times, birth and lineage, and the standing they gave in the social order, were unquestioned pointers to a man's worth—and Ghalib, it must be remembered, accepted this approach as valid. In getting his due as a poet, he was on much stronger ground and knew it. If there was one issue on which Ghalib was never in doubt, it was about his own talent. The thorough educational grounding of his early years had given his precocious intellect an erudition entirely out of keeping with his young years. And in Delhi, as we've noted, he was determined to win recognition for his poetic talent and knowledge, convinced that this was his right, and not something conditional on the efficacy of his efforts. Given his undeniable genius, this intellectual arrogance was perhaps justified. But Ghalib felt, to the very last, that he never got the acclaim rightfully due to him. This, however, never shook his conviction in his abilities. In the short shrift he gave to anything but the best in poetry—an attitude that was to embroil him in controversies throughout his life—he was, perhaps unconsciously, patterning himself on the legendary impatience and exactingness of his idol, the great Mir. However, his vibrant humour and compassion never did allow him to fully sustain the aloofness and exclusivity he would have liked to adopt.

On his arrival in Delhi, Ghalib rented a *haveli* in the heart of the Walled City, not far from Chandni Chowk.[7] Through his father-in-law, with whom he possibly stayed for a while on arrival, he got an *entrée* to the nobility and elite. His poetic debut was, however, far from smooth. Ghalib's early Urdu writing was highly Persianized. The attempt to overwhelm Urdu, within the straitjacket of classical Persian, was out of sync with the literary mood in which Urdu was replacing Persian as the *lingua franca*—and rapidly gaining confidence and popularity as the new literary medium. In addition, the thought structure of his compositions was complex to the point of being obscure. Ghalib appears to have been greatly influenced by the abstract writings of Persian poets such as Bukhari, Aseer and Bedil.[8] This was not surprising, given his philosophical inclinations and childhood interest in metaphysics. But the metaphysical content of his couplets was not easily intelligible to the average audience. Matters were made worse because he treated the existing stereotyped symbolisms and stock imagery in poetry with scant respect. He was impatient with the accepted grooves of poetic licence and chafed at the restricted repertoire of those who presumed to judge him. His search was for new imagery which would push back the horizons of literary experimentation. Along with such laudable pursuits was, very possibly, also entwined an irrepressible character trait: the desire to be different. One suspects that this was, in a sense, a mechanism to attract attention. As an aspiring poet Ghalib certainly wanted to be noticed. To write in a style completely off the beaten track would be a stratagem, in keeping with his intellectual arrogance and artistic confidence, and one cannot escape the impression that he seemed to derive a defiant pleasure in the controversial ripples he created. By the very 'unintelligibility' of his writings he sought to demonstrate not his own incoherence but the limited comprehension of his critics. Their criticism vindicated his conviction about his essential 'difference', and reinforced his desire to insulate his genius from the taint of plebeian association.

His self-assurance did not daunt the literati. In the literary effervescence of the times, it was not uncommon for a newcomer's ego to take a jostling, and Ghalib's was no exception. If Ghalib was present at a *mushairah,* a few poets would deliberately stand up and recite high-sounding but meaningless verse. On one occasion, Hakim Agha Jan 'Aish', a well known Delhi wit, pointedly recited a verse in which, throwing up his hands in despair, he said that only God and Ghalib himself could understand Ghalib's verse. Others were more subtle but equally devastating in their attack.

On one occasion Maulvi Abdul Qadir of Rampur said to Ghalib, 'There is one of your Urdu verses which I cannot understand,' and there and then made up this verse and recited it to him:

First take the essence of the rose
out of the eggs of buffaloes
And other drugs are there; take those
out of the eggs of buffaloes.

Ghalib was taken aback and said, 'This verse is certainly not mine, I assure you.' But Maulvi Abdul Qadir kept up the joke and said, 'I have read it myself in your *Diwan;* if you have a copy here I can show it to you here and now.' At length Ghalib realized that this was an indirect way of criticizing him and telling him that verses of this kind could be found in his *Diwan.*[9]

When similar criticism had been made in Agra, Ghalib had, with characteristic contempt, dismissed it. In Delhi his basic reaction was similar, and in a transparent attempt to conceal his hurt, he declared himself to be above the desire to please his disparaging audience.

I do not crave for praise,
For reward I do not hanker;
If my verses do not have meaning,
It really does not matter.[10]

He was also genuinely perplexed at some of the criticism, holding that some of his critics were not above non-literary considerations in running him down. In one of his Urdu *rubais* he writes sarcastically,

O, my heart, 'tis true my compositions are
extremely difficult!

On hearing them renowned and successful poets
Do plead that they be made easier;
But difficult it is for me to compose
Anything but difficult couplets.[11]

Although some of his most beautiful couplets are lyrical
in their simplicity, he made no secret of what his own
preference was.

O Ghalib, simple speech
Does not deceive my heart
Bring for me the quaint conceits
Of intricate diction.[12]

Of course, he was never in doubt of the quality of his
verse and, early on, annoyed several established literary
personages by stating his conviction immodestly:

Consider it a magical trove of meaning
Every word, Ghalib, of my writing.[13]

His instinctive intolerance to criticism undoubtedly
stemmed from a lifelong and unwavering belief in his
own poetic worth, and the consequent conviction that
there were few capable of judging him:

From the burning of my heart
Are my couplets alight;
None can place a finger
On a word of what I write.[14]

In the end, however, it appears that at a time when
he was still making his debut, he was not prepared to

jeopardize his literary acceptance by making an excessive virtue of his defiance. He knew where to draw the line. This was both a tactical compromise and a reluctant acceptance of some validity in the barbs of his critics. In a letter to a friend, a few years before his death, he confessed that his verse between the ages of fifteen and twenty-five had indeed been abstruse, and that once he had realized this he had torn up this fanciful *Diwan* retaining but ten or fifteen couplets for his next collection. Evidently, with the passage of time, Ghalib could write with greater equanimity about what had happened, but given his ego, one can understand that, at the time of its actual occurrence, bowing to his critics must have been a particularly difficult pill to swallow. Here Fazl-i-Haq—of whose literary abilities Ghalib had the highest opinion—played an important role. It was on Fazl-i-Haq's advice that Ghalib discarded the more obscure of his writings (practically two-thirds) from the first edition of his Urdu *Diwan* which he compiled in 1821.

Even so, the scars of this opening bout in Delhi took long to heal. One indication of this is that Ghalib almost stopped writing in Urdu for the next thirty years, switching to the rarefied climes of classical Persian, where he thought he would be better able to take on his critics. However, as events show, be it Urdu or Persian, Ghalib would, all his life, retain a remarkable facility of becoming the focus of the most bitter literary controversies.

The buffeting on the literary front did not prevent Ghalib from falling quickly into pace with the rhythm of life of the Delhi nobility. He considered himself a

member of the aristocracy and consciously adopted a
matching style. Hali has recorded that he never went
out except in a palanquin; he always returned visits of
those who called on him, and never called on those
who didn't. Soon he was not only accepted, but
acquired a popularity not entirely untinged with
notoriety. His ready wit and humour became
conversation pieces in the urbane circles of Delhi. The
art of intelligent repartee was then considered evidence
not merely of quick thinking, but of good education
and breeding. Even when it was practised at the expense
of somebody close, it was more liable to meet with
appreciation than be interpreted as a personal affront.
Thus, for instance, we have Ghalib's famous rejoinder
to Hakim Raziuddin Khan, one of his closest friends,
who did not share his love for mangoes. One day
when he and Ghalib were sitting in the veranda at
Ghalib's home, a donkey ambling along in the lane
below sniffed at some mango skins and passed on.
Hakim Raziuddin could not resist remarking that even
donkeys did not like mangoes. Like lightning came
Ghalib's reply: 'Of course, *donkeys* didn't like them!'
Once Ghalib was asked his opinion on the gender of
the word *rath*. His retort was that it depended on the
sex of the passengers, feminine if they were women,
and masculine if they were men. There was also the
incident when Ghalib himself carried the candle to
the edge of the carpet, to enable a friend who was
leaving to put on his shoes. When the friend protested
that Ghalib need not have taken the trouble, Ghalib
replied dead pan that he was doing so only to ensure
that his own shoes were not taken away by mistake.

In the compact elite circles of Delhi, incidents such as these acquired lasting anecdotal value and played a significant role in aiding the young poet's social debut. Besides, for all his intellectual arrogance and scalpel wit, Ghalib was both affectionate and accessible as a person. A friend always received a warm welcome at his home, and such was his charm of personality that those who met him once sought to keep up the acquaintance. The temperamental angularities of genius were there of course. He was good to his friends, could win friends easily, and had a large and devoted circle of friends. But his ego and complexity of mind, his vulnerabilities stemming from financial insecurity, and his touchiness in matters of social prestige, did not make for an entirely unruffled personality. A highly restless and sensitive mind allowed full play to the pull and push of opposing emotions and wide variations in mood and temper. Spontaneous joy and elation— not unnatural to a poet—could be dispelled in moments by a proclivity to brood and to nurse feelings of depression and alienation. Poetic melancholia could be dispersed, with equal felicity, by an irrepressible buoyancy of spirit and an earthy porousness to pleasure. Gregarious one moment, he could be aloof and withdrawn in the next; generous to a fault with friends, he could be unforgiving with his enemies; spiritually transcendent at one level, he could be very much the practical man of the world at another. He attributed the contrasting traits of his personality to the planetary contradictions in his horoscope.[15] In one of his Persian verses, in rather characteristic fashion, he admits:

I have no control
Over the turbulence of my nature;
The waves of lustre in my pearl
Have made me tempestuous.[16]

Throughout his life he remained extremely sensitive to criticism and—in spite of some very cherished associations—there is a discernible uneasiness in his relationships with the outside world. A poet's introspection only heightened his conviction that he was at the receiving end, in a milieu hostile to his talents and unable to comprehend his genius. On more than one occasion his writings reflect his sense of hurt at the hostility of his peers:

What can be said of the qualities
On which people of this world stood?
He did wrong to me
For whom I always did good.[17]

In personal lifestyle he had the habits and pursuits typical to the other members of his class. Thus he drank wine, and to shock the self-righteously virtuous, proclaimed his love for it, flaunting his indifference to religious proscriptions:

If the Imam of the city
Forbids me entry to the mosque
Then my place in the blessing of the tavern keeper
Will not be empty.[18]

Or again,

Once the tavern is renounced
Then for place what grouse?
A mosque, a house of learning,
Or just any other house.[19]

The story goes that once in his presence when a man
indignantly condemned wine drinking and warned that
the prayers of those who drank would never be
answered, Ghalib retorted that if a man had wine,
what else did he need to pray for? One of Ghalib's
Urdu couplets expresses the same sentiment:

That thing, for the sake of which,
I hold paradise divine
What else can it be except
Musk-perfumed, rose-coloured wine?[20]

For the *vayiz* he had little patience:

Preacher, you do not drink
Nor to others you can offer
How pure indeed is the wine
Of paradise you proffer.[21]

If there was one thing he hated, it was hypocrisy:

Ghalib cannot be stained
With the mark of hypocrisy
That patched robe is clean
Which has been washed in wine.[22]

To bring home his contempt for religious prohibition

he often used religious symbolism deliberately in references to wine.

> The Kaaba I need not circle
> At the Zam-Zam* do me consign,
> My garb** for the pilgrimage
> Is much too drenched in wine.[23]
> Drank wine, at the well of Zam-Zam
>   last night;
> Washed the wine stains from my pilgrim's garb
>   at the first light.[24]

For all his baiting of the orthodox, Hali maintains that Ghalib himself drank with self-restraint. He drank a little French wine diluted with two or three parts of rose-water every day, and tried, not always with success, to keep within the limits he had set himself. He would entrust the keys of the box in which the wine was kept to his steward, Kallu, with instructions that once he had had his fixed quota, the box should not be opened. Of course, there would be occasions when he would rail against Kallu for taking his instructions too seriously, but that good man would continue about his work unheeding. Apparently the amount he drank varied with the seasons. In a letter written in 1863 he recalled that when he was in his forties, his standard routine during the monsoons was to have three glasses of wine before lunch or towards the evening, in addition to his daily quota at night.

---

* A holy well near the Kaaba, where Haj pilgrims stop to drink water.

** The Jama-i-Ahram, worn by pilgrims before circumambulating the Kaaba.

Whether such quotas were strictly kept to in the days of his youth is debatable. However, there are verses in both Ghalib's Urdu and Persian collection in which he speaks disapprovingly of excessive or indiscriminate drinking:

> From a drunkard's company
> It is right to be removed;
> No fault of wine,
> Restraint in oneself must be imbued.[25]

> Ghalib, the wine-cup is unlawful
> For that drinker
> Who in his thoughtlessness
> Knows not the measurement of his speech.[26]

This being as it may, there is no doubt that Ghalib was fond of his drink. While he was not a heavy drinker, he could be acutely miserable if he was unable to have his daily quota, either because wine was not available—as did happen during the upheaval of 1857—or because he did not have money to buy it and none was available on credit. As a poet he had a ready rationalization for the craving to drink:

> Which sinner seeks to get
> Joy from his wine?
> A bit of oblivion is what
> I need all the time.[27]

> Our heart bears the wounds of affliction
> And wine is the only cure

For those who are wounded
What's this talk of lawful and unlawful.[28]

Although chronically in stringent financial straits he never considered it wrong to spend money on wine, or to purchase it whenever possible on credit:

For the morrow, do not today
Be miserly with wine,
That would be disrespectful
To the *Saki* divine.[29]

Sometimes his IOUs at the wine merchants could be very substantial. In a letter to his *shagird,* Tufta, in 1853, he confessed that the entire amount of Rs 100, sent by a friend, had gone towards paying the dues at the English wine shop:

The implements to distil wine
Were sold to pay for it;
These were the two accounts
And have thus been completed.[30]

His personal preference was French wine, and it was only much later in life, when there was a scarcity of wine, that he discovered the satisfying qualities of rum:

To the very dregs we drink
Even if 'tis Jamshed's cup that's filled
Shame on that liquor
That from grapes is not distilled.[31]

For a man of Ghalib's temperament, wine was an indispensable element of the gracious *mehfil,* an aid to refined conversation, a prop for the cultured way of life:

> Like flowers scattering down
> See how speech flows from me
> If only someone places
> A cup of wine before me.[32]

In Persian and Urdu poetry, cloudy days and moonlit nights were considered especially apt backdrops to wine-drinking, and Ghalib endorsed this sense of good taste:

> Ghalib, I gave up wine,
> But even now sometimes,
> On cloudy days and moonlit nights
> I confess I do imbibe.[33]

According to Hali, Ghalib often composed while drinking in the evening. Sitting alone, his fingers playing with a long sash, he would tie a knot every time he finished composing a verse; by the time he went to bed the sash would have several knots, and in the morning, untying the knots, he would recall the verses and write them down. Wine was an aid to his creative and imaginative faculties. In a beautiful Urdu couplet he writes:

> Wine the gaze fulfilled, *Saki* hope,
> the glance intoxicated;

In the realm of imagination
The tavern is sublimated.[34]

It is in this sense that he could say,

In the bare walls of the tavern
What attraction can there be?
He who drinks is drunk in thought
Of the flowers glory.[35]

The reference to wine, the *saki* and the tavern occur
repeatedly in Ghalib's poetry, but, in keeping with
the best traditions of Indo-Persian poetry, mostly in
symbolic terms. By the poet's touch the act of drinking
is transmuted. Infinite themes are woven in the clinkle
of the *shisha,* and the sparkle of the *bada*. *Saki* becomes
Divine Grace, wine the Almighty's offering of life,
and intoxication the bliss of the seer. In the integrity
of this vision wine does not debase man, but man
exalts it to the level of his own aspirations:

O Asad, the denier of wine-drinking
Is ignorant; but without the love
Of the *Saki* of paradise
Wine is forbidden.[36]

Gambling—playing *chausar* (backgammon) with
stakes—was another of Ghalib's *shauqs*. As usual he
made no secret of it. One day in summer, during the
Ramzan fast, Mufti Sadruddin Azurda, a close friend
and a noted poet and scholar of Islamic law, visited
Ghalib and found him playing *chausar* with a friend.

Seeing this he remarked that now he seriously doubted what the Books said about Satan being imprisoned during the Fast. Ghalib welcomed him in and said the Books were absolutely right; Satan was indeed imprisoned, right here in this room!

His irreverence towards the religious establishment often brought him close to harming his own interests. Hali records an incident when Ghalib deliberately provoked his father-in-law, Ilahi Baksh Maruf, a man known for his religious orthodoxy—although Ghalib was greatly dependent on his patronage at the time.

Maruf had asked Ghalib to prepare a copy of his family tree or line of spiritual descent. Ghalib prepared the copy, but only included every alternate name. When Maruf questioned him he said that the line of descent was but a ladder to reach God; the missing names only meant that the rungs were wider apart, requiring the spiritual aspirant to climb with greater agility! Maruf angrily tore up the copy.

Ghalib's contempt for established tenets went down well with the eclectic, Sufi mood of the times. He never kept the Ramzan fast, and, as usual, was prepared to admit it. He admitted his vices, ridiculed the sermonizers, and, in general, seems to have lived a lifestyle of considerable flamboyance. He was a handsome man and knew it. Many years later, in a letter to a friend, he recalls his attractive appearance with characteristic immodesty: '. . . when I saw your portrait and saw how tall you were, I didn't feel jealous because I too am noticeably tall. And I didn't feel jealous of your wheaten complexion, because mine, in the days when I was in the land of the living (a euphemism for his youth), used to be even fairer, and people of discrimination used to praise it.'[37] Hali bears this out. Ghalib was an old man when Hali first met him; but even then it was apparent that he must have been very handsome in his younger days, and several people who had seen the young Ghalib mentioned this to Hali. Predictably, Ghalib's dalliance with women[38] appears to have begun rather early, possibly in Agra itself. In a letter written much after he had left Agra, he describes Agra as having been 'the play-ground of my love-distracted heart . . . (in whose) soil only the mandrake grew, and, save the heart . . . trees would bear no other fruit . . .'[39] Delhi was no different. For the class to which he belonged there was nothing unusual in this. A young beau about town, and a budding poet to boot, would be expected to visit the *kotha* of the courtesan. There is no reason to presume that Ghalib deviated from this accepted code of conduct, and references to such matters do not display any sense of guilt on moral grounds. For instance, in a letter written in 1859, he recalled matter-of-factly his happy association with a courtesan by the name of Mughal Jan—whom he used to know extremely well, and in whose company he would often spend hours together.

Among the many casual liaisons, there was a serious one which apparently left a very deep scar on his psyche. Not much is known of this event, except for two references to it by Ghalib himself in later letters. In a letter to a friend, Mihr, whose mistress had died he wrote: 'The sons of the Mughals are incorrigible. When they love, they love with a vengeance and destroy the object of their passion. I, too, am the son of a Mughal, my ardent love proved fatal for a *femme fatale*. It happened over forty years ago, but still with a pang I remember her ravishing allure.'[40] This letter is undated but has been attributed to the year 1860; forty years earlier would mean that Ghalib was twenty-three at the time of the affair. That the event relates to his youth is mentioned by him in another letter written to a close friend, Muzaffar Husain Khan: 'In the days of my youth, when the blackness of my deeds outdid the blackness of my hair, and my heart held the tumult of the love of fair-faced women, Fate poured into my cup too the poison of this pain, and as the bier of my beloved was borne along the road, the dust rose from the road . . .'[41] It is clear that the girl was a *domni* (singing and dancing girl), and that the affair was short-lived as she died suddenly, perhaps in tragic circumstances, and certainly when still very young.[42] It is equally clear that the involvement, even if abortive, was highly intense. Ghalib pours out his anguish to Muzaffar Husain Khan: 'In the brightness of broad day I sat on sack-cloth and clad myself in black in mourning for my mistress, and in the black nights, in the solitude of sorrow, I was the moth that flew to the flame of her burnt-out candle. She was the partner of my bed, who at the time of parting my jealous heart could not consign even to God's keeping. What pain that her lovely body should be consigned to dust!'[43] Quite obviously, the affair was as much of the heart as it was physical, and its memory lived to haunt Ghalib throughout his life.

It appears that after her death Ghalib's instinctive reaction was to insulate himself, in the future, from the pain of a similar experience. At the same time he attempted—and this is typical of him—to subsume the trauma of the individual experience in a larger philosophical perspective. 'Truly, the candles radiant in the assembly are many, and roses bloom in the garden abundantly. Why should the moth grieve when one candle dies? When one rose fades and falls why should the nightingale lament? A man should let the world of odour and fragrance win his heart, not bind it in the shackles of one love. Better that in the assembly of desire he draw from within himself the harmonies of happiness, and draw into his embrace some enchanting beauty who may restore his lost heart to its place and once more steal it away.'[44] This was not a recourse to hedonism on the rebound; nor was it an attempt to exalt the casual, at the expense of the single, intense experience. It was more a desire to transcend personal sorrow by accepting the inevitability of pain, but even more so, the possibility of joy. The Almighty's benevolence cannot be restricted to one experience alone—it must be savoured in all its forms. The diversity of existence has philosophical validity; it is also an inexhaustible source of earthy, sensuous joy. We must know how to view it, not be blinded by the narrowness of our own vision:

A hundred visions will confront you
Should the eyelids rise;
But where is the strength to bear
The burden of the eyes.[45]

From this perspective he could joke about the transient ripples of grief, chiding his friend, Mihr, that if he loved bondage so much then a Munna Jan would be as good as a Chunna Jan. 'You should grieve someone's death only if you weren't mortal yourself,' he wrote. 'Be grateful for your freedom. When I visualize Paradise and think in case I am 'forgiven my sins (in the Hereafter) and granted a celestial palace—complete with a houri—the residence there would be permanent and eternity would have to be spent with the good lady—the very idea terrifies me. Ha, the Houri would become a pain in the neck—the infinite monotony, everlasting boredom. The same old emerald mansion. The same old branch of the Heavenly Tree. The same old Houri . . .'[46]

This was typical Ghalib humour, a shield to deflect morbidity, a sweetener to alleviate sorrow. However, there is no doubt that he could speak lightly to his friend of the death of a mistress only forty years after time had dulled the sharpness of his own loss. Even in his old age he confessed that the memory of his first love retained its sensitivity. At the time of her death, his immediate anguish was acutely mortal, unredeemed by any subsequent rationalization. This is clear from the moving elegy he wrote when she died (a few stanzas of which are produced below), which, as Professor Mujeeb points out, 'shows what rarely happened with him; a descent from the refined atmosphere of poetic love and grief to keenly felt earthly sorrow, a genuine outburst of purely physical emotion'.[47]

If your heart lacked the strength to bear my grief
Why did you sympathize with me, alas, alas
Why did the thought to share my grief come to
   you
My friendship became my enemy, alas, alas
So what if of loyalty you made eternal vows
Life itself is so fragile, alas, alas
Thy flower-scattering coquetry, where has it gone?
Now on thy grave flowers are laid, alas, alas
Love had not yet, Ghalib, matured to passion
Whatever desires were there, remained unfulfilled,
   alas, alas[48]

Apart from the unhappiness of this affair, Ghalib's early years in Delhi were not without their compensations. His reputation as a poet, though still controversial, was undisputed and was rapidly growing. He was accepted as a member of the feudal elite and, within it, enjoyed a lovable notoriety that at once set him apart from others. He had good friends, drank good wine, enjoyed regular gambling sessions and frequented the salons of courtesans. There was only one emerging problem: his increasing insolvency. Ghalib's only steady monthly income was Rs 62.50. This was his share of the hereditary pension that the British had agreed to pay the dependants of Nasrullah Beg Khan (Ghalib's uncle). Given the cost of living in those days, it was not an insignificant amount. But it was woefully inadequate to sustain the standard of living Ghalib chose to adopt. His tastes were expensive: French wine and gambling; and the love affair he had is noteworthy not only for its tragic poignancy, but

also for his readiness to spend money on the upkeep
of a keep. It is not that money did not have importance
for him; on the contrary, all his life he would be
acutely conscious of its need. Money did have
importance, but not sufficient enough to harness his
other predilections; its shortage never made him
compromise his convictions on the right way to live.
Throughout his life, it would be something he needed,
but not something he valued as an end in itself, and
he was speaking the truth when he confessed, later in
life, that he had always treated it as something of
lesser value than dust.

Inevitably, there was no recourse but to borrow;
and, equally inevitably, no way to repay. There is
evidence that in his early years Ghalib had fairly easy
access to credit: relatives were more obliging,
shopkeepers more indulgent, and moneylenders more
awed by his family credentials and general standing in
society. A few years before his death he nostalgically
recalled those years when he could take a loan with
ease from any number of moneylenders—Mathura
Das, Darbari Mal or Khub Chand—and happily give
them carefully sealed IOUs which they need not have
bothered to preserve for eventually they recovered
neither principal nor interest. Besides, at this time,
his aunt paid for his living expenses, Ahmed Baksh
Khan would often send ad hoc amounts from Loharu,
and his mother—who was still alive—would send
money from Agra.

But as his borrowings increased and he defaulted
on payments, his creditors' patience diminished. By
1826, this aspect of his affairs had reached a crisis

point. To his worries on this score was added his grief at his brother's mental derangement. Later, he would describe this period with characteristic flourish not unmixed with remorse. Speaking of the days of 'heedlessness' he said that, persisting with his reckless style of living, he stumbled from the tavern floor to be rudely jolted into reality by the emotional trauma of his brother's madness on one side and the unceasing clamour of his creditors on the other.

Clearly, therefore, it was time to think of some remedial measures; a change in habits or lifestyle was too difficult; the only other option was an increase in income. It was in such circumstances that he began to investigate his share of the pension granted by the British. Ghalib came to the conclusion that Ahmad Baksh Khan, who disbursed it, had deliberately deprived him of his rightful share by fraudulently having Ghalib's share reduced to Rs 5,000 from the designated Rs 10,000; also while excluding Ghalib's younger brother, a direct beneficiary, Ahmad Baksh Khan had included claimants such as Khwaja Hajee—who bore no relationship to Ghalib's uncle. His first reaction was to intercede with Ahmad Baksh Khan. 'In every way that I possibly could, I attempted to agitate the question of my claims, and time after time, both by writing and verbal remonstrances, urged my case to Ahmad Baksh Khan . . .'[49] In the beginning, concerns of kinship seem to have prevented an open dispute. 'Since Ahmad Baksh Khan was in two ways my elder and my kinsman, first, as my uncle Nasrullah Beg Khan was his son-in-law, secondly, as I was the son-in-law of Ilahi Baksh Khan his brother—

regarding these circumstances, I respected the seniority and affinity of Ahmad Baksh Khan, and devoured my own wrongs in silent mortification. I also prevented my brother from giving vent to his murmurs and from having recourse to Government.'[50] But then several things happened in quick succession. In 1822 Ahmad Baksh Khan abdicated in favour of his eldest son, Shamsuddin Khan. Shamsuddin was not well disposed to Ghalib, since Ghalib was closer to Shamsuddin's two stepbrothers, Aminuddin and Ziyauddin. In fact, Aminuddin was one of Ghalib's closest friends. In 1825, Ghalib's father-in-law died, thus removing one more restraining hand in the simmering family dispute. By now Ghalib's debts had become acutely troublesome. He became conscious of the need for more money just at the time Shamsuddin began to harass him about his regular pension payments. Even so, Ghalib remained hopeful that Ahmad Baksh Khan would intervene to set matters right. Quite obviously, the latter had no such intention, and was not above exploiting Ghalib's deference to him to adopt dilatory tactics. Ghalib describes an occasion when, after waiting for Ahmad Baksh Khan to redeem his promise, he went to Ferozepur and told him, 'You must now perform your promise and restore the lawful owners to their rights or else give me leave to go away that I may represent my case to Government.'[51] Ghalib writes that Ahmad Baksh Khan 'had then just risen from his sick couch in consequence of a wound and was in the greatest despondency on account of his loss of the *Mukhtaree* of Alwar, so he began weeping and sobbing before me and said—

"Boy, you are my child and the light of my eyes, you see how I have been wounded and knocked about, and have been defrauded of my dues. Moreover, there is no longer any friendship or cordiality between me and General Ochterlony. Have patience for some more time and your rights shall be at last restored in full."'[52] On Ochterlony's death, Ahmad Baksh Khan held out the hope that he would have a corrective *sunad* issued by his successor, Charles Metcalfe. Metcalfe was then stationed at Bharatpur, and Ahmad Baksh Khan asked Ghalib to accompany him there to meet him. Ghalib has recorded that, 'notwithstanding that I was all this time afflicted with the calamity of my brother's illness, and the clamour and importunity of creditors and was in no way prepared to undertake a journey, yet in hopes of paying my devotions (sic) to that gentleman, I left my brother in that state of fever and delirium, and having deputed four persons to watch and guard him, appeased some of my creditors with various promises, concealed and disguised myself from others, and without convenience of any sort . . . with much difficulty proceeded in company with Ahmad Baksh Khan to Bharatpur.'[53] To no avail. Ahmad Baksh Khan did not take up the matter with Metcalfe. Ghalib decided to proceed in the matter on his own. He had heard that the Governor-General was coming west and that Metcalfe would go to Kanpur to escort him. It was Ghalib's intention 'to go to Kanpur and return from there in his suite and in this way introduce myself to Sir Charles Metcalfe, explain to him my ignominious state of distress, helplessness and debt, and obtain justice'.[54] Ghalib left for Kanpur directly from Ferozepur, but unfortunately on reaching his destination fell ill, losing the opportunity to either meet Metcalfe or present an *arzi* to the Governor-General. But now the battle had been entered and he resolved to go to Calcutta itself to present his case.

The matter was important enough; if his claim was upheld he would, at once, be able to clear his accumulated debts and have more money to spend. He did not for a moment doubt the validity of his claim. Influential English friends in Delhi could help but the final decision would be made in Calcutta. The decision meshed well with his lifelong desire to travel. A change at this time, from Delhi and all its problems, must have also been tempting. Travel would entail expenditure; but people could be found to finance it in the hope that once he won his case these loans, and those taken earlier, would be repaid. He left for Calcutta sometime at the end of 1826 or the beginning of 1827.[55]

Travelling conditions were slow and arduous. He could not afford to go by boat and was forced to travel, most of the way, by horseback or by the *lurhiya* or cart, 'alone, with two or three servants, in a state of great exhaustion and debility without any equipage or comfort'.[56] From Kanpur, where he was unable to get a proper physician, he crossed the Ganga on a hired palanquin and reached Lucknow. Here he convalesced for several months. Lucknow, the capital of Oudh, was a cultural centre of considerable importance. Ghalib, the poet, was not unknown to its literati; his aim, now, was to get noticed by the apex centres of patronage—the ruling Nawab, Nasiruddin

Haider, and the most influential members of his government. In this endeavour, he was not very successful. He could not get an audience with the Nawab. Though he could have won over Agha Mir, the Prime Minister, or his deputy—Subhan Ali Khan Kanboh—he failed because he stipulated two preconditions to his meeting with them: one, that he should be greeted with 'due honour', and, two, that he should be excused from making the customary *peshkash*. Benefactors do not like preconditions being laid down by supplicants. It would appear that not having been able to meet the Nawab, Ghalib's heart was no longer in the venture: he had composed only a prose encomium for the presentation, not a *qasida* as was customary. The incident illustrates a perpetual tussle in Ghalib's life, between his financial condition which prompted deference to sources of patronage, and an absolute conviction of his worth—both as a poet and a member of the nobility—that considered any genuflection degrading. This tussle would often make him go through all the motions of kneeling, only to stand defiantly erect at the last minute. In the times in which he lived, he could not avoid writing odes—*qasidas*—in praise of the rich and powerful. But such odes were the weakest aspect of his creative life and art. In the preface to his Persian poems he regrets that half of his life has been wasted praising fools. For this reason the purely adulatory parts of the odes are the weakest while the poetic prologues are always powerful. Ghalib was keenly aware of his own superiority to the subject of his ode and often slyly found a way to put in a few, oblique words in his own praise.[57]

He left Lucknow in May 1827, and via Banda (its Nawab, Zulfikar Ali Bahadur, was known to him and gave him some monetary assistance), and Allahabad— a city which made a very poor impression on him— reached Banaras. Banaras made a very deep impact on him. He stayed there for about four weeks in a rented *haveli,* in the Naurangabad area. Ghalib's effusive reaction to the new places he saw indicates his genuine fondness for travel. This allowed him to maintain a difference between his personal experience in a city, and the city's worth in objective terms. Unsuccessful in his attempts to win royal patronage in Lucknow, he is full of praise for the city itself: 'By God, no words are equal to describe Lucknow,' he wrote, 'it is the veritable Baghdad of Hindustan.'[58]

Ghalib reached Calcutta in February 1828, almost a year after he had left Delhi. He was new to the city but not a stranger. On his entire journey he had friends in almost every important city, evidence both of his increasing fame as a poet and of the informal network of contacts—in spite of poor communications and long distances—between the feudal elite in north India. He took up comfortable living quarters in Mirza Ali Saudagar's *haveli* at Simla Bazaar, arranged at a rent of Rs 10 a month for him through a friend— Raja Sohan Lal. Nawab Ahmad Baksh Khan had died a few months ago; this only underlined the need for quick action. Ghalib called on the Chief Secretary, Andrew Sterling and on Simon Fraser, the Assistant Secretary. The meetings were cordial. The matter was taken up at the Governor-General's Council, and it was decided that it be brought up for decision through

the British Agent in Delhi which would procedurally
be the proper channel. Ghalib was not averse to this.
Sir Edward Colebrooke, the Agent in Delhi, was
known to him. Ghalib went personally to the post
office and at a cost of Rs 10, mailed a *mukhtarnama* or
power of attorney and all other relevant papers to
Pandit Hira Lal, his attorney in Delhi—with
instructions to secure the appropriate recommendation
from Colebrooke. For his expenses in Calcutta the
Nawab of Banda had sent him an additional loan. He
had three servants and one palanquin bearer in his
personal retinue. To augment resources he sold his
horse for Rs 150, and fixed his budget at Rs 50 a
month. Then, in a fairly optimistic mood, he settled
down to wait for the next round.

The period of waiting was far from uneventful.
Ghalib's stay in Calcutta is most notable for a prolonged
and vicious literary controversy of which he was the
centrepiece. A poetical symposium was held regularly
in Calcutta, on the first Sunday of every solar month.
Ghalib was invited to attend and recited two *ghazals*
in Persian. The gathering was large; according to
Ghalib 5,000 people were present. Some among them
took exception to certain constructions in Ghalib's
compositions and, in support, quoted the authority of
Qatil, the famous eighteenth-century Indian poet and
scholar of Persian. Ghalib was stung to the quick. In
his early years at Delhi, he had resented criticism of
his writings on grounds of conceptual obscurity. But
to be accused now of *linguistic* error, and that too in
Persian which he considered his forte, was intolerable.
He had learnt Persian by studying the Persian masters;

his knowledge of the language was vast and the result of years of painstaking study. 'In Persian, from the Bounteous Source, I received such proficiency,' he once wrote, 'that the laws and structure of the language are as deeply embedded in me as the temper is in steel. Between me and the Persian masters there are two differences: first, that their birthplace was Iran and mine India; and second that they were born a hundred, two, four, eight hundred years before me . . .,'[59] The authority of Qatil, an Indian, he dismissed out of hand. More than thirty years later his pen would still spit fire on this subject describing Qatil as the son of an owl, castigating Indians who claimed to be authorities in Persian, and making it quite clear, without any inhibition of modesty, that although an Indian himself, he was unlike the others because, thanks be to God, he held the very scales and balance of Persian in his hands.

Qatil was a convert to Islam. His original name was Dilwali Singh. He was widely respected as a scholar, and had a large following. Ghalib's angry and below-the-belt rejoinder to his critics was to contemptuously state that he would not accept the word of Dilwali Singh, the Khatri of Faridabad. The furore was predictable and not only restricted to Calcutta. In one of his letters Ghalib mentions that, in the ensuing literary scuffle, his chief opponents were well-known names like Maulvi Karam Hussain of Bilgram, Maulvi Abdul Qadir of Rampur, Maulvi Neamat Ali of Patna, and probably Maulvi Ahmad Ali Ahmad and Wajahat Hussain of Lucknow. His supporters included old friends in Calcutta like Nawab

Akbar Ali Khan and Sirajuddin Ahmad Khan, and significantly enough, Kifagat Khan, the Persian representative in Calcutta of the King of Herat.

While it lasted, the controversy kept Ghalib's name tossing in the spotlight; but at some stage he must have realized that this kind of publicity could cut both ways. Certainly, it was not the most useful thing in winning friends and influencing people. Probably Ghalib's feelings on Qatil's worth as a scholar were initially not so denunciatory or categorical. It was his acute sensitivity to even the remotest insinuation on his own Persian scholarship that had provoked a spontaneous reaction in unwarranted vituperative language. Unfortunately, after this controversy, the die was cast, and he would retain a lifelong antipathy to his detractors. But, for the moment, he had more than proved his point. A compromise would now be wise, in order to contain the bitterness and acrimony which could harm his other interests—including those relating to the pension matter. The advice of his friends was the same and, accordingly, Ghalib composed an Apology entitled *Baad-i-Mukhalif*—An Adverse Wind. But his Apology (like many of his odes) left no one in doubt about the real message. He craved forgiveness for his intemperate language but simultaneously asserted the validity of his stand; he praised his rivals in a language so excessive that its sarcasm was evident, and then said, matter of factly, that people hailed him as a second Saadi; he invoked their sympathy, by caricaturing a stance of exaggerated humility, only to say in the next instant, that he was not one to be daunted in battle; finally, he appealed to all to bury the hatchet. Not unnaturally, those to whom he appealed to forgive and forget, wondered whether he had done so himself.

Not all his literary activity was so controversial or high profile. On the encouragement of his friend Nawab Sirajuddin, he compiled a selection of his Urdu and Persian verse—*Gul-i-Rana*.[60] He had acquainted himself—thanks to the printing press which had come to Calcutta but would still take a few years to reach Delhi—with modern Persian and Urdu prose; and possibly the translations of English classics carried out by the recently established Fort William College. Calcutta had several daily newspapers—an institution yet to come to Delhi—and Ghalib picked up a life-long habit of reading them. Being the British capital and the largest port in the subcontinent, Calcutta, in general, offered a much larger stage than Delhi to observe the changes being ushered in by the British presence. Some of these, particularly those of the new technology—the printing press, the wireless, the steam engine—would make a lasting impression on Ghalib's mind. Nor apparently was the city lagging behind in other more traditional distractions. In a *nazm,* written at this time, Ghalib rhapsodized over Calcutta's excellent wines, its succulent fruits, its lush greenery, and not the least, the charms of its women. Its mangoes made a special impact; not all the fruits of paradise, he claimed, could erase the memory of their flavour and taste.

His efforts to get a favourable decision on the pension case—the reason for his going to Calcutta—did not, as we have seen, bear fruit. By the time the final decision was made he had returned to Delhi, angry and dejected at the turn of events.[61] Obviously, he was deeply bitter with the British:

> I said, 'Who are these moon-like people?'
> (She) said, 'The beautiful ones of the realm of London'
> I said, 'Do they possess any heart?'
> She said, 'They have, but of iron'[62]

Although he pursued the matter with continued and remarkable tenacity, he was never able to get a paisa more from the British than the original Rs 62.50. Yet his hope that he could, and his ceaseless efforts in this direction—spanning over two decades—form an important thread of hope, endeavour and frustration in his life. It left an indelible mark on his outlook and relations with others, and must be taken into account for any study of his life.

When he returned from Calcutta, Ghalib's debts stood at Rs 40,000—an astronomical amount for his times. The fate of his pension case was known to his creditors; they could no longer be foisted off with the buoyancy and swagger with which he had dealt with them before leaving for Calcutta. Patience was on a short leash; several creditors went to court—in 1835 as many as four decrees were issued against him. Ghalib was directed to pay or go to jail. He had no way to pay, but fortunately could avoid jail, since, in those days, prominent men had immunity from arrest while in their own homes. So long as he did not stir out he was safe—but this was hardly an acceptable or happy solution. For four months he remained a prisoner in his own home, not daring to step out. As he himself said, for a man of his temperament, this was twice the torture an infidel could suffer in a hundred years in hell.

It would appear that on one occasion he could not avoid being physically present in court. Mufti Sadruddin Azurda was the presiding judge. He asked Ghalib if he had anything to say in his defence. Ghalib then recited his famous verse:

Indeed I drank on credit but also knew for sure
My spend thrift poverty one day my ruin would procure.[63]

Azurda smiled, decided the suit against Ghalib, and paid the money due from his own pocket.

The wry humour of the couplet, or Azurda's generosity, could not blur the basic humiliation of the situation. The loss of the pension case connoted pecuniary loss. This was unfortunate, but not intolerable; the crisis would pass, something else could be pawned, new creditors found; besides, he was not the only Mirza Sahib to be indigent—this was the age of the 'bouleversement' of the nobility. What was really difficult to swallow was the loss of face: the petition of Ghalib, the distinguished nobleman, had been rejected, like that of any commoner, by those very people with whom he claimed both friendship and familiarity. His worth in their eyes was on public display. He was exposed to be a man without the requisite influence, the right contacts, without the nodding familiarity with the British, so essential for him to project his own standing in society. That the British, the new rulers, were responsive to his needs *in recognition of his status in society* was a myth he had nurtured with care. This myth was shattered. What was worse, his rival, Nawab Shamsuddin, had shown that he had better credentials with them. The loss of the pension case thus connoted a loss of standing in society. The Englishman's indifference to all his clamour demeaned him in the eyes of his own peers. It severely bruised his ego; angry and dejected he resolved to withdraw into himself, shunning the company of his peers, many of whom in their behaviour and casual conversation did not fail to remind him of his discomfiture.

In 1835, Nawab Shamsuddin, Ghalib's adversary, was publicly hanged for complicity in the murder of William Fraser, the British Resident at Delhi. It was the most sensational event in Delhi before 1857. Fraser was shot dead on 22 March 1835 while returning from a party at the house of the Raja of Kishangarh. The assassin—Karim Khan—was tracked down and confessed that he had been hired to do the job by Shamsuddin. Fraser had been supporting Shamsuddin's stepbrothers in the family dispute. The motivation for Shamsuddin to bump Fraser off was clear. Naturally, Ghalib was deeply involved in these dramatic developments. William Fraser was a good friend; Shamsuddin, an old enemy. Resentment against the British, after the pension case, had not made Ghalib oblivious to the importance of cultivating them if they were accessible. His grief at Fraser's murder appears to have been genuine. In a letter written at this time he writes of having experienced, afresh, a father's grief and of being plunged deep into sorrow. Even if we discount the hyperbole, one can understand his unhappiness at losing a patron as important as Sahib Bahadur. There is no doubt that he was involved in the investigations leading to Shamsuddin's arrest. He confessed as much in a letter where he mentions that the city magistrate was known to him and took his help in booking the murderer. This aspect could not have remained hidden from the citizens of Delhi whose loyalties were with Shamsuddin; the common belief was that Shamsuddin was an innocent victim of conspiracy and deceit; in the eyes of many he had become a martyr. Not surprisingly, Ghalib came in for a lot of flak for having colluded with the authorities in Shamsuddin's arrest, and his popularity and public esteem took a steep nosedive.

Public indignation with the British the arrest on and hanging of Shamsuddin is indicative of the stirrings—as yet embryonic—that would culminate in 1857. It is an incident which deserves to be studied in greater depth. It will, of course, be unfair to accuse Ghalib of toadyism. His response was conditioned by the limited framework of hostility to Shamsuddin and friendship with Fraser; the perspective of nationalism in the anti-British context was not yet an influencing factor. In any case, he emerged a loser from the entire episode: he lost in Fraser a useful friend and incurred the odium of his Indian brethren. And to no benefit. Even though his pension from now was paid directly by the British (Shamsuddin's estates were seized), he failed in all his attempts to have the amount increased.

In the aftermath of the pension case and the Shamsuddin incident, Ghalib kept increasingly to his home. His wife was an extremely orthodox lady, probably illiterate, and certainly not the type to look kindly upon his unorthodox style of living and frequent peccadilloes. It is said that she was so deeply involved in her routine of prayer and fasting that Ghalib took to jocularly calling his home the Fatehpuri Mosque. Certainly, in this respect, they stood in stark contrast, for Ghalib was the other extreme in his indifference to religious observances. It is for this reason that, according to Hali, the poor lady even kept her eating and drinking utensils separate from her husband's. They had no children—seven were born but none lived longer than fifteen months. Ghalib refers to this in passing in one of his letters, but the deep void and sense of inadequacy that it must have created cannot be minimized. The lack of common ground with his wife was not uncommon for the times. Men were educated, abreast of the affairs of the world, while women, mostly illiterate, and confined to *purdah* and the home were considered—true to stereotypical definition—narrow in outlook and concerned exclusively with petty gossip and the mundane problems of running a home. Between this divide children were the bridge. Their absence seriously eroded the anchorage and solace a home and marriage could traditionally provide.

References in Ghalib's letters to the institution of marriage would make it appear that he considered it an unredeemed burden. His advice to many a friend was that the wise fly does not get caught in a single pot of honey, but moves on from one lump of sugar to another. To others he quoted, approvingly, the old saying that a man should refrain from two things— marriage, even if the bride is the daughter of a king, and borrowing, even if there is time till doomsday to repay.

In a famous letter in which he recapitulated the main events of his life in symbolic terms, he spoke of his marriage in this way: 'Then, on the seventh Rajab, 1225 (1810, the year of his marriage), sentence of life imprisonment was passed on me, fetters were put on my feet . . .'[64] About another friend, who had probably lost his second wife, Ghalib commented: 'I feel sorry for Umrao Singh but envy him too. Imagine! He has been free of his chains twice over, and here I have been carrying my noose for over half a century . . .'[65]

One must resist the temptation to take Ghalib too literally; remarks such as these were largely tongue-in-cheek—part of conventional male deprecation of marriage—made more in the interests of style and *tarz-i-ada* than as serious complaints. 'His complaint that his marriage was imprisonment for life, would be scandalously untrue if he had made it seriously. But his letters are only conversation pieces, full of charming untruths.'[66] No doubt the fetters did chafe; but in time he got used to them. The lack of any meeting ground with his wife did reduce marital rapport, but did not obliterate it; in the course of a lifetime Umrao Begum and he accepted their differences, and agreed to drift together. For marriage to take such a turn was not entirely out of context with the times; and, within this framework, there is evidence that both were capable of caring. Ghalib would always find time, at some point in the day, to be with her in the *zenana,* and she, on her part, her religious preoccupations notwithstanding, never failed in concerning herself with his needs. Ghalib was not quite the merry rake, oblivious to family responsibilities, that he liked to portray himself as. The *domni* love affair was perhaps the last such episode. He did resent—particularly in times of economic stress—the burdens of family life; but it is unlikely that he ever thought of discarding his duties as a family man. On the contrary, he was happy to enhance his servitude. Having no children of his own, he adopted his wife's nephew, Zain-ul-Abidin Khan, as his son. The date of adoption is not known, but we know that Ghalib was extremely fond of him. Zain-ul-Abidin Khan was a good poet and wrote under the *nom de plume* 'Arif'. He was a source of enduring pride to Ghalib. Arif, his wife and their two children lived with Ghalib. Ghalib's letters provide enough evidence of his involvement with the family. Arif's two sons—Baqir Ali and Hussain Ali—were, in particular, the focus of a doting grandfather's attention. In fact, Ghalib's love for children is a little-known but very lovable aspect of his character. The children and grandchildren of many of his friends found in him an 'uncle', who never failed or forgot to enquire about their welfare. There is, for instance, this delightful extract from a letter to one such friend: 'How is my nephew and my dear little niece? You told me in an earlier letter that she takes her own pen and inkpot and sits down to write letters to me, and that when

she quarrels with you she says, "I'll go off to stay with
Mirza Sahib". Now you must tell her to stop calling
me "Mirza Sahib" and call me "Uncle".'[67]

Arif's premature death in 1852, at the young age
of thirty-five, was a shattering blow. The elegy Ghalib
wrote then will remain one of the most moving
testaments of a father's anguish at the loss of his son.

O, Eternal Sky,
Arif was still young,
How would it have harmed you
Had he lived a little more.

You were the moon-light
That illumined my home;
Then why could this happy picture
Not last a little more.

In innocence, Ghalib, you ask:
Why must I live on?
It was destiny that you would live
Seeking death a little more.[68]

Arif's wife had predeceased him by a few months,
victim probably of the same killer disease—
tuberculosis—that had taken her husband. A year
later, Ghalib lost an aunt to whom he was, obviously,
very deeply attached. She had always cared for Ghalib
as if he were a son, and Ghalib, from childhood, had
looked upon her as a mother. There is evidence that,
apart from affection, she was a source of monetary
support as well. Ghalib wrote that, with her death,

it was as though he had lost his father, his grandparents, three uncles and three aunts all at once.

In his personal life Ghalib's involvements, like others of his time, went beyond the nuclear family. The joint family maze of close attachments and obligations was an accepted way of life. It would be a fallacy to visualize Ghalib as a recluse, unhappy in marriage, issueless, without attachments, driven by grief into self-imposed aloofness. The poet's isolation was of course there; but his daily life was crowded by the impinging relationships of a *larger* family. Joy and tragedy came, but the framework was participatory, reducing the impact of sorrow if not enhancing that of joy, and providing the resilience to overcome. Ghalib again picked up the threads of familial existence by adopting Arif's sons as his own. The elder one—Baqir Ali— just five years old at the time of his father's death, probably left later, to stay with Arif's mother, but Hussain Ali, three years younger than Baqir, lived with Ghalib throughout. The boys were the 'apples of Ghalib's eyes' and their pranks and activities considerably enlivened his home. In one of his letters he complains that they disturbed him at dinner, walked barefoot all over his bed, spilled water here and raised dust there—but that he still did not lose his patience.

Most biographers tend to paint a picture of unredeemed bleakness on Ghalib's home front. Factual incongruence apart, such a picture would do injustice to the defiant and cheerful stoicism of Ghalib the philosopher and poet. 'If the fire is strong,' he once wrote, 'I fan it more. I fight with death. I hurl myself on unsheathed swords. I play with daggers and shower kisses on arrows.'[69] The acceptance of adversity, as but a facet of the divine immanence of the Almighty, gave him the strength to transmute personal loss into an 'understanding of the joyous splendour of agony'.[70] The result was an integral philosophical outlook combining, in enlightened proportions, the elements of surrender to and acceptance of the will of God. It manifested itself in a doughty sense of humour; where others succumbed, he could transcend:

If man is habituated to pain
Pain does not remain;
So many hardships fell on me
That they did not remain.[71]

The human situation had its agonies and its ecstasies, its ups and downs, its unions and its separations, its moments of elation and depression—but in all its facets there was an inherent vibrancy that only the insensitive could deny. Ghalib elevated the very act of experiencing to an ontological end in itself, to be savoured in spite of the existence of pain and sorrow, as long as one was alive:

O heart, consider even sorrow's song
To be a consolation;
For, one day, this body
Will lie without sensation.[72]

He believed that in the midst of the greatest tribulation the zest for life must prevail, and if man was too shallow a receptacle to absorb the range of experiences life could offer, he must enhance his sensitivity to compensate for capacity—a state of mind which allowed him to continue his literary pursuits, despite several ailments later in life:

> Desire regrets even the heart
> Can space no more apportion;
> In the pearl is interred
> The restlessness of the ocean.[73]

In this sense, Ghalib gave the meaning of the term *shauq* or desire a new resplendence and relevance. To desire was to affirm the validity of experience; to isolate oneself from experience was to negate it:

> A flower blooms and opens
> When by colour intoxicated;
> The drunk do not seek
> To keep themselves insulated.[74]

It was not necessary that desire be efficacious. It was an end in itself:

> By the sorcery of desire
> I too am mesmerized;
> But the aim of this is not
> That any aim be realized.[75]

In the resolve to be a participant—without aim or motive—considerations such as reciprocity and fulfilment, the lack of permanence of temporal

phenomena, could influence—but not circumscribe—
the inherent potential in every exposure for both joy
and reward:

> If the beloved does not care
> Let be; speak at least of her
> Alluring style and swaying gait.
> If the spring is fleeting
> Let be; speak at least of the
> Garden's freshness and the bracing air.[76]

One of Ghalib's oft-quoted couplets is best understood
in this context:

> The hand may be numb
> But the eye can still see;
> Let the wine and the cup
> Still stay before me.[77]

This is not simplistic hedonism, or, as some
constricted interpretations would have it, an exaltation
of profligacy. The divine relevance of *exposure* rather
than hedonistic annihilation, is the theme here. It is
an assertion of the validity of life's experience in any
circumstance, and, therefore, a proclamation of courage
to enjoy it, in spite of the grief and trauma that is
inevitably a part of it. As he wrote once, to be a
victim of the miseries of this world is itself evidence
of an inherent nobility. Not for Ghalib the hermit's
cloister. He would rather invite pain than build walls
to shelter himself from the colour and spectacle of
life in its plenitude:

If 'tis not already asunder
Plunge a dagger and tear the heart;
If thy lashes are not blood-soaked
Take a knife and pierce the heart.[78]

Or again,

The breast is ashamed
If the heart is not afire,
The heart is ashamed
If each breath is not on fire.[79]

Of course, the enlightened acceptance of pain could reduce, but not entirely dull, the cutting edge of grief and separation, or the weariness of daily strife and disappointment. Ghalib, the poet, internalized these a hundred times magnified, and could articulate his suffering with spontaneous simplicity:

A heart it is, not brick or stone
Filled with pain why can't it be?
A thousand times I shall weep
Why should anyone query me?[80]

Not the wine-cup am I
Accustomed to the endless fair;
Human am I, my heart
Of ceaseless strife despairs.[81]

The antidote was a philosophical anchorage for which he had shown an inclination very early in life. Even as a child, his favourite poets were those like Bedil or Nazir, whose writings were steeped in complex and even obscure metaphysical thought. Later in life he could not remain uninfluenced by heated debates on such metaphysical questions as the Nature of Reality, the Unity of Godhood, or the validity of temporal phenomena. His writings confirm that he was often dragged into such controversies. But apparently, in spite of a very thorough grounding in the various schools of philosophical thought, he had little taste for sterile academic debate, and even less respect for theologians who spent a lifetime splitting hairs on such questions. In a Persian couplet he writes sarcastically:

O passion for unity, pull Ghalib
From the assembly of the debate
Our simple Turk cannot successfully
Compete with these doctors of theology.[82]

Throughout his life he retained an eclectic openness and was proud to admit it. Aware of the debate, he was not prepared to restrict his search to the tenets of any one sect or group, or to allow his queries to congeal through acceptance of any one person as his spiritual guru:

With every passing swirl
Some distance I go;
A guide for the journey
I do not yet know.[83]

The exhilaration of new horizons, not the fixed vision of the unquestioned destination, the enquiry, not the preconceived answer seemed to have been the guiding tenets of his philosophical search. Not unexpectedly he was often assailed with doubt and this was the motivation for some of the finest poetry he wrote incorporating concepts that were, quite often, far ahead of his times. If the Apparent was not the Real, and yet the Real was manifest in the Apparent—how did one unite the opposing spectrums of belief and yet chart an unwavering path of conviction? If the world was a playground for the manifestation of His grace, how did one deal with the discordance of one's own pain and grief? If His unity was the only reality, what was the need for this bewildering plurality?

When except you, none else exists
Then, O God, what is all this tumult about?
Who are these fairy-faced ones?
What is this coquetry and blandishment about?
What is this aroma of cascading tresses?
What these dark-eyed enticing glances?
From where have come the flowers and trees?
What are clouds, and what this breeze?[84]

Or, in a somewhat different mood:

The reality of the sight of God,
The one who sees, and what is seen,
All in effect are one; I am amazed
Then, what is all His witnessing?[85]

However, doubt and query never hardened into disenchantment. They only heightened his almost child-

like awe and wonder at the magnitude of the human
dilemma, in the face of His eternally fascinating
inscrutability. The unanswered could also be laid at
His feet, as one more manifestation of His *leela,* as
one more indication of the limitation of man's reason
in the face of His ingenuity:

Who can say
Whose magical revelation this is?
He has dropped such a veil
That cannot be lifted.[86]

Only Thy perfection
Knows how to comprehend Thy perfection
To realize Thine existence in thought
Thine own existence is the only guide.[87]

This spiritual porousness allowed Ghalib to pick
and choose elements to evolve *a personal* philosophical
vision. At one level he could detach himself from the
temporal experience by the Vedantic assertion of the
non-existence of anything, except the Real.

Asad, do not fall a victim
To existence's deception;
The world is a snare
Of thought's conception.[88]

In dreams did thought
With you a bond feign
There was, on awakening,
Neither loss nor gain.[89]

In the deception of existence
Do not get caught,
Even if they say it is
In reality it is naught.[90]

That which appears emergent
Is in fact concealed;
He still is in a dream
Who awakes in a dream.[91]

At another, he could imbue with divinity every aspect
of the mundane, seeing in each atom both the
manifestation and proof of His grace:

That Glory, which suffuses
From earth to sky, all creation—
Drunk in the same resplendence
Is the tiniest grain and atom.[92]

Or, as he put it in a Persian verse:

The clue of His unity
Is found in His diversity,
To all the countless numbers
The common figure is one.[93]

From this stemmed his view of the Absolute as
benevolence incarnate—like the rays of the life-giving
sun, in whose radiance the brittleness and struggle of
the individual ego was reduced to naught:

From the rays of the sun
The dew learns of its demise;

I too am until
A benevolent glance does me surprise.[94]

This effulgent light is the basis
Of thine subsistence;
A speck, not caught in the rays of the sun,
Has no existence.[95]

God, then, was not to be found in the idol in the temple or through obeisance in the mosque. The orthodox sought to ensure divinity in the constricted realm of ritual and practice, right and wrong, sin and reward. Ghalib's concept of morality was liberated, precisely because of his counterpoised and transcendent view of His benevolence:

Nothing strange, if in His mercy
He accepts it;
Through remorse do not deny
Sins committed.[96]

Right and wrong in the 'religio-moralist' sense were the creation of the divisiveness of man's intelligence. But the world had been created by Him for man to revel in; the truly spiritual could not be constrained by such narrow categorizations, and Ghalib flaunted his irreverence of conventional morality, especially for the benefit of the orthodox:

The river of sin ran dry
For lack of water;
Not yet wet even
The edge of my trousers.[97]

If for sins committed
I am to be punished,
What about justice for desiring
Those uncommitted?[98]

It needs to be reiterated that statements such as these
were not a plea for unenlightened wallowing in the
pleasures of the senses. Ghalib had a word of warning
for those inclined to take him too literally:

You who tangle with Ghalib—remember
Inwardly he is a saint, if outwardly a sinner.[99]

The assertion of moral freedom was a stance with
Ghalib, linked to the poetic and philosophic perception
of joy—in the widest possible sense—as the basis of
creation—very much in tune with the Upanishadic
injunction: 'Where there is joy there is creation. Where
there is no joy there is no creation: Know the nature
of joy.'[100] Such joy could be of enduring value only in
the perception of the real essence behind transient
phenomena. In several of his couplets, Ghalib articulates
this perception with beautiful and startling clarity:

Stems and leaves emerge and grow
Because of the root;
From silence alone emerges
What we seek to moot.[101]

The theme recurs in his Persian collection:

The drop, the wave, the foam, the whirlpool—
All are aspects of the river

The boast of this 'I' and 'Mine'
Is no more than a curtain.[102]

In the light of this perception, Ghalib could proclaim
His existence in unequivocal terms:

When nothing was, God was;
God would still be, if nothing had been;
Being born, I was damned;
What loss would it have been
Had I not been?[103]

The negation of the individual ego and the assertion
of its complete futility in the presence of His
immanence, may—at a simplistic level—appear to
be both paradoxical and hypocritical for a man of
Ghalib's hypersensitive ego. But this only illustrates
the complex personality of Ghalib the man, sublimely
spiritual at one level, earthy and human at another.
Perhaps his moments of spiritual transcendence
stemmed from the realization that he was so wrapped
up in the tinsel of daily struggle and ambition and so
far from the spiritual liberation he yearned for:

O God, how long must I endure
The lowness of the nature of desire
Grant me the height of hands
Raised up in prayer.[104]

It is undeniable, however, that he did have reservoirs
of spiritual solace. From the many strands of his
philosophic vision, two elements are easily identified

as, probably, providing the greatest strength to him in tragedy and disappointment. The first was a willingness to surrender—whenever a crisis came to a pitch—to the will of the Absolute; a stoical acceptance of the futility of struggle beyond a point, and an equally stoical conviction that such acceptance would provide the resilience to overcome:

> Glory it is for the drop
> To merge with the ocean;
> Pain ceases to be
> Once beyond redemption.[105]

The second was an ability to detach himself from the immediate context: to become a transcendent observer of his own situation, even as he remained, to all apparent purposes, an intense participant and witness. In doing so, he was able to retain a sense of perspective, and even more importantly, a sense of humour, and on occasion, experience the most lofty, soaring sentiments of joyous abandonment.

> Like the reflection of an arched bridge in the torrent,
> Dance in delight at disaster;
> Separating thyself from thyself,
> Balance thyself, and dance.

> There is no faith in the keeping of promises;
> Whatever happy moments come, consider thy good fortune;

At the time of making promises,
If the fair ones offer blandishment, then dance.

There is delight in the search itself,
So why talk of finishing thy journey?
At the sound of the camel-bell
Lose thy balance, and dance.

The flower-garden was verdant,
When we walked there proudly;
In the burning of our straw and rubbish,
O flame—dance.

Even the hooting of an owl
Should be heard as a kind of melody;
Even in the breeze
Of the phoenix's fluttering wings—dance.

The delight of the desert-waste
Cannot be found in love;
Become a whirlwind of dust,
And, rising in the air—dance.

Put aside the outmoded customs
Of thy honoured friends;
Mourn at the wedding feast,
And in the assembly of mourners—dance.

Unlike the anger of the devout
And the friendship of hypocrites,
Be not self-centred,
But before everyone—dance.

Seek not distress in burning,
Or delight in blossoming;
On the edge of the *simoom,* and in the gentle breeze,
Frivolously dance.

Ghalib with this exultant joy,
To whom art thou bound?
Wax great in thyself alone
And with the shackles of disaster—dance.[106]

Over the years, Ghalib's fame as a poet had steadily grown. He had first compiled his Urdu verse in 1821.[107] In 1825, at the request of friends, he collated the general principles of Persian letter-writing in a popular booklet called *Panj Ahang.* In 1828, he compiled a combined selection of his Urdu and Persian verse—*Gul-i-Rana.* His Urdu *Diwan* was first published in 1841, and sold out immediately. It was reprinted in 1847, but obviously, was grossly unable to meet popular demand. As late as 1855, Ghalib complained that he could not lay hands on a copy for himself because the publishers had committed copies, in bulk, to booksellers in advance. The collection of his Persian verse was published in 1845.

Literary pre-eminence imposed its own obligations. The desire to withdraw from his fellowmen, after the humiliation in the pension case and the bitterness of the Shamsuddin incident, must have been short-lived and largely unfulfilled. Much of his time was taken up in correction work. This was a labour of love expected from a literary figure. Ghalib never refused anyone and, as his fame increased, so did the number of people keen to have his comments on their verse. He took this work seriously and expected others to appreciate this. In a letter he gently chides Munshi Hargopal Tufta, his most prolific *shagird,* to read corrections carefully. Apart from correcting the metre and construction of the verse, he would also append detailed advice and comments. His criticism was always frank, and often blunt, but never cursory. In a long letter to Tufta he discusses in detail a certain line written by him, but ends by saying that nothing could make that line make sense. On occasion his critique could be devastating. Commenting on certain lines written by Tufta, with whom he appears to have corresponded the most on such matters, he stated: In all these verses there is nothing wrong—and nothing of interest.'[108] Of special interest was the degree of intellectual eclecticism that guided him on any question of correct usage. Once, when a *shagird* sought to justify a particularly literary usage, by quoting a couplet of the classical Persian poet Hazin, his answer was that Hazin was but human; even if the angel Gabriel had written the couplet it would not be correct.

Ghalib was a prolific writer of letters and expended a great deal of time and effort in their composition; he considered this to be a literary pursuit. His innumerable letters read effortlessly, like flowing conversation, full of details and charming *obiter dicta,* with minimum stylization and transparent spontaneity. 'I have invented a style,' he once wrote to a friend, 'through which correspondence has become conversation. From a distance of a thousand miles you can speak through your pen, and enjoy company despite separation.'[109] Letters took time to reach, but, until the institution of the newspaper was introduced— and in many ways even after that—remained the most important instrument for the dissemination of news. For Ghalib, keeping up a correspondence with his many friends, all over northern India, was a major occupation. Waiting for letters to arrive or sending his servant Kallu to the post office to dispatch some was a daily routine. A collection of his letters was printed during his life-time. His vocation was not only the writing of poetry; but in a much broader sense it was the mastery of all attributes of literary excellence. Very frequently, he was asked to write introductions or prefaces to the work of other authors. He took great pains over these. 'My friend, is it an easy matter to write an introduction?' he once asked Tufta. 'It is a heartbreaking task. To write prose is just as hard as to write verse.'[110] There was no fixed time for him to write his own poetry, but it would appear that he wrote more in the quieter hours of the late evening. *Mushairahs* were much in vogue, and provided a highly popular institutional forum for the literary effervescence of the times. The palace regularly organized at least two formal *mushairahs* a month at the Diwan-i-Am but there must have been many more informal gatherings in the salons of the nobility. Ghalib was a major attraction at these. He had a powerful voice and he used it to telling effect. In recognition of his poetic eminence his turn to recite usually came at the very end. Sometimes, impatient of waiting, especially if the calibre of poetry was lacklustre, he would excuse himself for a while, take a stroll in the city, have some wine, and then return to the *mehfil* which would go on till the light of morning could be seen on the horizon. His close friends included Munshi Nabi Baksh (Haqir), Fazl-i-Haq, and Mustafa Nawab Khan (Shefta), who had become a close friend after his return from Calcutta. All of them were accomplished poets and scholars in their own right. His *shagirds* included Tufta and Alai (Allauddin Ahmad Khan of the Loharu family). These and others formed a literary circle that met and corresponded almost daily. Ghalib's daily life was, thus, not very unlike that of a celebrated literary don today—involved in correction work, the writing of poetry, essays, critical commentaries, prefaces, participating in debates, symposiums, seminars and poetry reading sessions, giving much-sought-after opinion on any issue of literary controversy, editing, presiding over tutorials— with this difference, that in an age of unprecedented literary efflorescence the milieu was, if anything, even more vibrant and demanding. This integral literary experience, lived day in and day out, was the most striking weave in the texture of Ghalib's life, and cannot but be taken into account.

With the opening of the Delhi College, Ghalib was offered the professorship in Persian in 1842. Thompson, Secretary to the Government of India, asked him to come for an interview. When Ghalib alighted from the palanquin he expected Thompson to come outside to receive him. This was customary courtesy when a member of the nobility was calling. Thompson did not do so because, as we've seen, he saw no reason to follow custom as Ghalib was coming in the capacity of an applicant for a job. Ghalib was cut to the quick. He told Thompson that he had expected that the job would add to his prestige, not detract from it. Thompson said that he was bound by the rules that govern such matters. Ghalib then begged to be excused and left. Ghalib needed the money, of course; but there were certain values by which he sought to define his image, in his own eyes, which he was not prepared to sacrifice. Besides, a salaried appointment in a college was still a new concept; a poet of renown was supposed to be supported by royal patronage and the discerning among the rich. In any case, literary activity outside the college was both satisfying and sufficiently time-consuming. Money was the only consideration, but then one could not have everything.

Life thus went on in much the same way as before. During the hot seasons he spent the days in a darkened little room over the main entrance to his house. In winter, he sat in the adjoining veranda where the sun came in. A bit of wine in the evening, and chess and *chausar* remained unchanging recreations, mangoes the unchanging addiction. Literary preoccupations kept him busy. The ups and downs of family life were equally demanding, a source of joy, but perhaps more often, a cause of grief. The shortage of money remained a constant irritant and there were some problems emerging on the health front, largely a result of lack of physical exercise 'combined with a diet consisting almost entirely of meat and bread'.[111] In this pace the years rolled along until an event which shook him—his arrest for gambling—occurred. I have touched on this briefly earlier but it deserves to be looked at in depth.

Ghalib liked to play *chausar* with stakes; it is possible that financial stringency had made him a trifle reckless, but his house was not, as some authors allege, a gambling den. He played with friends and did not consider it morally wrong. British officials at this time were becoming the harbingers of a new morality, evangelical in its zeal and inflexible in its smug sense of the need to reform 'native' habits. They considered gambling a social vice that had to be eradicated. Ghalib had received a warning, in 1841, when his house had been raided and he had been fined Rs 100 for gambling. What happened in 1847 is not very clear. In one of his letters Ghalib mentions that the *kotwal* of Delhi—Faiz Hasan Khan—was hostile to him. (It is this kernel of fact which the otherwise enjoyable commercial Hindi film on Ghalib uses with generous additives of fiction.) By one account, the *kotwal* sent his men disguised as ladies in *burkas* to raid Ghalib's house. Ghalib was caught gambling—red-handed. Probably he was still confident that the matter would be contained: after all he was a distinguished member of the nobility, the acknowledged Poet Laureate of the city, not unknown to British officials. But he was in for a rude shock. The magistrate—Roberts—was newly appointed and did not know Ghalib's background; nor did he consider it necessary to find out. According to Ghalib, he was excessively influenced by the *kotwal*. Ghalib was sentenced to six months' imprisonment with hard labour and a fine of Rs 200; if the fine was not paid, the term of imprisonment was to be extended, but for an additional payment of Rs 50—over and above the fine—he could be excused the hard labour. The sessions judge, who knew Ghalib well, confirmed the sentence.

Predictably, the judgment created a furore. The harshness of the sentence provoked outrage. A contemporary newspaper protested that it was manifestly unjust, that, for such a minor crime, a nobleman and respected public figure should be given a punishment so harsh that it could well endanger his life. The king, Bahadur Shah, intervened with the British authorities; but the *angrezi sarkar* remained unmoved. His Highness was informed that the matter was *sub judice*. The law must be allowed to take its course.

Ghalib did not serve the full six-month sentence. He was released after three months. In prison he did not have to perform hard labour. He was allowed to eat food sent from home, wear his own clothes, and receive visitors. But it was the hot season, and he must have suffered. In fact, he was probably released earlier on the advice of Dr Ross, the Civil Surgeon. The really wounding aspect was the humiliation of it all. Ghalib, the aristocrat, the intellectual, the sensitive poet of sorrow and joy, was incarcerated like a common criminal. Any illusions about his worth, in the eyes of the new rulers, were severely eroded. The impotence of the Mughal king, the Shadow of God on Earth, and, in inverse proportion, the power of the *feringhees,* was vividly demonstrated. Efforts to cultivate the latter had proved unavailing; it was a new value system, a new inexorable scale of right and wrong buttressed by a new political framework, which one either accepted or suffered—and in this suffering no one stood with you. At the personal level, this was the greatest revelation for Ghalib. Most of his friends in Delhi, and even close and loved relatives, deserted him and displayed rather finely honed sensitivities on how to remain on the right side of power. Aminuddin Khan of Loharu, who was one of Ghalib's closest friends and a kinsman, publicly sought to remove the taint of this association, by having it published in a newspaper that he was related to Ghalib only by marriage. Ziyauddin, his brother, was no less hostile.

The one noteworthy exception was Mustafa Khan Shefta. Shefta did his very best to have the prison sentence waived. He defrayed the expenses for the trial and appeal, and when these did not succeed, he (in all probability) paid the fine. During Ghalib's imprisonment he continued to meet him almost daily. For this behaviour, in such stark contrast to that of others, Ghalib remained indebted to him for the rest of his life. In his famous poem—*Habsiyya*[112]—written in prison he pays him tribute, referring to him as God's mercy and compassion incarnate in human form. With friends like Shefta, Ghalib exclaimed, a man could die ungrieving. The same poem also has stanzas full of bitterness and deep sarcasm on the 'loyalty' of other friends. Their behaviour, Ghalib said, made the prison a better place than the free world.

On his release, Ghalib's frame of mind was one of intense dejection. The thought of returning to the same society, which—in a moment of need, support and solace—had dropped him like a hot brick hardly appealed to him. There was also the shame and humiliation to live down. Perhaps he wrote the famous couplet that portrayed the callousness of society at this time:

> Let us remove to such a place
> Where none else should be,
> None to speak one's tongue
> Or share one's thoughts should be;
> Build a house sans walls or floor
> No neighbour, no person, close by should be;
> If one is sick, none need be there to care,
> And if one were to pass away
> Nobody to mourn should be.[113]

A Persian letter, quoted by Hali, echoes similar thoughts: '. . . It is my desire no longer to stay in this world, and if I must stay, then not to stay in India. There is Rum; there is Egypt; there is Iran; there is Baghdad. But these too I pass by. The Kaaba itself is the sanctuary of the free . . . I await the day when I shall gain release from this bondage of wretchedness, which wears away my soul more than the bondage I have undergone could do, and shall set my face towards the wilderness, not caring where I go.'[114]

The prison sentence must have brought about a major upheaval in his domestic arrangements. We can infer this by the fact that on his release he did not return to his old home, but moved into one provided by a friend—Fakir Miyan Kale Sahib, whom the king, Bahadur Shah, regarded as a spiritual preceptor. It was Miyan Kale Sahib's relations with the king that now helped Ghalib to get official access to the Mughal court—for the first time. The king's physician, Hakim Ahsanullah Khan, who was a close friend, must have also put in a good word. Ghalib's reputation as a poet had not been affected by the prison term. In any case, people in general—notwithstanding their callous behaviour—had never looked upon him as a criminal. The *feringhee sarkar* was the ruler, and its whims had to be obeyed. Once Ghalib was released there were many who found the courage to express their dormant sympathies. The king had officially intervened with the British for a waiver of the sentence. This was his duty to Ghalib, the distinguished poet and nobleman. But at the personal level his relations with Ghalib were not particularly good. Bahadur Shah came to the throne in 1837, but as we know he was not the choice of his father Akbar Shah II, who kept appealing to the British to recognize Prince Salim, a younger son, as the heir apparent. Ghalib had written a *qasida* in honour of Akbar Shah II, in which he also praised— with rather excessive eloquence—the qualities of Prince Salim. When Bahadur Shah came to the throne he did not forget Ghalib's backing of his rival. It took Ghalib 'thirteen years and fifteen *qasidas* to live this down'.[115] Finally, in 1850, the king at last conferred on him the titles of *Najm-ud-Daula, Dabir-ul-Mulk, Nizam Jang* (Star of the Realm, Scribe of the State, Marshal of War) and awarded him a commission to write a history of the Timurid dynasty, at a salary of Rs 600 a year.

These developments helped rehabilitate Ghalib emotionally. His social standing received a much-needed refurbishing. But the initial sense of achievement soon lost its glow. The writing of history was a research exercise of which he appears to have tired quickly—and with which he persisted only because of the money. In the first six months—July to December 1850—he was not able to get beyond Babur.

It had been decided that his remuneration would be paid six-monthly; Ghalib, whose financial liquidity was always precarious, preferred to be paid monthly, and in the beginning he decided that if this was not done, he would get rid of the entire project. In his inimitable fashion he raised the question of receiving monthly remuneration in a *nazm* addressed directly to Bahadur Shah:

> The salary fixed for me
> Has for payment a strange practice;
>
> A ritual for this corpse six-monthly
> Amazed the world is at such tactics;
>
> A one-third partner in my salary
> Has become the money-lender;
>
> Make my salary payable monthly
> So that life for me is easier.[116]

He succeeded in getting paid monthly but never succeeded in taking the historical narrative beyond Humayun. By 1851 his reactions had become much more blunt and he looked upon the whole business as a headache. The project died a natural death. The court lost interest and Ghalib made no effort to revive it. What he had already written was finally published, in 1854, under the title *Mihr-i-Nimroz* (The Sun at Mid-day). The only significant outcome of the whole business was that Ghalib, fatigued by the long hours of writing stylized Persian, reverted—after a lapse of over two decades—to Urdu as the medium of his letters.

The nature of the work assigned was not the only reason for his lukewarm relations with Zafar's court. The choice of Sheikh Muhammad Ibrahim Zauq as the king's *ustad*,[117] Ghalib felt, reflected poorly on Zafar's literary discernment. Ghalib was the acknowledged Poet Laureate of the city, Zauq was the official *numero uno*. His resentment and hostility were understandable. The story goes that one day Ghalib was sitting in a tavern when he saw Zauq coming down the street, *en route* to the palace. As he passed by, Ghalib remarked loudly: 'But a courtier of the king, he struts about so.' The taunt was blunt and, as expected, Zauq complained to the king. Ghalib was still at the tavern when an *abdar* came with a message that His Exalted Highness wished to see Mirza Nausha immediately. A convincing explanation would have to be given as it was an attack on the king's *ustad* and denial would be futile. On the way to the Red Fort, Ghalib composed the following poem which, while subtly chiding the king for his partisanship, completely changed the context of the insult addressed to Zauq:

> To all I say, you rejoin:
> Pray what is this?
> You tell me, for conversing,
> What style is this?

When the body was burnt
The heart too must have;
You rake the ashes now,
What search is this?

My envy is but this,
That he has your ear;
Fear of the enemy's mischief
What else—except for this?

I have no strength for speech
And even if I did
With what hope would I say:
My desire is this

But a courtier of the king
He struts about so
Ghalib's prestige in the town
What else—if not this?[118]

In the changed context there was nothing which His Highness could take umbrage at; but he and the entire city knew the truth. A more serious incident took place in December 1851. The occasion was the marriage of Bahadur Shah Zafar's son—Prince Jawan Bakht. Jawan Bakht's mother—Zinat Mahal—was Zafar's favourite wife and exercised great influence on him. On her instigation, Zafar was trying to get the British to recognize Jawan Bakht as the heir apparent, though he was much younger than the other princes. Not surprisingly, the arrangements for Jawan

Bakht's marriage were very elaborate and there was much excitement in the city. Ghalib was asked by Zinat Mahal to write a *sehra* on the occasion. He complied promptly, writing one on traditional lines but for the last verse, which, in the context of his well-known rivalry with Zauq, was deliberately provocative:

Not biased towards Ghalib, in poetry we have insight
Let us see if someone else a better *sehra* can recite.

The king did not appreciate the insult to his *ustad*. He asked Zauq to pick up the gauntlet, and compose a fitting rejoinder. Zauq then wrote his own prothalamion in which the last verse (in the same vein as Ghalib's) challenged the ability of those who made a claim to be poets to equal his writing of a *sehra*.

Zauq's prothalamion was given very wide publicity by the professional singers in the palace, and the next day it was published in the local newspaper. In the beginning, Ghalib assumed that his controversial verse had been resented by Zauq alone. Although he was privately prepared to concede that he had perhaps pushed the boundaries of poetic licence a little too far, his initial reaction was to ignore Zauq's rejoinder. But the considerable publicity being given to it made him realize that the king himself was annoyed. He then presented his famous Apology to the king:

I accept that facts as they are must be narrated
'Tis not my desire to project any qualities in me.

For generations my ancestors have been warriors
I do not seek respect on account of poetry.

Free in spirit, my way is friendship with all
To fight with others is not my mentality.

Glory enough the opportunity to serve Zafar
Even though in this I have neither prestige nor
money.

To think I could ever cross swords with the royal-
tutor!
This temerity, this daring, this strength is not in
me.

Urdu is not my forte, yes this I will say
I had no other purpose but to please Your Majesty

The last couplet has become the subject of dispute
My goal was never a break in amity.

A sinner, if in speech against another I insinuate
So bereft of my senses I just cannot be

My fate may be bad, not so my temperament
Happy am I with the place assigned to me

Honesty is my creed, Ghalib, God is my witness
By habit, I do not lie, I speak the truth
unreservedly.[119]

The entire incident became the talk of the town
for days to come. Ghalib's Apology, through

exaggerated protestations of meekness and humility, ostensibly craved forgiveness. But its *double entendre,* so exquisitely tongue-in-cheek, defiantly proclaimed that he was *above* competition with anyone in Urdu— his forte being Persian, the language of the glorious rulers of the past—and that, in any case, his personal standing rested on his noble lineage (Zauq, everybody knew, was of humble origin) and not on writing. The last verse delivered the knock-out punch. The assertion that he did not lie was made as a general statement, but it was obvious to all that it sought to reiterate the validity of his original boast in the prothalamion! This delectable play on words must have amused, if not mollified, the king. It certainly provided tremendous entertainment to the people of Delhi who eagerly followed the literary thrust and sparring.

Zauq died in 1854. Ghalib succeeded him as the king's *ustad.* The king was a distinguished poet himself. His predilection towards Zauq had never blinded him to Ghalib's intrinsic worth as a poet. The three presiding poets of the poetic efflorescence in the first half of the nineteenth century were Ghalib, Zauq and Momin. Momin had died in 1851. On Zauq's death three years later Ghalib was the obvious choice. It is likely that Ghalib was not overly enthused by the appointment. The recognition had come too late— Ghalib was fifty-seven—and even now, was not accorded the formal title—*Malik-ush-Shuara* (Poet Laureate)—which had been given to Zauq. The king's financial position was such that there was little to expect in terms of material benefit. The appointment was not linked to any increase in stipend. More importantly, Ghalib could never really forgive or forget Zafar's initial choice of Zauq as *ustad*. This not only devalued the assignment, but, in Ghalib's eyes, also tainted the king's literary abilities. He could never overcome the suspicion that Bahadur Shah was incapable of understanding the worth of Ghalib, the poet.

It would appear that he could dispose of corrections of the king's verse with a minimum of effort and a casualness reflective of the feeling that the verses *required* only that much effort. An eyewitness once saw him correct a sheaf of Zafar's verses in just a few minutes—as he chatted in the Diwan-i-Am. Once the corrections were over, he told a footman to deliver the papers to Zafar and expressed great relief the work was done.

The implication is clear: the corrections were done not only casually but also reluctantly. However, as the royal *ustad* there were certain formal requirements which he could not avoid: these included the presentation of odes on celebrations—such as the two Ids—or on other occasions when the king so desired. Ghalib found these obligations increasingly irksome. In 1855, on the occasion of Id, he did not write an ode, a *qata* or a *rubai* but recited two or three couplets, composed on the spur of the moment, of which he did not even keep a copy. A similar attempt at evasion on the next Id was strongly objected to by Hakim Ahsanullah Khan, who insisted on a full-length *masnavi*. It was not only the compulsion and the sterile formality of it that Ghalib resented. By this time, he found the task of serious verse writing too effort-consuming—even though he could compose with minimum effort—because by temperament and training he took a great deal of pain over formal poetic compositions. He mentions this in a letter perhaps of 1855 or 1856: '. . . my heart no longer holds its former strength, nor my pen its former power. The one talent that remains to me is the gift of facile composition. I can write—without thought and without delay—whatever fancy comes into my head. The labour of poetic creation I cannot now sustain.'[120]

The king required him to be present in his court almost daily. In several of his letters Ghalib mentions that by nine in the morning he would set off to the Fort. Depending upon the whims of the Jahanpanah. the schedule could become fairly demanding. There would be stretches when Bahadur Shah would hold court every day; this meant that Ghalib would leave for the Fort between eight and nine, return at mid-day for a hurried lunch, rest a while, and often be back in attendance again in the evening. The king's requests were inviolable; after a full day, for instance, he would invite Ghalib to join him for kite-flying in the evening, which was a favourite pastime for the nobles at that time. It was not possible to refuse. Ghalib, who had never been formally employed, was unused to a routine of this pace and grumbled to his friends that he fell asleep each night as exhausted as a labourer. It was perhaps at this time that he wrote the lines:

Ghalib you are a pensioner
Give blessings to the monarch

> Those days are gone when you could say
> A servant I am not[121]

But there were redeeming features about the job too; in spite of the inherent unease in their relationship, both the king and Ghalib often enjoyed a relaxed informality at a personal level. The king, in deference to his *ustad's* reputation, his years, and his status as a nobleman, allowed him considerable leeway in personal behaviour and the performance of official obligations. Ghalib was aware of this, but never misused the situation to become excessively familiar. In their interaction there was that correct mix of restraint, subtlety, respect, humour and urbanity that best symbolized the cultural sophistication of the period. On one occasion, when the king was present in court the conversation turned on the close relations that had existed between (the medieval Muslim saint) Nizamuddin and (the Persian poet) Amir Khusro. Ghalib who was renowned for his mental dexterity and ability to compose verse at a moment's notice, at once composed and recited the following verse:

> Two holy guides; two suppliants. In this God's power we see.
> Nizamuddin had Khusro; Sirajuddin has me.[122]

Sirajuddin was the real name of the king; he changed it to Bahadur Shah only after he came to the throne. He could not but have found this spontaneous demonstration of his *ustad's* sparkling wit most diverting. Indeed it was this shared sense of humour which in course of time allowed them to build bridges of tolerance and adjustment even on issues where their views were fundamentally at variance. The king was a devout Muslim who prayed and kept the fasts most meticulously. Ghalib was impatient of ritualistic religion and never kept the Ramzan fast. At the end of Ramzan the king once asked Ghalib how many fasts he had kept. Without batting an eyelid, and with an absolutely straight face, Ghalib replied: 'My Lord, I did not keep one.' This could mean he had failed to keep only one or failed to keep a single one. The king knew the latter was true. But he smiled and let the matter pass. In a similar vein Ghalib once recited the following lines to Zafar:

> That sovereign whose throne is the sky
> And who, on this earth, reigns like the sun
> He should certainly keep the fast.
> But he who does not even have
> The means to break the fast
> What else can he do
> Except to eat the fast[123]

The fact that Ghalib could address the king in such terms, on a subject on which his views were doctrinaire, speaks volumes for Zafar's tolerance and the special relationship the king and his tutor had come to enjoy.

In temporal terms, 1854, the year he became the king's *ustad*, was the best period for Ghalib. Earlier that year the king's son and heir apparent, Mirza Fakhruddin, whose poetic *nom de plume* was 'Ramz',

had also become his *shagird* on an annual stipend of
Rs 400. Mirza Fakhruddin was married to the widow
of Nawab Shamsuddin. Given the fact that Ghalib was
suspected of helping the British convict Shamsuddin,
the fact that Mirza Fakhruddin could appoint Ghalib
his *ustad* is tribute both to the young prince's
magnanimity and to Ghalib's reputation as the
undisputed presiding poet of the city. At about this
time, Ghalib's persistent efforts to impress Nawab
Wajid Ali Shah, the ruler of Oudh, also bore fruit.
Wajid Ali granted him an annual stipend of Rs 500.
For Ghalib, always hard pressed for money, this
accretion to his income was most desirable. But this
happy state of affairs was all too fleeting, a momentary
flash on the peak before the long and final decline.
Ghalib was, by now, an old man; his health was
deteriorating fast. The traditional Delhi diseases—
malaria and the Delhi Sore—had taken their toll. He
had become increasingly prone to vicious attacks of
colic. His eyesight had weakened and he was partially
deaf. In the foreword to *Mihr-i-Nimroz* he wrote that
the joints in his fingers had become stiff, making it
difficult to hold a pen. His letters of this period carry
frequent descriptions of his failing health: loss of teeth,
increasing deafness, wrinkles on the face, the trembling
of limbs, and loss of hair.

The death of Momin and Zauq had come as a shock
to him. Even though Zauq was a literary rival, and
this rivalry often spilled into personal acrimony, he
was also a fellow poet and a contemporary, witness to
an era spent together, a symbol of the continuity of
a certain milieu. His death suddenly brought home to

Ghalib his own advancing years. When Momin had
died three years earlier, he had written to a friend:
'Just see, my friend, one after the other people of our
own age die; the caravan moves off, and we ourselves
are waiting with one foot in the stirrup. Momin Khan
was of the same age as I, and was a good friend too.
We got to know each other forty-three years ago
when we were no more than fourteen or fifteen years
old . . . And, my good sir, you'd be hard put to it to
find even an enemy of forty years' standing, let alone
a friend.'[124] However, despite his melancholia, he still
showed signs of his irrepressible buoyancy; brief
moments of exhilaration were quick to be seized and
deliberately articulated. In a letter to Tufta in 1853,
very soon after Momin's and Arif's deaths, he exclaims
with childlike glee: '. . . All my miscellaneous debts
are paid and I feel greatly relieved. I now have forty-
seven rupees cash in my box, and four bottles of wine
and three of rose-water in the store-room. Praise be
to God for His kindness!'[125] But these sparks occurred
less and less and Ghalib began to gradually realize
that the best part of his life was over and that the
inexorable decline had begun. His thoughts now began
to be more and more taken up with the question of
death, of how much longer he had to live, of how
much longer he could expect to keep up his writing.

In 1854, it became common knowledge that the
British proposed to further clip the powers of the
titular Mughal king. In 1856 the British deposed Wajid
Ali Shah and annexed Oudh. In the same year the
Mughal heir apparent, Mirza Fakhruddin, died. Ghalib
was deprived of his income from these sources. More

disturbing was the uncertainty about the king. The horizon was becoming increasingly dark and ominous. Ghalib was worried that with the death of Mirza Fakhruddin—who was his *shagird*—his ties with the Mughal court were ensured only as long as the king lived. Apparently, Ghalib's relations with Fakhruddin were very cordial; the prince used to pay, over and above the fixed stipend, Rs 10 every month to buy fruit for Ghalib's grandchildren (Arif's two boys). This income also stopped.

But Ghalib need not have worried about such minor losses. The upheaval of 1857 would soon overwhelm almost all the familiar contours of life, as he had known it. In its aftermath, he would live on to witness an entire social system—which alone gave meaning and relevance to his values—being dismantled, bit by bit, before his very eyes. Neither Ghalib, nor Delhi, nor the *tehzib* which bound the two so inextricably, would ever be the same again.

FOUR

The Trauma of 1857

The year 1857 marked the end of a historical phase. In its aftermath, the painstakingly built, centuries-old, socio-cultural edifice of the Mughals came crashing down. It was Ghalib's fate to live till 1869, a forlorn and heart broken witness to the end of an age. The mature and self-assured *tehzib,* composite in outlook, urbane and sophisticated in form—that gave his life and work anchorage and sustenance—would never be the same again. He would live to see the Red Fort—the Qila-i-Mualla—converted into a barracks. He would live to see His Exalted Highness, the Shadow of God on Earth, exiled from the land, unsung and unheralded, never to return again. And he would live to see his beloved Delhi systematically brutalized almost beyond recognition.

The objective reasons which led to the Revolt of 1857 are well known and have been analysed in detail in several works. I will, therefore, not recapitulate them here. At the subjective level, however, there is little evidence to show that Delhi was overtly anticipating or expecting the upheaval. It is true that there was some vague unrest. But this was primarily focussed on speculation about the future of the monarchy. It was widely known that the British were planning to remove the Mughal residence from the imperial backdrop of the Red Fort to somewhere outside the city, near the Qutab Sahib, and to designate Zafar's successor as 'prince', not 'king'. There were at least some in the palace and in the city who believed that the Shahanshah of Persia or the Czar of Russia would intervene to drive the *feringhees* out and restore the Mughal dynasty to its earlier glory. A poster announcing that the Shah of Persia would come to the aid of his oppressed Muslim brethren had, in fact, been found pasted, for a few hours, on the walls of the Jama Masjid two months earlier. Some astrologers and soothsayers, including one within the palace, Pirzada Hasan Askari—'an attenuated prototype of the Russian Rasputin[1]—were also active in predicting ominous developments. But these were the normal eddies and ripples in the flow of Delhi's gossip and rumours. Certainly, on 11 May 1857 when the Revolt started at Delhi, there was little that could have warned Ghalib that the day would so radically change the settled pace of his life.

The sepoys from Meerut were first spotted by Bahadur Shah Zafar as they came cantering across the bridge of boats. Zafar was seated in his private apartment gazing out across the Jamuna. He immediately summoned his trusted aide—Hakim Ahsanullah Khan—who was also a close friend of Ghalib's. The time was about seven in the morning and the city, as yet, was unaware of the approaching storm. The students of Delhi College were in their classes, the paper from Calcutta had arrived as usual, the Collector's court was in session, and Ghalib was probably getting ready to go to the Fort: Delhi had woken up to the routine pursuits of a normal summer day. The troops soon reached the ramparts of the Red Fort and beseeched Zafar to let them in. Zafar was not appreciative of the tumult; he summoned Captain Douglas instead—the British Commandant of the Palace Guards. The *sowars* rode on and gained entry to the city through the Rajghat gate near Daryaganj. From then on it was only a matter of time before the city and the troops stationed in Delhi joined them. The British and Anglo-Indians were slaughtered without compunction—one of the first victims being Dr Chaman Lal, the well-known convert to Christianity. Ghalib has kept this record of the happenings: ' . . . at noon on Monday, the sixteenth of Ramzan 1273 AH which is the same as the eleventh of May 1857, the walls and ramparts of the Red Fort shook with such force that the vibrations were felt in the four corners of the city. Swarming through the opened gates of Delhi, the intoxicated horsemen and rough foot-soldiers (from Meerut) ravished the city like madmen. They did not leave their bloody work until they had killed officers and Englishmen, wherever they found them, and had destroyed their houses . . . Shut up in my room I listened to the noise and tumult and I heard it shouted that the guardian of the Red Fort and the British agent there had been murdered. From all sides one could hear the foot-soldiers running and the hoof-beats of the horsemen . . .'[2] By nightfall, sepoy leaders and excited Mughal princes were all over the gardens adjoining the Diwan-i-Khas, haranguing Bahadur Shah to give his blessings to the insurgency. The king was reluctant, but then he had little option and perhaps there was something to gain out of it after all. He gave his blessings. Delhi had raised the banner of Revolt. For more than four months the banner would be held aloft until, on 13 September 1857, the British recaptured the city.

What was the nature of Ghalib's involvement in the Revolt? This is a matter of some controversy. For Ghalib and scores of others of his class, the Revolt was the ultimate nightmare, given the penumbra of divided loyalties in which they lived. The British were the *de facto* rulers. The Mughal king was the *de jure* symbol of reverence. In the political twilight of the years before 1857 it was possible to somehow harmonize obeisance to both without bringing into sharp focus the fundamental incongruence of this stance. But 1857 abruptly put an end to the shadows. It called for a dramatic choice: you were either against the British and for the king, or against the king and for the British. Ghalib wrote a book, the *Dastanbuy*[3]— which is ostensibly a diary, written spontaneously as events unfolded in those traumatic months. The book is intensely pro-British and ruthlessly condemnatory of the Revolt. If we take this book literally we have no option but to conclude that Ghalib had, on 11 May 1857 itself, made *his* choice unequivocally: the British were the only legitimate rulers of India. Those who rebelled against them were uncouth *namak-harams;* and victory over the rebellion was the harbinger of the return of justice and well-being.

But the question is: can we take this book literally? Available evidence would caution us from doing so. The *Dastanbuy* is hardly a spontaneous record of 1857, or a genuine expression of Ghalib's beliefs. It was written after the British recapture of the city, or, at least, after it had become clear—towards the very end—that the rebellion was a lost cause. Its limited purpose was to help establish Ghalib's innocence in the eyes of the British.[4] To do so was not a matter of intellectual toadying; it was a matter of survival. The British were ruthless in victory; the slightest suspicion was sufficient for a man to be hanged. Ghalib's purpose was two fold: first, to avoid any reprisal against him, and second, to establish his bona fides sufficiently to persuade the British to resume his pension. As we shall see, this too was a matter of survival. With the Mughal court wound up, Ghalib had no other source of income to hope for and he was in desperate straits. The *Dastanbuy* was thus a means to an end. Although in form a narrative, in style it was something similar to the *qasida* or the panegyric, the time-tested instrument of poets in feudal times to win favour from the ruler. It was not expected that a poet actually believe the lavish encomiums and related *obiter dicta* contained in his panegyric. The purpose was a limited one: to influence the powerful. The *Dastanbuy* formed part of just such a genre; as a poet and writer in a feudal milieu, this was the only way that Ghalib knew to protect himself. We shall see that he himself looked upon the *Dastanbuy* only in this light. And there is other evidence that shows his involvement in the Revolt, and that his real views were quite in divergence with what we would expect from the author of so emphatically pro-British a book as the *Dastanbuy.*

Ghalib's praise for the British in the *Dastanbuy* is expressed with the same blatancy as in a *qasida,* and with equally transparent insincerity. To preface every mention of the British with laudatory adjectives was not difficult for a man who once admitted having spent half his life praising fools. Thus Queen Victoria is described as 'splendid as the stars'. Lord Ellenborough as 'that administrator who is magnificent as Alexander, splendid as Faridum'. Sir John Lawrence as 'glorious as the sun and exalted as the stars'. 'Brave', 'good-natured', 'courageous', 'lion-hearted', 'just' are other commonly used adjectives for the Englishmen, while Englishwomen who were killed by the rebels, are described as, 'those fairy-faced, slim-bodied (women) whose faces shone like the moon and whose bodies glittered like raw silver'.[5] At one point he rhetorically proclaims: 'Do you not see the similarity between the protecting *daman* and the enslaving *dam,* and between *dad* and *dad* ? *In truth one cannot perceive of justice under other auspices than those of the British.*'[6] This from a man who had spent a fortune and half his life trying to invoke British justice to no avail! The ability to mechanically churn out flattering verbiage was commonly mastered by a poet and writer in nineteenth-century India. It was a matter of livelihood and survival, in no way incompatible with creativity; in fact, a necessary prerequisite, in order to have the wherewithal to sustain creativity. For Ghalib the more difficult part was to justify, or gloss over, British savagery after the recapture of the city. He could not avoid some reference to this aspect; it was essential to attempt to give his narrative the garb of authenticity. But his attempt is far from convincing. He writes: 'I have told you that when the angry lions (the British) entered the town, they killed the helpless and the weak and they burned their houses. It may be that such atrocities always occur after conquest.'[7] A few pages later: 'it is widely known that although looting was common, killing was generally abjured . . . although the (British) were full of the fire of fury, they restrained themselves.'[8] But on the same page: 'The hearts of the helpless inhabitants of the city . . . are filled with sorrow and they are afraid of mass slaughter.' And again: *The victors killed all whom they found on the streets.* Those of noble birth and position, in order to protect their honour, which was all that remained to them, stayed inside their locked houses.'[9] In the same vein: 'At noon on Friday, the twenty-sixth of Muharram, which is the eighteenth of September . . . the victors captured the city and the Fort. *The horror of mass arrests, assassinations, and slaughter now reached our lane* and the people shook with fear . . . Beyond the (Chandni) Chowk *mass slaughter was rampant* and the streets were filled with horror.'[10] (Emphases mine) The truth inadvertently comes out in spite of his best attempts to conceal it. His real views were reserved for his letters to his friends. As we shall see later, here too—for fear of his life—he was extremely circumspect.

A primary concern was to devalue his association

with the Mughal court. The British were hunting out all those suspected to be in the inner circle of the court with special zeal. Ghalib, as the king's *ustad* in poetry, was under suspicion. It was essential to pre-empt any reprisals. It would be unintelligent to completely deny his connections with the palace. But he could water down the relationship, minimize its importance and reduce its content, projecting himself as a mere employee on the fringes of the king's circles. This he proceeds to do in the very first pages of the *Dastanbuy*:

> Readers of this book should know that I . . . have eaten the bread and salt of the British and, from my earliest childhood, have been fed from the table of these world conquerors.

> Seven or eight years ago the Mughal emperor of Delhi summoned me to his palace and asked me to write a history of the Timurid dynasty, for which he proposed to pay me six hundred rupees annually. I accepted his offer and began the work. Eventually the emperor's master of verse died and I was also appointed as the one responsible for the correction of the royal poems. (Notice the dexterous manner in which he casually brings in his becoming the royal tutor).

> I was aged and weak and had become used to my corner of loneliness and quiet. Further I had developed a deafness which was a source of great inconvenience to my friends and I could only watch the lips of those who spoke. Twice a week I visited the royal palace where, if it was his will, I would remain for a while in the presence of the king. If

Behind Ghalib's condemnation of the sepoys there is, therefore, a kernel of class antipathy towards the unbathed masses. Somewhere in his mind is the notion that the breaking of the covenant of loyalty to their masters by *such* people was unethical—against the feudal dictum of fealty to the salt-giver—*namak-halali*. But the shell is deliberately padded and embellished to strengthen the pro-British content of the *Dastanbuy*. His views against the sepoys could not, *ab initio*, have been so bluntly articulated, for the simple reason that when the Revolt began British victory was far from being a foregone conclusion. The sepoys and their leaders could well emerge as the new focus of power; and they were extremely intolerant of pro-British sentiment—killing scores of people on the slightest suspicion of being British sympathizers and agents. Would Ghalib have made the mistake of committing his views on paper while the Revolt was on, as the *Dastanbuy* would have us believe? The battle for Delhi was not a walkover for the British. They did win the first direct skirmish near the river Hindan on 30–31 May. They also won the battle of Badli a week later. But there was little demoralization in the city. On the contrary, in spite of the confusion of a multiplicity of leaders and acute shortage of resources, the general mood was one of buoyancy and optimism. The meagre British presence, clinging to the Ridge, was in a miserable condition. Its numbers were small, supplies were dwindling and reinforcements were remote. It was the height of the hot season—poor living conditions, dysentery and malaria were taking a heavy toll. In the city, what was lost in poor organization

he did not emerge from his chambers I would sit briefly in the Hall of Private Audience before returning to my home.

During this time I used to take to the emperor whatever writing I had completed or send it by a messenger. This was my connection with the court and the nature of my work. Although this small position gave me some restfulness and peace *and was free from courtly entanglements,* it assured me neither prosperity nor happiness.[11] (Emphasis mine)

But this was not enough; if he did not support the Revolt, could he not have done something to oppose it? The possibility of such an accusation is also quickly taken care of:

A few poor reclusive men, who received their bread and salt by the grace of the British, lived scattered throughout different parts of the city, in lanes and by-lanes, but quite distant from one another. These humble, peaceful people did not know an arrow from an axe; their hands were empty of the sword; and even the sound of thieves in the dark night frightened them. These were not men who could do battle. They could do nothing but sit, helpless and grief-stricken, in their locked houses; for no blade of grass can stop the swift flow of the running water. I was one of these helpless, stricken men.[12]

He is particularly scathing in his criticism of the chief actor in the *dramatis personae* of the Revolt: the sepoy. One suspects that here expediency coincided with belief. Ghalib was not egalitarian. His loyalty was to the feudal pyramid, in which he believed his rightful place was towards the apex. This ordained

order of things was increasingly under threat from
the British; but it could as easily crumble from the
onslaught of the 'rough foot-soldiers', the 'rabble',
the 'lawless multitude'. If, therefore, he held no brief
for the arrogant British, he had little sympathy for
the swagger of the sepoys either. There is evidence
that when the Revolt began, the sepoys, emboldened
by a new sense of power and dignity, became less than
careful about the obsequiousness expected from them
by the feudal aristocracy. The king was the first to
notice this change of behaviour and publicly voiced
his resentment. In a speech to his officers, he
complained strongly that the sepoys' uncouth
demeanour in his presence was most objectionable. In
a letter to his son, Mirza Mughal, he continued the
refrain: '. . . they (the sepoys) come riding on horseback
into the (palace courtyards) improperly dressed,
without turbans . . . even though whenever an officer
of the British government came into the palace, he
dismounted from his horse at the gate of the Diwan-
i-Am and proceeded on foot . . .,'[13] The sepoys were
brave patriots, but not many among them were above
the common weakness of indulging in plunder and
loot. Bahadur Shah complained: '. . . the sepoys have
plundered the bazaars . . . by day and night. On the
false pretence that an Englishman is lurking inside,
they dash into people's private dwellings and plunder
them. They break open the locks and take away the
shutters and doors and plunder the goods inside most
shamelessly.'[14] Ghalib, the feudal patriarch, resented
the brashness and tyranny of the rabble. His lament
on the situation has the ring of genuine revulsion:

How can I describe the lack of judgement, the
indifference of these times? These *rough labourers*
who spend their days digging and selling mud, have
now found in it pieces of gold. And those others
whose assemblies were illuminated by the blaze of
flowers are plunged into failure and despair.
With the sole exception of the wife and daughter
of the police chief, the ornaments of all the young
women of Delhi have been seized by the black-
hearted, cowardly robbers. Bereft of their
embellishments, these women have been further
debauched of their remaining charm and grace by
the *newly rich sons of beggars,* and they have no choice
but to satisfy the conceit of the *rabble.* Those loving
and courteous people who shattered the coquetries
of the young women with their respect and
affection, can do nothing now but bow beneath the
wickedness of these newly rich, vile-natured ones who
are so filled with pride that to see them you would
say they were not men but whirlwinds puffed up
with conceit. These lowly men, engrossed only in
their own self-importance, are but small blades of
grass floating pompously on the wide water.
Noble men and great scholars have fallen from
power; and the *lowly ones, who have never known*
wealth or honour, now have prestige and unlimited
riches. One whose father wandered dust-stained
through the streets now proclaims himself ruler
the wind. One whose mother borrowed from
neighbour's fire with which to light her kit
declares himself sovereign of fire. These are
men who hope to rule over fire and wind.
(Emphases mine)

was at least initially more than made up for by revolutionary zeal and the will to win. Popular opinion considered it a matter of time before the beleaguered British were vanquished. A day after the defeat at Badli, the Indian side regrouped and launched a strong attack on the Ridge. The assumption of leadership by Bahadur Shah Zafar was real. His eldest son, Mirza Mughal, was appointed Commander-in-Chief. Jawan Bakht, the younger favourite, was appointed *Vazir*. The *kotwal* was instructed to go about his business as usual. The basic administrative model was retained, although the titles were now in Persian. Some old institutions, such as that of the *Sadr-us-Sadr*, the Chief Interpreter of Muslim law, were revived. Some innovations were made, the most notable being that of the Administrative Court. 'Its function was to control both civil and military affairs, and its membership of ten included six military and four civil representatives . . . In intention it would seem to have been a war cabinet, with the widest powers . . .'[16] Some improvisations, demonstrating quick flexibility and responsiveness to changing power equations, were also in evidence. For instance, Muhammad Bakht Khan, the competent but arrogant leader from Bareilly, who commanded a large body of loyal troops and had money to contribute, was accommodatingly given a title hitherto uncommon in the Mughal court: *Sahib-i-Alam Bahadur* or Governor-General. The problems to be tackled were daunting. There was much confusion and even more intrigue; but all contemporary accounts and records bring out, unambiguously, that Bahadur Shah Zafar's court was in charge and functioning actively.

In such a situation it is highly unlikely that Ghalib, the king's *ustad* and a daily visitor to the palace, could have kept himself aloof. That he was fully *au fait* with the intrigues in the court is revealed, ironically enough, in the *Dastanbuy* itself. One of his closest friends, Hakim Ahsanullah Khan, was the king's most trusted aide and chief adviser. The Hakim was suspected by some in the court of being a British agent. Ghalib refers to the incident in passing in the *Dastanbuy*, without giving details of the controversy. But the language he uses to condemn the man, who was probably in the forefront of the anti-Ahsanullah lobby, is hardly that of a remote or casual observer: 'Unless he was a bastard, the meanest slave would not behave in such a manner. This contemptible man, this wretch untrue to the salt, with cheeks pitted by small pox and a gaping mouth, whose eyes stare in shamelessness considers himself a Venus. He walks with swaying hips and believes his gait lovelier than that of the partridge. I have purposely not mentioned his name as he is the infamous son of a tramp.'[17] Only an insider to the controversy could be so personal and harsh in his denunciation.

In January 1858, in a letter to the Nawab of Rampur, Ghalib makes a very guarded and cautious admission of his role. 'In those turbulent days I held myself aloof (from the court). But I feared that if I completely severed all connection with it my house might be destroyed and my very life perhaps endangered. Thus I continued inwardly estranged, but outwardly friendly.'[18] The Nawab of Rampur was avowedly pro-British; the times were extremely tense;

British savagery was at its peak. Ghalib could hardly be expected to state the entire truth—especially in a letter which could well be intercepted. That he was prepared to admit being 'outwardly friendly' to the court is significant enough. The British were rightly suspicious that his involvement was much deeper. He was lucky that nothing really incriminatory about his role was found in the palace records. In a letter to Tufta in March 1858 Ghalib heaved a sigh of relief that a search of the royal papers had so far failed to implicate him. It is probable that many of the records were deliberately destroyed just before the British recaptured the city. But he could not completely escape incrimination. During the Revolt a newspaper claimed that the inscription on Bahadur Shah Zafar's coinage was composed by Ghalib. The British had a copy of this news item, and the Commissioner, after questioning Ghalib, came to the conclusion that the report was true. Ghalib tried to deny it. His defence was that the king himself was a poet; many in his court were poets; and certainly some of his sons were. Thus, the inscription could have been composed by anyone. His strength was that as yet no piece of paper had been found in court records directly implicating him. Important court functionaries, such as Hakim Ahsanullah Khan could, he argued, testify to his innocence. To his friends, however, he was prepared to concede that if he did write it, he did so because he had no other option and, therefore, had done no wrong. If an amnesty could be proclaimed for the mutinous soldiers, why couldn't two lines of a poet be pardoned, he asked? Professor K.A. Faruqi writes:

'. . . there is no doubt that Ghalib sided with the Mughal emperor, and presented a versified *sikka* (inscription) on the joyous occasion of Bahadur Shah Zafar's assumption of full authority, in 1857. This *sikka,* hitherto unknown, was quoted by Munshi Jiwan Lal in *Roznamcha* (his original diary), and left out by Metcalfe in his English translation. It is reproduced below:

Bar zari aftab O nuqra-i-mah
sikka zad dar jahan Bahadur Shah

On the gold of the sun and on the silver of the moon Bahadur Shah has struck his coins.[19]

His regular involvement with the court is borne out by other evidence as well. Munshi Jiwan Lal's court diary has this entry on 13 July 1857: 'Mirza Nousha (the name by which Ghalib was known) and Mukarram Ali Khan read a *qasida* in praise of the king's victory over the English.' There is further evidence that Ghalib was honoured by a *khillat* from the emperor in August 1857, and on that occasion he had presented another *qasida*.

Syed Mubarak Shah, the Chief of Police under Bahadur Shah during the Revolt, has in his narrative (as is the case in other narratives written by Indians during the period) done his best to establish his own innocence in British eyes—and that of other Indians prominent at this time. He writes: 'The Hakim (Ahsanullah Khan) was anxious to discover some means of preventing the mutineers' regiments coming to Delhi. But had he made his wishes known he would have been instantly put to death. On the occasion he flew into a passion and abused the sepoys calling out to them, "Why do you come here making mischief? If you want to fight why don't you go out and do so?" From this the whole of Delhi suspected the Hakim to be at heart a friend of the British. Similarly Nawab Aminuddin Khan and Ziauddin Khan sons of Nawab Ahmad Baksh an old *jageerdar* of Lord Lake were really well-wishers of the British government; but how could their innermost thoughts and feelings be known? People could only judge by outward acts—these men did not take any part with the rebels or join the king's sons— and their loyalty on the occupation of Delhi by the British army was clearly established. In the same category may be placed Mufti Sadruddin Principal Sadr Amin of the city who was repeatedly, both by princes and troops, called on for a *fatwa* that the crusade they were engaged in was lawful and right, and pleasing to the Deity. The Mufti always avoided doing so . . .'[20] About Ghalib's involvement, Mubarak Shah writes: 'A report was indeed current in the army that Mirza Nousha and Mirza Ilahi Baksh were also friendly to the British and there is no doubt that they earnestly desired the overthrow and utter discomfiture of the mutineers *but the story was only partially believed*. Had the princes or the troops really believed it during the siege they would have destroyed them root and branch, and spared neither age or sex—wives and infants, everyone belonging to them would have been slaughtered—subsequent to the capture of the city the conduct of these men became known.'[21] (Emphasis mine)

In a narrative, so transparently intended to whitewash the involvement of important personages in the Revolt, the fact that Mubarak Shah is prepared to say that reports about Ghalib were only partially believed by the princes and the sepoys, indicates that Ghalib's involvement with the court, during this period, was much too active to be totally discounted. Mubarak Shah was also not prepared to jeopardize the attempt at authenticity, in the case of other people, by writing in the same categorical vein about Ghalib.

Thus the more emphatic the pro-British sentiment of the *Dastanbuy,* the more it is revealed to be what it was: an ingenious cover to hide Ghalib's real involvement in the Revolt. He was afraid to record his real views, but he gives enough indication of them in letters to friends. The extracts quoted below are from the same period of which the *Dastanbuy* is supposed to be a record and has Ghalib singing paeans in praise of the British:

• December, 1857 to Tufta: *'I am afraid to write you a detailed account.* Those who were in the service of the Fort are being drastically dealt with . . .'[22]

• December 1857 to Hakim Ghulam Najaf Khan: 'I got your letter . . . You say that I've never written to you. Be fair! What am I to write? What can I write? *What news is there that can be put in writing?* What did your letter amount to? And what does this letter of mine amount to? Nothing more than this, that both of us are still alive. And *more than this neither you nor I can write.'*[23]

• January 1858 to Hakim Ghulam Najaf Khan: 'So far we are still alive—I and my wife and the children—

but no one knows what may happen from one hour to the next. *When I take up my pen there is a lot I should like to write. But I cannot write it. If we are fated to meet again I will tell you all about it.* And if not then—verily we are for God and verily to Him we shall return . . .'[24]

• February 1858, again to Tufta: 'These are evil days my friend and I cannot see them ending well. *In short, everything is finished.*'[25]

• February 1858 to Majruh: 'If I live, and the day comes *when we can again sit you shall hear my story.*'[26]

• February 1858 to Saqib: 'If we survive . . . and are fated to meet again I will tell you everything. *Otherwise to put it briefly, everything is finished. I am afraid to write anything, and what is there, anyway, that one would feel any pleasure in writing about? . . .*'[27] (Emphases mine)

The compulsion which drove Ghalib to write the *Dastanbuy* is hinted at, characteristically enough, in the book itself. 'I am,' he writes, 'merely a slave to my belly and seek only bread.' He quotes a couplet of Saadi:

The slave must bow his head before the master
The ball has no choice but to follow the swing of the mallet.[28]

In the text he skilfully blends the details of his pension case. In the typical format of the *qasida,* at the end he makes the request for which all the preceding pages have been but a build up: 'Even if I now receive the balance of my pension the film of sorrow caused by my debts will not be wiped from the mirror of my heart. However, if I do not receive the arrears of my pension my heart will be broken in pieces as a mirror by a stone . . . I long for orders from the auspicious sovereign concerning the three petitions about which I have written in this book—that is, for title, for robe of honour, and for pension.'[29] When the book is ready for publishing his anxious instructions leave no doubt about the purpose for which it is written.

Tufta, who is helping in the printing, is asked to get the job done quickly for copies have to be urgently presented to the Governor-General, and through him, to the queen in London. He wants 'Nausha' to be removed from his name, for while people in Delhi are familiar with it, British authorities in Calcutta and England, for whom the book is meant, are not. He wants just 'Asadullah Khan' to be given as the author's name, for while his full name was 'Muhammad Asadullah Khan', the British authorities did not use the latter in addressing him. When there is a delay in the printing of the book, he berates Tufta and says that at this rate all that he expected to gain from the book would be lost. He asks that five deluxe copies be made and sent off to the Chief Commissioner of Punjab, the Governor-General, Queen Victoria, and the two concerned Secretaries in the British government. Ultimately, his investment paid dividends. In March 1859, the first sign of his rehabilitation in British eyes became visible with the Lieutenant Governor sending a letter of appreciation. The sales of the book were also encouraging. Ghalib was proud of his prose and was pleased at this development. But he was never in doubt as to who the book was meant for. To a friend who had sold off some of the copies, he wrote: 'I am glad that *Dastanbuy* has been sold. Who bought the copies—Englishmen or Indians? *Bhai,* the light has gone out of India. The land is lampless. Lakhs have died and among the survivors hundreds are in jail. Those outside cannot afford to buy books. I think the English must have bought its copies and it must have been sent to the Punjab. (Strongly pro-British)'[30] As to the contents of the book, he had, in a letter to the Nawab of Rampur, made as candid an admission as was possible: '. . . please be sure to read the book. *I have used the utmost care and circumspection in everything I have written.*'[31]

From the point of view of twentieth-century nationalism, Ghalib's cultivation of the British would seem a compromise which no mitigating circumstances could justify. At one level this point of view is valid, but the question is whether it has any relevance in judging Ghalib. Ghalib was a product of a feudal order in which obeisance to *de facto* power was a socially accepted norm. He wrote in the *Dastanbuy:* 'Since it has been my practice to send a panegyric to *whosoever comes as ruler of India, and particularly of Delhi,* I composed a *qasida* of congratulations and welcome in praise of his lordship Sir John Lawrence.'[32] (Emphasis mine) In his time, nationalism in the modern sense was as yet an embryonic force; anti-British sentiment had yet to be harnessed into a coherent or identifiable nationalist ideology. After the British recaptured Delhi, survival was the most immediate and overriding motivation for all sections of the people. The king, Bahadur Shah, himself sought to prove that his loyalty to the *angrezi sarkar* was never in doubt.[33] Hakim Ahsanullah Khan sought equally hard to rehabilitate himself in British esteem. Ghalib's chief patron outside Delhi, the Nawab of Rampur, had of course openly sided with the British. Once the Revolt was defeated—and with no credible opposition to foreign rule as yet existent—pragmatism demanded acceptance of the situation and restoration of as much past benefit as possible. In Ghalib's case, the question of survival was etched in particularly sharp profile: he was under active suspicion and had no other source of income except his British pension. People with much less at stake had made the compromise with the inevitable. It would be unfair, therefore, to judge him in hindsight, against the inflexible criterion of modern patriotism. What is really significant is that in spite of the feudal temper of his times, his instinctive anti-colonial bias was remarkably well developed. In February 1857 he wrote to a friend commenting on the British annexation of Oudh: 'Although I am a stranger to Oudh and its affairs, the destruction of the state depressed me all the more, and *I maintain that no Indian who was not devoid of all sense of justice could have felt otherwise.*'[34] During the Revolt, in spite of his reservations about the newfound swagger of the hoi polloi, he remained actively associated with the Mughal court. And in the *Dastanbuy,* for all its tactical praise of the British, his true feelings are, on occasion, but thinly camouflaged. At one point he writes:

Nothing more can be said of the fate of the Mughal princes than that some were shot and devoured by the dragon of death; and some were hung by their necks with ropes, and, in their twisting, their spirits left them. A few unfortunates are imprisoned, others have fled, wretched and disordered, into the wilderness; and the aged and fragile Mughal emperor is under trial by the court.

The *jageerdars* of Jhajjar, Ballabhgarh, and Farrukhnagar were executed separately on different days. Their lives were ended in such a manner that none could say blood had been spilled.'[35]

The sarcasm in the last line is dangerously evident; the brevity and casualness of tone hardly hides the anguish and sense of injustice of the author. And when, in November 1858, the news came that the East India Company had been superseded by the British government itself—final evidence, if any was needed, that the struggle was all over—Ghalib, in a letter, made little attempt to conceal his reaction: 'In Shahjahanabad (Delhi) a comet was seen several evenings over the western horizon after sunset. I only know that it means God's wrath and destruction of the country. On the first of November, on Wednesday, the city was officially illuminated. The Company handed over India to the Queen. Governor-General Lord Canning Bahadur was appointed her regent in this land . . . Allah. Allah. Allah.'[36]

Ghalib's personal suffering during the Revolt, and immediately after it, was considerable. In the *Dastanbuy* he laments the looting and breakdown of administration. A prolific letter writer, he was particularly upset by the breakdown of the postal system. 'The postal system is in utter chaos and service has virtually stopped. It is impossible for postmen to come and go: thus letters can neither be sent nor received.'[37] The regular supply of newspapers had also been disrupted. More importantly, French wine was no longer accessible. He writes in the *Dastanbuy*: 'To conceal the truth is not, in fact, the practice of honourable men. I am only half-Muslim, and quite free from the rigidities of religion . . . It has always been my habit, at night, to drink a foreign wine and if I cannot have it I cannot sleep. During these days the price of wine has become prohibitive and I have no money at all.'[38] He was lucky that for a while a friend sent him a stock of what seems to have been some kind of rum. The liquor was made from sugar-cane; to Ghalib's parched throat its bouquet appeared superior to foreign wine, and he described it as the very elixir of life for which Alexander the Great had been in search!

The shortage of money was a very major problem. His pension, which was paid by the British Collectorate, had stopped in May 1857—the month the Revolt began. His income from the Mughal court had also stopped. He had an entire household to support—wife, two grandchildren, and several servants—with absolutely no income. Borrowing money was not easy in those troubled times. Apparently, he somehow managed by selling his household effects. With grim humour he wrote that he managed to stay alive by selling his bedding and clothes; thus it could be said that where others ate bread, he ate cloth and would die from hunger when all the cloth was eaten. He was desperate. In one of the most moving lines in the *Dastanbuy,* he writes of his two grandchildren, raised with so much love and care, who ask him for milk and fruits and are met with silence.

Until the rains came, the unusually hot summer of 1857 added to the suffering. May and June are the hottest parts of the year and, by all accounts, 1857 was one of the hottest years in memory. To Ghalib, the suffering on account of the heat seemed more pronounced because a lot of people he knew who were used to spending the hot months in the comfort of their sheltered and well-ventilated homes, were now homeless. The dust and din of battle was a constant backdrop to the heat. The smell of cannon powder pervaded the air, and the noise of gunfire and cannon shots was never-ending. There was an acute shortage of basic commodities and services. 'The joint influences of increased demand within the city accompanied by a collapse of credit, a rival market on the Ridge (where the British were ensconced) backed by plentiful funds, and increasing reluctance on the part of the country people to bring in supplies, had produced a general shortage. If the city had not been taken by storm, by the end of September, it might have been reduced by famine in the course of a few months.'[39] Ghalib complained that shops were no longer open, grain was in acute shortage, and basic services—such as that of the sweeper, washerman and barber—had just vanished. In the days of rampant killing and looting by British troops after the recapture of the city, even water became a scarce commodity. People were afraid to stir out of their homes. Like others, Ghalib took to rationing water, and consuming it, he wrote, as though it came from a well dug by a fingernail. At one time all supplies dried up, and for two nights and days he and his family remained without water.

Fortunately for Ghalib he lived on a street which soon came under the protection of the Maharaja of Patiala. The Maharaja had ranged himself from the beginning with the British. The famous *hakims* who lived on Ghalib's street—Mahmud Khan, Murtaza Khan and Ghulamullah Khan—were associated with the Patiala court and enjoyed its patronage. When British victory seemed certain, the ruler of Patiala extracted a promise from them that the *hakims* would come to no harm; soon after the city was retaken he posted his own men at the entrance of the lane to protect its residents.

The Maharaja's soldiers were in position at the street on the third day after the British victory; its inhabitants then mustered enough courage to go out for food and water. But they were warned that to venture beyond Chandni Chowk would be to invite slaughter. With great trepidation they opened the gate of the lane and, with whatever utensils could be carried, a man from each house and two of Ghalib's servants, ventured out to the nearest well. Unfortunately, its water was brackish, but since sweet water wells were too far away, they had to quench their thirst with what was available.

Ghalib's house was not looted; but as ill-luck would

have it, he lost his most valuable possessions. When the Revolt broke out, his wife, a cautious lady, collected her jewellery and valuables, and sent them off secretly for safe keeping to the house of Kale Sahib, Zafar's spiritual mentor and a widely respected *fakir*—with whom Ghalib had stayed after his release from prison in 1847. Her reasoning was that in troubled times, these things would be safer in the house of a religious person who enjoyed the king's protection. The valuables had been duly deposited in a cellar whose entrance was concealed by a wall of clay. However, when the British recaptured the city, Kale Sahib's house also fell victim to the rampant looting. Ghalib apparently learnt of what his wife had done only at this time; nothing could be done and he consoled himself with the thought that perhaps it was best that the valuables had not been there, to be looted from his own house.

A much greater loss was that of his entire collected verse when the libraries of the Fort and that of his pupil and relation Nawab Ziyauddin Khan were looted. Ziyauddin kept a copy of whatever Ghalib wrote in prose or verse; he had spent a considerable amount in having the entire collection—900 pages of prose and 1,500 to 2,000 of verse—bound handsomely in leather with ornamentation in gold and silver. One of Zafar's sons—probably Mirza Fakhru who was Ghalib's *shagird*—had then had a copy made of Zia's collection for the palace library. Ghalib was content that his entire literary output was preserved suitably for posterity for he had never taken the trouble himself to systematically keep what he wrote. But when the looting began, both libraries were vandalized—the gold and silver work on the volumes must have been an attraction—and destroyed. Ghalib was extremely distraught. 'Now I yearn for my own poems,' he wrote. 'The other day a beggar, who has a good voice, got hold of a *ghazal* of mine from somewhere. When he showed me that piece of paper I wanted to cry.'[40]

Another cause of great anguish and pain was the plight of his mentally deranged younger and only brother. Mirza Yusuf lived with his family about a mile away from Ghalib. A quiet, introverted man, he had, at the age of thirty, become insane and never responded to treatment. When the city fell to the British, his wife, children and maidservants ran away leaving him unattended except for two aged servants. This news came to Ghalib but in the prevailing conditions it was not possible for him to leave his home. His sheer inability to do anything, even though he knew of his brother's condition, was a daily trauma.

On 19 October 1857, Ghalib got the news that his brother had died. Professor K.A. Faruqi has asserted that he was shot dead by British soldiers, a fact which Ghalib deliberately omits in the *Dastanbuy*.[41] By another account he was inadvertently killed, when, attracted by the tumult outside, he strayed into the street. Mainuddin Hasan Khan, *kotwal* of Delhi for a short period during the Revolt, has noted in his narrative, 'Mirza Yusuf Khan, brother of Mirza Asadullah Khan, who had long been out of his mind, attracted by the noise of the firing, wandered out into the street to see what was going on; he was killed'.[42] Ghalib's account in the *Dastanbuy* is that his brother

G H A L I B   229

died of illness. He had had high fever for five days,
and expired a little after midnight on 19 October
1857. The almost insurmountable problems of
arranging his burial now came to the fore. No shop
was open to buy cloth for the shroud; no grave-
diggers were available; there was no way to get four
men to carry the corpse to a graveyard. Finally, some
neighbours took pity and came to Ghalib's assistance.
Escorted by a Patiala soldier, they journeyed to Yusuf's
residence, wrapped his body in a few used sheets, and
interred him in a mosque next to his house.

When the city fell, Ghalib's name figured high on
the British suspect list. People everywhere were being
summarily executed on the most flimsy evidence.
Immediately after the recapture of the city, he had
been called for questioning by a Colonel Burn. Ghalib
mentions this in the *Dastanbuy*, but obviously, tries to
make light of it, 'Monday, the fifth of October, was
a day of calamity. Suddenly, at noon, white soldiers
scaled the wall near the closed entrance of our line,
climbed over the rooftops, and from there jumped
down into the street. The guards of Raja Narendra
Singh (of Patiala) tried to intercept them but were
unsuccessful. Ignoring the small houses nearby, the
soldiers entered directly into my house. They did not,
in their consideration, touch my possessions, but took
me, my two children, two or three servants and a
few good neighbours to the wise and experienced
Colonel Brown* who was staying in the merchant

---

* Ghalib is mistaken here. The Colonel's name was Burn not Brown.

Qutubuddin's mansion situated on this side of the Chowk at a distance of some furlongs. Colonel Brown talked with me gently and humanely, asking of me my name only, but of the others their profession, and so dismissed me politely. I thanked the Lord, praised the courteous Colonel Brown and returned home.'[43]

In a situation where the British were shooting first and asking questions later, the rounding up of Ghalib, his family, and the entire establishment for questioning, must have been a terrifying experience. But apparently Ghalib still retained his wits about him. According to Hali, the Colonel asked Ghalib, in broken Urdu, whether he was a Muslim. Ghalib said he was half a Muslim. The Colonel was surprised and queried what this meant. Ghalib then gave his famous reply: 'I drink wine but do not eat pork.' The Colonel was amused. Given British suspicion of all Muslims Ghalib's flippancy towards his religious affiliations, quite apart from reflecting his real views, was also expedient. He had also taken the precaution of carrying one of the few—perhaps the only—acknowledgements he had received from London, to the many odes he had written and dispatched in honour of Queen Victoria. It appears, however, that the Colonel was not one to be swayed by such testimonials. He wanted to know why Ghalib had not turned himself in when the British recaptured the city. Ghalib replied that given his standing in society, he travelled only in a palanquin; since the palanquin bearers had run away, he could not have come. Colonel Burn finally allowed Ghalib and his family to leave, although it is doubtful that he would have done so, as Hali says, with all courtesies. As we know, British suspicions were finally allayed in Ghalib's case because of the lack of evidence to convict him and also because he published the *Dastanbuy*.

***

British rule after 1857 irrevocably changed the political, social, physical and psychological profile of Delhi. Ghalib internalized every nuance of this cataclysmic metamorphosis. Before 1857, the city had an internal rhythm oscillating between fixed and familiar points of reference. The presence of the *feringhees* had brought in a discordant note, but had not altered the basic pattern. The increasingly obvious political impotency of the emperor was unsettling; but somehow it had been assimilated. There were other compensating factors, such as the all-pervasive passion and pursuit of the poetic muse. But the aftermath of 1857 brought in a new pace, a new rhythm. Ghalib, and countless others of his generation and background, were doomed to remain hopelessly out of step.

On the night of the fall of the city, General Wilson, the Commander of the British forces, celebrated his victory with a festive dinner laid out in the Diwan-i-Khas—the *sanctum sanctorum* of more than three centuries of Mughal power. In the days that followed, the palace was systematically ransacked. The few semi-precious stones that remained in the engravings and mosaics were prised out by bayonets. Exquisite chandeliers were, laughingly, smashed by drunken troops. Every scrap of gold inlay in the ceilings was vandalized. The gold plate, on the domes of the Moti Masjid, was removed and sold for the upkeep of the army. When the pillaging was over, little was left except some old clothes, medicines and a few books. The Diwan-i-Am was converted into a hospital. The other 'fairy like pavilions and courts and gardens of Shah Jahan' were converted into barracks, messes and canteens.[44]

Twenty-one princes of the imperial family were 'condemned, hanged and carted off'[45] in one day. Several more were shot in cold blood after they had surrendered, and their corpses displayed in Chandni Chowk—with only a loincloth to cover their nakedness. Bahadur Shah Zafar surrendered and was incarcerated within the Red Fort, in a small, dingy room with a low roof and plain whitewashed walls. He became an object of curiosity, 'a peep-show for any European who chose to stand and stare, from the wife of the Commissioner downwards'.[46] One of those who saw him gave this account of the condition of the Jahanpanah: '. . . there on a low *charpoy,* cowered a thin, small old man, dressed in a dirty white suit of cotton, and rolled in shabby wraps and *razais* . . . At our entrance he laid aside the *hookah* he had been smoking, and he, who had formerly thought it an insult for any one to sit in his presence, began salaaming to us in the most abject manner, and saying he was *burra kooshee* (very glad) to see us.'[47] Others recorded that 'not a word came from his lips; in silence he sat day and night, with his eyes cast on the ground, and as though utterly oblivious of the conditions in which he was placed'.[48] Some others 'heard him rambling on about his dreams and quoting some verses of his own composition . . . ,'[49] It is known that not having paper or pen he wrote poetry on the walls of his cell with a burnt stick. In October 1858 he was exiled for life to Rangoon.

Ghalib was Bahadur Shah's *ustad*. Their association was several decades old; their friendship, not without its tensions, was one of considerable respect and affection. It is significant that, in the *Dastanbuy,* Ghalib refrains from saying anything against the king. These were generational ties: Bahadur Shah's son was Ghalib's *shagird*. For many years now, Ghalib had been a visitor to the palace. He had begun his career as a poet within the precincts of the royal *mushairah*. For more than half a century he had looked upon the Qila-i-Mualla as the pivot, the unchanging backdrop to his life. He was, of course, aware of the enfeeblement of Mughal power. Indeed he was a first-hand witness to it. But he was unprepared for such an abrupt termination of its role, or such a violent desecration of its sanctity. The humiliation of the king, the vandalizing of the palace, and the insensitive conversion of some of its most exquisite buildings into barracks, must have lived with him as an abiding trauma.

While General Wilson sipped champagne in the Diwan-i-Khas, Delhi was a deserted city. The majority of its inhabitants—both Muslim and Hindu, rich and poor—had fled to escape the wrath of the British troops. Many camped, throughout the winter, outside the city in makeshift shelters or in the open. Their suffering was terrible, but the British would not allow re-entry. The jails were filled to capacity and mass slaughter had disposed of those not imprisoned. An eerie silence hung over the city. A British officer has recorded: 'There was something so strange and weird in every sound made in those silent streets which echoed to our footfalls like a city of the dead. Here and there a dog lay crouching at a body, or a vulture, completely gorged and unable to rise, flapped aside at our approach . . .'[50] Ghalib was among the few who had not left. He voiced his anguish in the *Dastanbuy:* 'In the entire city of Delhi it is impossible to find more than one thousand Muslims; and I am one of these. Some have gone so far from the city, it seems as if they were never residents of Delhi. Many very important men are living, outside the city, at a distance of two to four *kos,* on ridges and thatched roofs, in ditches and mud huts, as if their fortunes were sleeping with blindfolded eyes.'[51] In November 1858 the British declared a general amnesty, but entry to the city was still strictly regulated by the issue of permits. In February 1859 Ghalib wrote to a friend: 'As if the English soldiers were not enough, the *thanedar* of Lahori Gate now sits on his stool by the roadside. Whoever gives the Tommies a slip and comes out is at once arrested: five lashes or two rupees fine. Tickets (i.e., permits) are being checked at every police station. The other day a *jamadar* came over to question me. According to a rumour five thousand tickets have been printed; any Muslim who wants to live in Delhi must give a *nazrana* to the British officials and get the ticket to live within the city . . .'[52] Not content with this, the British ordered that those camping outside the city walls had no right to construct a shelter.

Ghalib recorded with indignation that orders had been issued to demolish all such constructions and prevent any coming up in the future.

The entire process of resettling was both sporadic and frustrating. Ghalib keenly followed the tortuous ups and downs. Right in the beginning, after the permits had been printed and the public proclamation for return of residents made, Edgerton—the Delhi Magistrate— went off without any notice to Calcutta leaving all the people—as Ghalib said—hanging about like idiots. For some time the resettling exercise went completely into abeyance. It revived in fits and starts with one set of orders often inexplicably rescinded by another. Ghalib caustically commented that if God Almighty willed one *mohalla* would be settled in three or four years— what was the hurry!? It was not until November 1859—almost two years after the original exodus— that general permission was accorded to return; but the population of Delhi, till as late as 1863, was at levels far below that of the pre-1857 period.[53]

During this period, it is interesting to note the increasing bluntness of Ghalib's comments on the British authorities. The comments are made in letters to friends but stand in sharp contrast to the tone of the *Dastanbuy*. A letter of 1858 has this poem enclosed without comment:

Each soldier of England is now a potentate
Men are mortally scared to go out in the bazaar,
The Chowk is the execution ground, the house
    dungeons.
Each speck of Delhi dust

Is thirsty for the Muslim blood . . .
Ev'n if you meet your woeful friends—
Oft bitterly,
Oft a-weeping
They describe their sorry lives and bruised hearts.[54]

In May 1858 he informed a friend that in Delhi the
authorities could do what they wanted, there was
neither law nor constitution. British insensitivity and
arbitrariness comes in for devastating comment in an
incident recounted in a letter of July 1859. An
acquaintance, Hafiz Mammu, had been acquitted of
all charges, and his property, already verified, was to
be finally returned to him. When the file came up
before the Commissioner the latter asked: 'Who is
Hafiz Muhammad Baksh?' Mammu replied: "I am."
'And who is Hafiz Mammu?' "I am," said Mammu,
explaining that while his formal name was Hafiz
Muhammad Khan, he was commonly known as Hafiz
Mammu. This required too much effort for the
Commissioner to grasp. He rejected the case and
Mammu returned empty-handed. A letter of the same
month has Ghalib again expostulating that in the
awarding of compensation and the return of properties,
total arbitrariness was the norm; no law, no rules, no
precedent or arguments had any effect. Sometimes
his comments have an unexpectedly sharp political
tone. In a letter to Tufta in December 1859 he remarks
'. . . I hear that it is proposed to establish in Lahore
a department to award compensation to ten per cent
of its value, to citizens whose property was looted by
the blacks (sepoys). That is, a man who asks a thousand

rupees will be given a hundred. As for the plundering which the whites did that's all pardoned; there will be no compensation for that . . .'[55]

But basically his bitterness welled from a deep sense of personal trauma and expressed itself, less in anger, than in an abiding sense of grief and sadness. Deteriorating health and property had not crushed Ghalib's keen sensitivity to the change of seasons, the varying moods, the joys and diversions of the city, and the enjoyment of the company of his wide circle of friends. In the aftermath of 1857, confined to his room in the bruised and battle-scarred city, we get an inkling of his despair and misery from a moving letter written early in 1858, wherein he laments the fact that the month of *Farwardin** and *Nauroz*** had come and passed, unheralded that year, without joy in a city deadened into silence; and weeps over his fate that he cannot be outside to welcome the spring, take in the greenery and flowers, and smell the rose. Loneliness and ennui were major problems. On 25 April 1858 he wrote plaintively to Tufta that alone, without company, he had nothing to do all day long. There is a similar refrain in the *Dastanbuy,* 'Ghalib who had thousands of friends in the city and acquaintances in every house, now in his loneliness, has none to talk with except his pen and no companion but his shadow.'[56] The aloof yet essentially gregarious Ghalib, the elegant conversationalist, the humorist who never let the opportunity for repartee to pass

---

* The first month of the Persian calendar.

** The Persian New Year's Day.

by, the litterateur who revelled in long discussions on the merits of this poet or that, the raconteur encouraged by a large and appreciative audience, the loved *ustad* of admiring *shagirds* available at his beck and call, the presiding poet of the city used to repeated calls of *mukarrar mukarrar* in impromptu gatherings or at formal *mushairahs*—this Ghalib was left bereft and forlorn with the violent disruption of the pre-1857 setting.

In particular, he acutely missed the company of his friends, many of whom had been his companions since childhood. Fazl-i-Haq, perhaps his closest friend, was sentenced to transportation for life. Ghalib would never see him again. Shefta, another very old friend, was sentenced to seven years' imprisonment.[57] Countless others had been executed or had fled to escape British reprisal. Their absence was a void in Ghalib's life, since his daily life and routine was inextricably linked to their presence. In letters of this period he refers again and again to his sorrow on this account. 'Once I was surrounded by friends all the time,' he wrote in June 1858. 'Now among my friends only Shivji Ram Brahman, Balmukund Das and his son visit me often . . . No news of friends in other cities . . .,'[58] Each time the name of a friend cropped up in correspondence, nostalgia would grip him, and he would be immersed in the memory of those days when his circle of friends was intact and they could meet and laugh and talk. His letters provide an endless list of those whose absence he mourned: Muzaffaruddaula, Mir Nasiruddin, Mirza Ashur Beg, Ahmad Mirza, Hakim Raziuddin Khan, Mustafa Khan,

Qazi Faizullah, Hussain Mirza, Mir Mahdi, Mir Sarfaraz Hussain, Miran . . . The manner in which they had been summarily executed or forced to flee, leaving behind home and possessions, haunted him day and night. At his age these men were irreplaceable; it was impossible to even think of building such relationships again. Grief on this account left him inconsolable till his death. Much after 1857, he still recreated for himself the days when all his friends would drop in and there would be banter and diversion: 'It is the same upper floor,' he wrote in a letter in 1863. 'I look at the staircase. That's Mir Mehdi coming, and Yusuf Mirza, and Miran, and Yusuf Ali Khan . . . Allah. Allah. I am mourning thousands. When I die who is left to mourn me?'[59]

What ate Ghalib's heart away was not only the absence of friends and familiar faces, but, in essence, the absence of *hum zaban o hum sukhan log*—people who could speak his language in intellectual and emotional terms. The artistically refined with whom a bond of friendship and respect had been chiselled over decades of interaction, and with whom he could effortlessly converse in a known idiom. 'My good Sir,' he wrote to one such friend in 1861, 'Delhi people now means Hindus, or artisans, or soldiers, or Punjabis or Englishmen. Which of these speak the language which you are praising? . . . Oh, my friend . . . where is Nizamuddin Mamnun? And where is Zauq? And where is Momin Khan? Two poets survive: one, Azurda—and he is silent: the other Ghalib—and he is lost to himself, in a stupor. None to write poetry, and none to judge its worth . . .'[60]

Delhi was changing physically too. Immediately after its recapture many of the British felt that the only way to deal with the traitorous heathens was to raze the entire city to the ground. Others seriously advocated that the Jama Masjid be pulled down and the Red Fort demolished, and a cathedral and Victoria Palace be built in their place. More restrained counsel finally prevailed: the Fort was not dynamited; its Lahori and Delhi gates were (incongruously enough) renamed Victoria and Alexandra gates, and the palace was converted into a barracks. A host of other buildings, including the Jama Masjid, and that hallowed sanctorum of learning—Ghaziuddin *madrasa* (Delhi College)—were similarly converted into barracks. The exquisite Fatehpuri Masjid was sold to a Hindu merchant as private property, and the Zinat-ul-Masjid was converted, by order, into a bakery.

The first and foremost concern of the conquerors was to make Delhi more amenable for governance. Delhi's labyrinthine lanes and alleys, its narrow winding streets and unexpected cul-de-sacs, and its structure of separate yet interconnected *mohallas,* had provided ideal cover to the rebels and made the recapture of the city a most arduous task. The British decided that this dense, organic structure would have to change. Like clinical incisions of a surgeon's knife, new roads and boulevards would have to be built— that ran broad and straight across the historically evolved character of the city. Clear spaces would have to be created to make the city more transparent for the ruler's gaze. Town planning would have to proceed on the basis that Delhi become a secure, garrison city, where any incipient rumbling of revolt could be quickly detected and efficiently crushed.

The new imperatives of town planning made it logical for the Red Fort to replace the Kashmiri Gate guard, as the focal military point in the city. This in turn required that in front of the Fort a clear field of fire be carved out. Accordingly, it was ordered that all buildings within a radius of 448 yards from the Fort walls be demolished. Initially the famous shopping centre Dariba was also included within the demolition zone. But later, on a representation from leading citizens, it was spared. A clear space was ordered to be cleared around Jama Masjid as well. All structures in the way of two new roads and a railway line were also to be demolished. Ghalib wrote in anguish, 'Large areas will be cleared around the Jama Mosque. Shops and houses will be demolished. Darul-baqa* has been pulled down. Only God's name remains. Spades are active on either side.'[61] The demolitions were carried out with ruthlessness, in disregard of the feelings of the affected population. For the British, the task was not merely functional but also appropriately retaliatory. In Lucknow, where a similar exercise was under implementation, the Chief Commissioner wrote a memo which described 'how demolition squads arrived in an area destined for clearance and proceeded to engage in their work, often without taking even the clementary precaution of making sure that the houses about to be razed were empty'.[62] Large tracts of land

---

*The famous seminary established by Azuda for the study of literature, medicine and theology, where education was imparted free.

had also been acquired—'mostly by virtue of right as conquerors without being too finicky about the right of original owners'—for the creation of a cantonment planned to occupy one-third of the total area of the walled city.[63] Ghalib suffered to see the hardship of the thousands who were dispossessed of their homes overnight. His anguish was not for Muslims alone, but for the plight of the Delhi citizen and for the sheer magnitude of human suffering. At another level, he was acutely conscious of what the new town planning was doing to the soul of the city. When the British destroyed a *kucha* or *gali* or *mohalla,* and built a broad and straight boulevard over the debris, they were dismantling a way of life, in consonance with which the city had acquired its physical contours. Streets in old cities in India were rarely either broad or straight. They 'served principally as areas where people milled, mingled, and socialized, where itinerant hawkers lined the curbs, where goods and services were bought and sold, and where traffic—which chiefly comprised pedestrians or beasts of burden—was slow-moving and yielded to those who were standing and transacting business. The street was a public space with social and recreational functions . . . the custom was often to go to the street not to get anywhere; the street *itself* was a destination and an event.'[64] Similarly, the cul-de-sacs which had no place in the schemes of British town planners, were 'structurally very important to keep a *mohalla* compact and private, to control and limit traffic, and to preserve the community spirit and integration that was typical of the city's neighbourhood'.[65]

For all its physical irrationalities, so apparent to an outsider seeking to govern it, Delhi provided a much-loved, functional and reassuring setting to its citizens, both for business and for pleasure. The poets of Delhi were unabashedly sentimental about its charms. It was Ghalib's fate to remain a helpless witness to its systematic mutilation. When the demolitions had begun, he had written angrily: 'I should rejoice in the desolation of Delhi, when its citizens have gone, then to hell with the city.'[66] But anger soon gave way to a deep despondency, and his letters of this period recount, in detail, every aspect of the manner in which his beloved city was being savaged. One by one he saw some of the most famous bazaars of Delhi—Khas Bazaar, Urdu Bazaar, Kharam Ka Bazaar— disappearing in the dust, and entire *mohallas* and *katras* vanishing without a trace. Familiar landmarks and oft-visited mansions—the *havelis* and *kuchas* of friends—were razed to the ground before his eyes; the accumulated debris everywhere gave Delhi the look of a barren waste. Delhi, Ghalib wrote, had become a desert, all the more so because, in the aftermath of war and the frenzy of the demolitions, the neglect of wells had led to an acute water scarcity. 'From the Jama Masjid to Rajghat is all wasteland', he wrote. 'If the debris were removed the place would look haunted—And the people are still proud of Delhi's language! What a laugh. Where is Delhi? It is now a military camp.'[67]

A British visitor, visiting Delhi a few years after 1857, noted with bland, but telling accuracy, 'Since the Mutiny . . . the native town has been much cleared

away, and what remains but very imperfectly
represents the extent or population of the place as it
existed ten years ago.'[68] The demolitions irrevocably
changed the physical contours of Delhi. They disrupted
vital aspects of the lifestyle of its citizens.
Simultaneously, they were instrumental in bringing
about 'one of the most remarkable revolutions in the
ownership of urban property'.[69] Extensive property
belonging to those who had participated in the
rebellion, or were suspected to have done so, had
been confiscated by the British authorities. They now
decided that those whose houses had been demolished
could be compensated by allotments of similar value
from this confiscated property. To implement the
scheme, tickets indicating the value of the demolished
property were given to the owners who could then
exchange them for the new allotments. At first glance,
it was a simple and ingenious scheme. But schemes
such as these do not operate in an inert socio-economic
milieu. The tickets were bought from the original
assignees by a handful of rich merchants and bankers
who, operating through an informal cartel, cornered
vast properties at a time when the price of land was
exceptionally low. The alternative British scheme, of
auctioning confiscated property, also helped these very
people, who in any case had already appropriated
considerable portions of it by claiming that the original
occupants were their mortgagees. The entire operation
thus acted as a catalyst for the organized emergence
of a new mercantile class, and the further
pauperization of the old feudal elite.

Both these classes had suffered in the plunder of the

city after the British had recaptured it. Prize agents had then been appointed, and official 'digging tickets' given to treasure-hunters. British officers, soldiers, their wives and relations went to work with pickaxes, shovels and an enthusiasm and cheerfulness that contrasted grotesquely with the desolate condition of Delhi's inhabitants. The plunder, recovered daily, was described by one British enthusiast as 'more than enormous. It is almost incredible.'[70] Much of what was found was appropriated on the principle of finders keepers. Some was also kept on display for sale on— ironically enough—the roof of a house near the Diwan-i-Khas.

The merchant–banker class was seriously affected by this organized plunder. During the rebellion it had suffered equally by the arbitrary and excessive extortions of the sepoy leaders. It is a tribute to its economic resilience, entrepreneurial vigour and ideological flexibility that it survived. The feudal aristocratic class was less agile. There were essential differences in lifestyle between both. The former with its traditional emphasis on thrift had, for generations, been engaged in the task of capital accumulation. The latter preferred to borrow, to maintain lifestyles which it did not have the means to sustain. In the face of British plunder, the large-scale confiscation of property, and the web of transactions linked to the demolitions, it was left hopelessly defeated. Of course, its economic decline had begun much earlier. Even before 1857, with the exception of a few leading *zamindars*, the *sahukars* had the money power. But, until 1857, their economic strength and social primacy were not in congruence. After 1857, the emergence of the *Lalacracy* was self-assuredly overt. People like Chunna Mal, Sahib Singh, Ramji Das, Narain Das, Mahesh Das, Janki Das, Meher Chand and Mirza Ali claimed social leadership, and the British—suspicious of the loyalties of the feudal elite, and desirous of seeking new partners for the next phase of their rule—conferred it on them.

Ghalib was quick to note this shift in political and social equations, the dip in the balance of power away from him and the old nobility. He may not have been aware, in ideological terms, of the socio-economic forces behind the process, but he certainly had a glimmering of comprehension of what was happening and there was no ambiguity in the articulation of his distress. In 1858 he wrote to a friend who was looking for subscribers to a newspaper in Delhi: 'Sahib . . . where are the men who would buy newspapers? *The traders and the mahajans who live here now,* go around looking for cheaper rates of wheat. If they are very generous they would give you the correct measure of grain, why should they spend money on mere paper?'[71] (Emphasis mine) In a similar vein he wrote a little later: 'The *sahukars* are rolling in money and jewels. What difference does it make to me?'[72] In November 1859, giving voice to the lament of an entire class, he wrote to the Nawab of Rampur that he knew no one in authority; the very profile of things had changed. The Governor-General was to visit Delhi in December 1859. During his visit the customary ceremonial durbar was to be held. Lord Hardinge had held the last Governor-General's durbar at Delhi. Ghalib had a place of honour in it, occupying the tenth place to the right, and distinguished by a ceremonial robe, seven gifts of cloth, a turban with an embroidered velvet band and jewelled gold ornaments to wear in it, a string of pearls and a cloak. But now many among the nobility who had been given places of honour were not even invited. Ghalib was one such and recorded with bitterness: 'Nawab Governor General Bahadur will arrive on 15 December . . . In earlier durbars the seven *jageerdars* (of the seven states near Delhi) held their own court. They were Jhajjar, Ballabhgarh, Farrukhnagar, Dojana, Pataudi, and Loharu. The first four states were wiped out during the Mutiny. Dojana and Loharu are now under the administration of Hansi-Hissar. Pataudi remains. If the Commissioner of Hissar brings along the two nawabs it would mean three. Among the Muslims (nobility) only three survive: Mustafa Khan in Delhi, Maulvi Sadruddin in Sultanji (Nizamuddin) and in Ballimaran this dog of the world called Asad. All three condemned, doomed, despondent and grief-stricken.'[73] A little later, displaying uncanny insight into the irrevocability of the social transformation under way, he advised a friend to forget that he was ever a member of the nobility, had rank and wealth, drew an honourable pension and held property.

Ghalib's specific mention of Muslim members of the nobility should not lead us to assume that he was conscious only of the grievances of Muslims. In fact it was at this time that he wrote with deep conviction to Tufta that he held all men, whether Hindu, Muslim or Christian, to be his brothers. The Mughal nobility at Delhi was constituted preponderantly of Muslims;

the emergent *Lalacracy* was dominated more by Hindus.
This led Ghalib to, sometimes, contrast Muslim and
Hindu in his comments on the new order. But there
is not the slightest doubt that he was basically
articulating the grievance of his *class* and not of his
community. In this role he was capable of showing
anger and anguish at the economic ruination and
humiliation of the erstwhile wealthy and influential,
some of whom he counted as his closest friends. Hakim
Ahsanullah Khan, he sarcastically commented, had
converted his main hall into the *zenana* and was himself
living where the stables used to be; an Englishman
had moved into the rest of the house. Even the rubble
left behind after the demolitions, he angrily wrote,
did not belong to the owner; the government had
demolished its own seized property.

In November 1859 he recorded: '. . . Helplessly I
watch the wives and children of aristocrats actually
begging from door to door. One must have a heart
of steel to witness the contemporary scene!'[74] Two
years later this sight remained a continuing trauma.
'If you were here . . .,' he wrote to Tufta in April
1861, 'you would have seen the moon-faced Begums
of the Red Fort wandering around in the streets in
filthy clothes, ragged pyjamas, and broken shoes.'[75]

In a hazy sort of way—more poetic than
analytical—Ghalib probably had an inkling, in 1857
itself, that the old order had vanished forever. In a
remarkable letter written to Tufta as early as
December 1857 he categorized all that used to be—
the order that was under the Mughal king, the way
of life they were familiar with—as but a mirage, a

dream, the remembrance of a former birth; in the present birth, some of the people were possibly still the same, but nothing else could ever be the same again. The city's changed physical and social features gave concrete corroboration to this emotional perception. 'Delhi meant'—Ghalib wrote in December 1859—'the Fort, the Chandni Chowk, the daily bazaar near Jama Mosque, the weekly trip to the Jamuna Bridge, the annual Fair of the Flower-sellers. These five things are no more. Where is Delhi now? Yes, there used to be a city of this name in the land of Ind.'[76]

This was the epitaph of Ghalib—the quintessential symbol of Delhi's pre-1857 life and culture—to the passing of an era. Not surprisingly--except for what was written spontaneously—he had little inclination left to compose verse. In April 1858 he had confessed to Tufta that he had stopped writing completely and was amazed at his ability to do so in the past. Often, during these days, he was seized by a profound sense of transcendence, a perception of the futility of man's incessant struggle and of the hollowness—in the ontological sense—of all his ambitions and desires. In 1859 he wrote to Tufta.

. . . I find both (the learning of) Avicenna and (the poetry of) Naziri to be futile. To live one's life one requires just a little happiness; philosophy, empires, poetry are all nonsense. If the Hindus had their *avatars* and the Muslims their prophets, so what? If you lived as a famous man or as a non-entity, what of it? One should have some means of reasonable livelihood and good health. The rest is all illusion

. . . In this silence in which I find myself now, I am not aware either of myself or of this world or the hereafter. I duly answer questions, continue my dealings with others, but know that all this is delusion, not a river, but a mirage, not life but vain glory. Both you and I are fairly good poets. Agreed that some day we might become renowned like Saadi and Hafiz. But what did *they* gain that we wouldn't?'[77]

He was convinced that he would not live very much longer. Old age, failing health, and an overpowering sense of weariness at the unending vicissitudes of daily existence contributed to this philosophical disenchantment. To a friend he wrote in December 1859, 'How much life is left to me? Then. . . I shall go to my Master, where hunger and thirst and piercing cold and raging heat will be no more. No ruler to be dreaded, no informer to be feared, no rent to be paid, no clothes to be bought, no meat to be sent for, no bread to be baked. A world of light, a state of pure delight.'[78] Behind this glorification of the other world, there was undoubtedly a genuine spiritual anchorage, an intellectual detachment, a real urge to go beyond the turmoil and trauma to which flesh is heir. In a Vedantist tone he wrote to Tufta in January 1861, 'The greater part of life is already gone, some is left—that too should pass well. What did Urfi achieve through his *qasidas* that I should advertise mine? What did Saadi get out of his *Bostan* that you would out of your *Sumbalistan* (the title of Tufta's collection of Persian verse)? Apart from Allah all is vague and non-existent. There is no poetry and no poet, no ode and no ode-writer. Nothing exists except God.'[79]

And yet, this was the paradox of Ghalib the man that his most sublime philosophical perceptions co-existed with a continuing preoccupation with self, privilege and the normal accoutrements of a more than life-size ego. At a time when he could tell Tufta that all his faculties were intent only on obtaining oblivion, he could also confess to be consumed by incessant anxiety about whether he would get an invitation to the Governor-General's durbar. The co-existence of two opposing mental states did not render the one false or the other hypocritical. On the contrary, together they provide the real clue to the complexity of Ghalib the man: aloof, spiritual, transcendent, detached at one level, possessive, proud, vain, egoistic, at another.

Ghalib would live on for twelve years after 1857, but he would never recover from its trauma. When the sepoys had come cantering into Delhi on that morning in May 1857 he had been taken by surprise. But when the British were expelled from the city he had, as a member of Bahadur Shah's court, been more a participant in events than he would have ever liked the British to know when they recaptured the city, four months later. The *Dastanbuy* was a timely hedge against likely British reprisal. It cannot be interpreted as a record of his true feelings. His personal suffering and loss during the Revolt was great. He was, by now, no longer young and his health was failing. But it would be ignoring both his personality and the other evidence—including most importantly his letters to his friends—to conclude that he remained a withdrawn, disinterested or indifferent observer during the tumultuous days when the Mughal king ruled again from the Red Fort. He was not a nationalist in the modern sense, but—although he would very much have liked the British to think so—he was not a collaborator either. He was not particularly appreciative of some of the excesses of the sepoys, but he was far from being unsympathetic to the cause they had ignited. The British terror in the aftermath of the Revolt pulverized him emotionally. An entire way of life was permanently destabilized. Many of his dearest friends were executed or exiled. Scores of Delhi citizens were hanged daily at the Chandni Chowk. His king was sent into exile in distant Burma. Much of the old feudal class was dislodged from its self-assured niche in society, and compelled to fend for itself in poverty. Large parts of his beloved city were demolished. Perpetually unsure of his own fate, he remained, without his old pension, a beggared, lonely and mute witness to this continuing upheaval. It was perhaps at this time that he wrote his famous lines:

An ocean of blood churns around me—
Alas! were this all!
The future will show
What more remains for me to see.[80]

FIVE

Last Years

The city was still badly battered and demoralized when, in 1859, the Delhi Bank reopened. Three years later, the troops were evicted from the Jama Masjid and it was restored for worship, although the Fatehpuri Masjid bought by Lala Chunna Mal, in the cataclysmic property changes after 1857, remained his private property till 1877. The Phoolwalon ki Sair was revived in the 1860s; in 1864 classes in the Delhi College were resumed; and in 1867 the Delhi Canal began to flow again. But as the old shakily sought to regain a footing, it continued to be jostled by the arrogant emergence of the new. The first train chugged into the city in 1867 much to the excitement and amazement of its citizens. The construction of the railway line and two new boulevards—Queen's Road and Hamilton Road—caused the demolitions to continue in fits and starts late into the 1860s. When the picks and axes took a pause, silence would possess the city, and it would appear, Ghalib said, as though Delhi was a city of the dead. Cheek by jowl with the past emerged the symbols of the future and the new order. The Town Hall was built opposite the railway station, and within its premises—a new focus of influence—the Town Municipal Committee was inaugurated in 1863. In the northern part of the walled city, towards Kashmiri Gate, a Post and Telegraph Office and a *dak* bungalow were constructed. A British staple, the clock tower, was erected in Chandni Chowk. The new buildings, built in the Victorian style, stood in incongruous contrast to the rest of the city. Beyond Kashmiri Gate the fledgling Civil Lines, of the pre-1857 period, was rapidly expanding to accommodate the enlarged British presence—with colonial-style bungalows and new roads dotting much of the landscape between the walls of the city and the Ridge.

Amidst these changes, fresh troubles continued to jar the beleaguered Delhi citizen. The years 1860 and 1862 were ones of severe famine. The shortage of grain was accentuated by the richer merchants resorting to large-scale hoarding. Widespread demolitions, and the British preoccupation with making the city more amenable to better military governance had led to a neglect of the municipal infrastructure, and, in particular, the wells which naturally resulted in contamination of potable water and insanitary conditions. This caused a rampaging epidemic of the Delhi Sore, a rash of undiagnosed fevers—and, more seriously, the outbreak of cholera, a disease hitherto unknown in Delhi. Ghalib remained a weary witness to this fresh outbreak of misery but, as always, the indefatigable chronicler. In 1860 he wrote that Delhi had been ravaged by five successive invading armies—that of the rebels when the Revolt began, that of the British when they recaptured the city, that of famine, that of cholera, and, last but not least, that of the fever epidemic which showed no signs of abating. The shortage of essential commodities was chronic; millet was selling for thirty-two pounds to a rupee, and lentils for sixteen. Death is cheap, Ghalib wrote, and grain dear. In 1862 havoc was caused due to excessive rain. Conditions in the city were pitiable. Many thousands were homeless, others—in the general tumult and under the threat of demolitions—had been unable to devote attention to maintenance, and, still others, freshly paupered, had no money to do so. While new and broad boulevards were being constructed and proud Victorian buildings being built, hundreds of houses in the city were caving in daily. Ghalib's house was no exception. In July 1862 he wrote to Allauddin Khan Alai, his *shagird* and kinsman from Loharu: 'Miyan, I am in great distress. The walls of the *mahalsara* (ladies' apartment) have collapsed, so has the bathroom. The ceilings are dripping incessantly. Your aunt feels she'll be buried alive any moment. The *diwankhana* (men's apartment) is worse . . . The ceiling has turned into a sieve. If it rains two hours the ceiling trickles for four.'[1]

Foliage grows from the floors and walls Ghalib,
In desolation am I and spring has come to my house.[2]

According to Ghalib the floods caused by the

unrelenting rain had led to the collapse of thousands of homes and hundreds of lives had been lost. The earlier famine had occurred due to lack of rain; the second due to an excess of it. The shortage of food and general pauperization contributed to a marked deterioration of law and order. The British had dispensed with the old system of *kuchabandi* wherein at night one *mohalla* was locked off from another. The city gates were not always locked as before, and in any case, the construction of the railway line had made ingress into the city much easier. The old *chowkidari* system had been abolished and the new police force was both numerically weak and inadequately established. Not a day would pass, Ghalib wrote, when several burglaries were not reported. He himself invested in a *chowkidar*.

In the British concept of 'reconstruction' after 1857, Indians of the right background were allowed to associate, as subsidiary partners, in the pursuit of municipal concerns. Indians were represented on the municipality and the Jama Masjid Committee. In general, members of the traditional Delhi nobility— and particularly those who had been associated with the Mughal court—were kept out. Those of the old nobility who did manage to retain some peripheral influence were people like Nawab Ziauddin, Ghalib's kinsman from Loharu. They had satisfactorily given an account of their loyalty during 1857, so their association was useful on tactical grounds. The Jama Masjid Committee consisted of ten members. Ghalib took note of its functioning in one sentence. 'The Jama Mosque has been released from military custody.

Kababias have set up shop on its stairs; eggs, chicken
and pigeons are being sold.'[3] The municipality was
decisively swamped by wealthy representatives of
the newly powerful, loyalist mercantile class. Five
merchant families who acquired particular influence
were: the 'Saligram and Girdhar Lal families—both
Jain—and the Chunna Lal, Gurwala, and Naherwala
families—all *khatri*'.[4] The Municipal Commission
assembled in decorous meetings, in the newly built
Town Hall. Beyond its Victorian façade, and beyond
the distraction of the Clock Tower, stood the Red
Fort, silent and barrackized—a constant reminder of
what once was, and what now had irrevocably ended.
When news came of Bahadur Shah Zafar's death in
Rangoon, Ghalib informed a friend about it in a
satirical manner: 'On Friday 7 November 1862
Abdulzafar Sirajuddin Bahadur Shah was released from
the prisons of the British and of his mortal body.
From God we come and unto Him we return.'[5] But
we get a glimpse of his continuing sense of hurt, of
the trauma below the surface of controlled emotions
through snatches from letters written at this time.
He is particularly resentful of any suggestion that
Delhi is back to normal. As early as 1858, he scolded
Tufta for making this assumption. 'Mirza Tufta, you
can be cruel. You have no pity on the destruction
of Delhi and seem to think that the city is still
flourishing. Here one can't (even) get hold of a *hookah-
maker* . . .'[6] In 1863 he berates another friend.
'Bountiful Master, do you think that Delhi still
prospers, and that the Fort thrives and that the Empire
continues. "The cow ate all this up, and the butcher

killed the cow, and the butcher died on the road." All these things lasted only so long as the king reigned.'[7]

The king did not reign any more. The court had been wound up. The old order had ended. For Ghalib, what remained at the practical level was the continuing need for monetary support. His British pension had been discontinued since May 1857. In its absence he knew of only one framework for pecuniary sustenance—the patronage of the rich and powerful— which in his time mostly meant the patronage of royalty. Even before 1857, he had tried to come to the notice of the house of Jaipur and the Nawab of Oudh. One association that came to fruition now was with Nawab Yusuf Ali Khan, the ruler of Rampur. In 1855 Ghalib had presented a *qata* in Persian to him which had gone unreplied. However, in 1857, Ghalib's friend Fazl-i-Haq, who was close to the Nawab, interceded on his behalf. On Fazl-i-Haq's advice Ghalib promptly presented a *qasida* in the Nawab's honour. This time the seed fell on fertile ground; the Nawab accepted Ghalib as his tutor in poetry, and, along with verses for correction, began to enclose occasional gifts of money. In July 1859, on Ghalib's request, he fixed the sum of Rs 100 as the poet's regular monthly honorarium. This financial arrangement provided the right framework for the relationship to grow. In January 1860, responding to the Nawab's repeated requests, Ghalib, accompanied by Arif's two sons, paid a visit to Rampur—leaving Delhi after an almost unbroken stay of nearly three decades. He was treated well in Rampur; the Nawab received him cordially, a large house was put at his disposal, and arrangements were made to have his meals sent daily to his residence.

Ghalib returned to Delhi after a little over two months. Soon after his return his British pension was restored (April 1860). It is almost certain that the Nawab of Rampur's influence with the British had helped in obtaining this decision. In several of his letters from Rampur, Ghalib alludes to the likelihood of the Nawab speaking to the Lieutenant Governor of the North-Western Provinces in the matter. Ghalib had not slackened in his own efforts, and there had been indications that the British were relenting. The Lieutenant Governor had sent an encouraging acknowledgement on receiving the *Dastanbuy;* an ode addressed to him had also been acknowledged by a communication in which Ghalib was called 'Khan Saheb'. The Lieutenant Governor of Punjab, Robert Montgomery, to whom a timely panegyric had been dispatched had also written back to express his pleasure. As it turned out, all this was not unintentional. The pension was restored with the arrears due from May 1857. It was (by the prevailing standards) a sizeable sum, but nothing was left after payment to creditors. Ghalib's annual pension was Rs 750. The arrears for three years came to Rs 2,250 from this Rs 100 was deducted for an adhoc grant-in-aid given earlier; another Rs 150 was deducted on miscellaneous charges—probably taxes remaining unpaid. That left Rs 2,000 his current debts were Rs 600 more.

In 1863, Ghalib's robe of honour and ceremonial place in the Governor-General's durbar were also restored. The hand of the Nawab was probably instrumental here as well—and apparently the instructions came from Lord Elgin the Governor-General himself. This was a development of great satisfaction to Ghalib. The restoration of the pension signified the renewal of British favour and helped to ease his perennially precarious financial position. But the restoration of his ceremonial standing helped fill a crucial psychological void. It betokened a renewed recognition of his place in the social scale. He had received this recognition from the Mughal court; and had asserted his rights with the British—especially in the protracted dispute over the pension case—on the strength of it. The Mughal court was no more. The Revolt of 1857 was short-lived, and the hopes it had raised stood thoroughly defeated. In the new order of things, Ghalib, along with the bulk of the old nobility, had been ignored and humiliated. The British were now the unchallenged, paramount power in India. When they decided to reconfer the ceremonial honours that Ghalib never doubted belonged to him, his acceptance was not a matter of ideological compromise, but of personal vindication. Not only did it help rehabilitate his own esteem—although he was never in doubt that it was but a symbolic gesture—but in the eyes of his peer group it contributed to the restoration of due status. The mistake some critics make is to transpose the modern nationalistic context on to Ghalib's times; the mistake others commit is to see his pursuit of such recognition out of context. A sampling of the latter is the following comment: 'Ghalib's self-esteem sometimes bordered

on the comic. I wonder if there is any other poet of
equal fame or merit who . . . took such a childish
delight in titles, distinctions, robes of honour,
invitations to durbars, or plumed himself so much on
his contacts with the outside world.'[8] It is undeniable
that Ghalib was pleased with titles and robes of honour.
But he considered his pleasure in such conferments to
be justified—and did not expect to be judged by
posterity, by some superhuman and transcendent code
of behaviour. His pursuit in such matters was not
merely that of a child blinded by the glamour of
baubles. It was more the tenacity of a man who was
human, and who—quite justifiably in the context of
his times—believed his status to be worthy of
recognition; and who had nothing left to cling to in
the face of its negation. Nor did British conferment
of such recognition convert him overnight into a
fawning acolyte. His personal views on what was
happening in Delhi, and his nostalgia for the days
when the king ruled remained unchanged. The
restoration of honours was not so much a proof of his
unwavering loyalty to the British, as it was a reluctant
and delayed British forgiveness of past disloyalty. Ghalib
once reminisced that an ode he had sent to Lord
Canning, soon after 1857, had been returned with a
reply that the British government did not want to
have anything to do with a man who was in league
with the Mughal king. But persistence paid; a second
ode, sent after a gap, was acknowledged by the Chief
Secretary to Government—as used to happen in the
past. The goal of getting due recognition of *status*
from the British was, in Ghalib's eyes, an end in

itself. About the means he never had any illusions. 'I was the government's hired bard,' he wrote with characteristic candour in July 1860. 'I wrote my panegyrics and got my robes in reward.'⁹

Nawab Yusuf Ali Khan of Rampur died in 1865 of cancer. In the period between 1859 and 1865, Ghalib, though not resident in Rampur, functioned virtually as his court poet. The Nawab would regularly send his verses for correction, and Ghalib would give them his prompt attention. In a sense, the court of Rampur replaced the court of Delhi by continuing the familiar framework of royal benefactor and court poet. The Rs 100 the Nawab sent every month was vital to Ghalib. His British pension of Rs 62.50 a month had never sufficed for his style of living; even before 1857 he had sought to supplement it by other incomes. With the all-round increase in prices, after 1857 this pension had become hopelessly inadequate. Both the boys—Baqir Ali and Hussain Ali—had grown up. Baqir Ali had, in fact, married, and although he later got gainful employment at Alwar, initially, Ghalib had to provide for him and his wife. Even the Rampur allowance was not really sufficient to cover his expenses. (In addition to the upkeep of his family, there were, Ghalib complained, all kinds of expenses to be met: income tax, the *chow-kidars'* pay, servants' wages, repayment of principal, and that of the interest.)

In the circumstances, he was fully aware of his stark financial dependency on Rampur. In one of his letters of this time, he expresses a desire to wander about in poverty and freedom; but this was wishful thinking. In practice he was unable to curtail his expenditure and disinclined—at this late stage of his life—to change his style of living. 'I am not afraid of dying,' he wrote, 'but the lack of comfort unnerves me.'[10] To be fair, once in 1862, when things got really uncomfortable, he did try to change his habits. He gave up his morning drink, halved his meat consumption, and, through a miracle of will-power, renounced his lifelong daily quota of wine in the evening. More than him, his friends were amazed at this performance. However, even before a month had elapsed a little money, over and above his fixed stipend, came from Rampur. The most pressing debt repayments were somehow met; the old routine was resurrected with relief and life went on as always.

There is evidence that Nawab Yusuf Ali Khan was quite responsive to Ghalib's repeated requests for money—over and above his stipend. There seems to have been a genuine feeling of respect between them. But, as in the relationship with Bahadur Shah Zafar, Ghalib's relationship with the Nawab was not without its occasional unease. In the benefactor–beneficiary nexus, Ghalib was prepared to accept being the weaker partner; but his quick ego and assertion of personality chafed at such a weakness being taken as abject or mute servility. On occasion he could introduce just that degree of calculated levity, take just that much licence, to transmute his role from supplicant to that of near equal. In 1861, the Nawab was celebrating the marriage of his second son with great pomp. Ghalib was unable to attend, but received Rs 125 in lieu of the robe of honour, tray of food and gifts normally distributed at such events. Ghalib wrote back to thank the Nawab; the money, he said, was in lieu of a feast and a robe of honour. But since he was starving, if he spent all the money on feeding himself, would the Nawab, he jokingly asked, still owe him money for the robe? Ghalib knew that his financial dependencies were such that he was in no position to alienate his benefactor; but his sensitivity to any suggestion of slight always made it difficult for him to act fully in accordance with such a realization. In 1861 there was noticeable tension when the Nawab did not act on two recommendations for employment which Ghalib had forwarded to his court. Ghalib patched up the misunderstanding by a clarificatory letter in which he maintained, however, that both the men recommended were able and intelligent. A letter to a friend at this time reveals that he was genuinely hurt at the Nawab's action. Apart from these incidents, Nawab Yusuf Ali Khan gave Ghalib the respect due to his years and his poetic reputation. And Ghalib, on his part, respected him for that.

On his death, Yusuf Ali Khan was succeeded by his son Kalb Ali Khan. Ghalib journeyed to Rampur a second time for his coronation. Quite apart from the royal invitation, there were two motivating factors for his attending the event; first, he was anxious to ensure that the new Nawab continued his father's practice of sending Rs 100 every month; second, he was hopeful that during the coronation the Nawab, as was customary, would make a suitable gift. Kalb Ali Khan treated Ghalib with honour and respect if not with particular warmth. He continued the practice of the monthly stipend. At the time of Ghalib's departure he gave him an adhoc gift of Rs 1,200. The amount was not small but Ghalib was a trifle disappointed. Apparently, the Nawab had bestowed greater largesse on people who, Ghalib felt, had less claim to his generosity. The Nawab also largely discontinued the practice of acceding to Ghalib's requests for money over and above his stipend. Between Yusuf Ali Khan and Ghalib there had been greater contemporaneity and literary compatibility; Kalb Ali Khan did not write much verse and consulted Ghalib mostly on his Persian prose. Ghalib's financial dependency on Rampur was, if anything, greater now. He was also fully aware that he could not expect the same indulgences from the new Nawab as he had from the father. But, characteristically, he was unable to curb his proclivity to fight to preserve his independence, in spite of his financial vulnerability. Relations were severely strained when Ghalib, rather brusquely, dismissed the Nawab's views on the validity of Persian usage as followed by Persian writers in India—but disapproved of by classical Persian writers. The Nawab was a traditionalist—and Ghalib must have known this. He took serious umbrage and Ghalib, afraid that his stipend would be terminated, tendered an apology. The controversy died, but the fact that Ghalib was prepared to take on the Nawab—fully aware of the thin ice on which the Rampur patronage now rested—speaks both of his lack of pragmatism and his intellectual courage. Although his unredeemable state of dependency made him ultimately bend in such situations, he liked to believe that, whenever possible, he had tried to maintain his intellectual freedom. In literary matters he considered intellectual compromise particularly unacceptable. Flattery has not been my practice, he wrote with some inaccuracy to a friend in 1366; but he meant what he said when he added that where matters of poetry were concerned it was something he had scrupulously avoided.

Ghalib stayed in Rampur for less than three months, returning to Delhi in December 1865. On his first visit, in 1860, he had not stayed much longer. At that time there had been a definite incentive for him to do so because the previous Nawab had offered to double his stipend if he remained in Rampur. When he returned this time, there was speculation that either the Nawab had turned him down, or the British had intervened with the Nawab to terminate the relationship. But Ghalib had cited the two boys—Baqir's and Hussain's—homesickness as the reason. The truth is that he himself missed Delhi. Delhi may have become a 'camp' but it was still the known and familiar; he had passed a lifetime in its *galis* and *kuchas;* it symbolized a way of life which was the only one he knew. 'Who could have told you anything so contrary to the facts?' he incredulously asked a friend who thought that he had left Delhi. 'I have always stayed here in Delhi with my wife and children—swimming in this sea of blood.'[11] It was too late now for him to make a home anywhere else. Perhaps he also lacked the energy to continue as an active court-poet-in-residence. Delhi allowed him to retain his familiar setting and the freedom to live his own lifestyle, without losing his stipend or access to the Rampur court. In monetary terms it was a loss, but from his point of view there could have been no other decision. There was also the question of his wife. She had not accompanied him to Rampur and probably had no intention of ever doing so. Ghalib's letters from Rampur shed a lovable light on his concern for his wife. He insisted that the two boys write regularly to their grandmother, and, since she could not read, made arrangements for friends to read out the letters to her. He also made elaborate arrangements to ensure that in his absence she had enough money for the household—and the servants were paid on time.

Of course, Rampur could never replace Delhi as Ghalib's preferred stage for literary concerns, in which—in spite of his age—he continued to be very active. In 1861, a fresh volume of his Urdu verse was printed. In 1862, an edition of his collected Persian verse was published. The same year also saw the publication of his prose work, *Qate-i-Burhan,* a commentary on the Persian dictionary *Burhan-i-Qate.* In 1863, his friends finally persuaded him to have a collection of his letters published; one collection, entitled, *Ood-i-Hind* was published in 1868 and a second, *Urdu-i-Mualla,* after his death. Of course he continued to receive an incessant flow of the prose and verse of others for correction—and not just from Delhi. These came from as far away as Bareilly, Lucknow, Calcutta, Bombay and Surat, and, to the best of his abilities, he continued to give each of them his personal attention.

For all this, failing health compelled Ghalib to almost give up the labour of writing serious verse himself. He probably wrote his last Persian *ghazal* in 1865 and his last Urdu *ghazal* in 1866:[12]

In Ghalib's fiery pen
We too believe in;
But has he any strength
Still left in him?[13]

In 1863 he was seriously affected by the Delhi Sore.
Boils erupted on both his hands and his right leg and
quickly became wounds. When traditional medication
failed, an Indian surgeon trained in Western medicine
was summoned to cauterize and excise the putrified
flesh in and around the sores. There was some
improvement, but then a virulent swelling affected
his foot. He could not wear his shoes and walked with
the greatest difficulty. The infection persisted for almost
a year. For the greater part of 1864 he remained in
constant pain, unable to sleep at night, with bandages
and ointment all over his body. By the end of the year
there were signs of recovery, but his weakness was
such that it took him, he wrote, as much time to
stand up as it would to build a wall up to a man's
height.

The analogy had a dollop of truth in it. He could
walk now only with the help of a staff. His hearing,
poor for many years now, was failing rapidly. His
eyesight was becoming progressively weaker, and he
had problems with his memory. He often misplaced
verse or prose sent to him for correction, or mailed
them incorrectly. This always pained him, but he did
his best to inform people of his diminishing faculties.
'Exalted sir, the *ghazal* your servant has brought has
gone where I am going—to oblivion. That is, I have
lost it . . .',[14] he wrote with some exasperation to a

friend in 1864. When people persisted in asking about their work he would lose his temper, but it was apparent that this was really at his own helplessness than their reminders. 'I have told you already that I do not remember the quatrains you want,' he wrote to *shagird* Allauddin Khan of Loharu. 'And again you ask me to send them to you as though I have been lying—*Bhai,* I swear by the Quran, the Gospels, the Torah, the Psalms, the Four Vedas, the Zaud, Pazand and Avesta, and by the Guru's Granth that I do not have either that wretched ode or those quatrains with me. . .'[15] He spent most of the day now confined to his room in the *mardanah* section of his home. He preferred to remain lying down, getting up only when visitors made it essential for him to do so. He was not afraid of death:

A day is fixed for one's death
Why pass then the night unslept?[16]

As per his own astrological calculations he expected to die in 1861. That was the year of the great cholera epidemic. When 1861 came and passed, and he had survived it all, he could joke that it was below his dignity to die in a general epidemic!

Illness inconvenienced him more than it frightened him, and he went through a severe depression when he was bedridden from sores and swellings all over his body. There was also a sadness not unmixed with nostalgia for the days when he was younger and more capable of enjoying the distractions life could offer. Several of his couplets tellingly encapsulate this frame of mind:

Ages have gone by
Since I last hosted my beloved,
And since with brimming cups of wine
A gathering was illumined.[17]

Again I feel stifled
By this policy of restraint;
Years have passed since
I last abandoned all constraint.[18]

Where now the intoxication of that wine sipped at
   night
Come, get up, the joy of early morning slumber
   has gone.[19]

Ghalib, the turn of time has taken a heavy toll
Where now those hopes, that youth—where has it
   gone?[20]

Even so, when not in pain or disabled, he retained
snatches of his irrepressible buoyancy, the poet's sense
of seizing a moment, living it, chiselling and refining
it, and recapitulating it with the translucent clarity of
total experience. 'Now it has stopped raining . . .' he
wrote in August 1862. 'The open terrace, the moon,
a cool breeze, Mars visible in the sky all night. In pre-
dawn Venus glimmering. As the moon sets in the
west, Venus appears in the east. The delight of a sip of
wine, the glowing night.'[21]

He liked to think of himself now as *a fakir,* or
darwesh, confined to his room, still an observer but
much less a participant. The challenges were less, but

in a sense watching the mainstream from the bank
had its own compensations:

> No arrow is in the bow, no hunter is at hunt
> Such ease have I, in my imprisonment.[22]

He knew he did not have the physical strength to take
centre stage any more, and so there was less of the
chafing and striving, less ambition, less rancour and
greater reconciliation:

> When the boat has drifted to the shore, Ghalib,
> Why complain to God of the boatman's injustice?[23]

Lying in his room he wrote endless letters describing
daily events, his problems and his health, but also
dwelling on larger issues of life and death, human
triumphs and foibles. He offered advice when
writing to younger relatives and friends, and
was often contemplative and introspective with
those contemporaries and friends that remained of
his generation:

> I too caroused in dizzy youth
> 'mid riotous revelry;
> But now, at last, the thrill is past
> and all the ecstacy.[24]

One of his strengths now was his deep spirituality,
untainted as before by the mechanics of religion.
'. . . I have drained the heavy goblet of the pure wine
that teaches, Nothing exists but God,' he stated with

certitude in 1862, 'and I sit here above the radiance of religion and the fire of infidelity alike.'[25] Many character traits, which earlier remained less articulated due to the efforts and preoccupations of a more embattled life, were now stated with deep conviction: 'How I wished,' he wrote with feeling in 1865, 'that if not in the entire world, at least in the town where I lived, none should go ragged or hungry . . .'[26] He had tried to be of help to his friends and acquaintances in the past, too; but now—when he could do much less—there was an emphasis and passion in his interventions which were redolent of genuine humanitarian concern. Pandit Jai Narain was a young man whose father and grandfather had worked for the house of Loharu; in 1865, he approached Ghalib for assistance in obtaining employment in Patiala. Ghalib immediately wrote to Hakim Ghulam Murtaza Khan in Patiala. 'I have never bothered you about anything. Pandit Jai Narain comes to you with this letter . . . I swear upon my head that if you do your best to get him a job . . . I would think as if you had given me that position. I shall be infinitely grateful . . .'[27]

Even in his younger days, he had never found it difficult to wallow in a bit of self-pity. Now he had more time and more reason to do so: he would often refer to himself as one despised by men and punished by God and would, in his letters, dwell at length on his ailments and abject impoverishment. What had always saved him from sinking into self-pity was a sense of humour and a resilient stoicism. He would always emerge from such bouts of depression to stress again that life, for all its pain and sorrow, was worth living and enjoying. But there was one issue on which his regret neither vanished nor diminished: the firm conviction that—in his time—his poetic worth had not received the appreciation—both in material terms and intellectually—that was its due. As he wrote in a Persian verse:

In eternity without beginning,
My star has reached the zenith of acceptance;
But in this world, the renown
Of my verses will be after me.[28]

In the last years of his life this gnawing regret was only further accentuated and he mentions it in several of his letters. In one written in 1864, obviously composed in deep depression, he sums up his life's literary output: one Urdu *Diwan,* one in Persian, three small books all unawarded and unappreciated. 'I did not get the acclaim for my prose and poetry that they deserved,' he wrote again in 1865. 'My poetry was composed for myself alone . . .'[29] It is not that Ghalib was unaware of the recognition and fame he had achieved; it was characteristic of the man that he considered his achievement too little in relation to what he felt he had to offer. His was not the case of the average, fretting ego remaining perennially dissatisfied. It was more an instance of a larger-than-life ego, an exalted ego, using its *own* standard to judge the measure of achievement. His was not the regret of a man hostile to competition or envious—in the twilight years of his life—of the achievement of others. His was the regret of a man who had never been in doubt that he was the best, and who genuinely felt that, in his age, very few had the literary discernment to appreciate his poetic work—or the material wherewithal to befittingly reward it. As he writes in his Persian *Diwan:*

Ghalib, thou should'st take thy poetry
Outside India, since here no one discriminates
Between a stone and a jewel,
Or sleight-of-hand and a miracle.[30]

When he started his poetic career his poetry had seen derisive rejection by many in the literati on grounds of being too obscure. He had then changed his style—more out of deference to the comprehension of his critics, than to any real conviction that his style needed revision. Later he had found it difficult to gain access to the Mughal court, whose *mushairahs* under Bahadur Shah Zafar were the ultimate stage for every aspiring poet. When he did gain access, he had to accept Zauq—a poet whom he considered but average—as the court poet. On Zauq's death he had been made court poet, but it was an honour which he felt had come too late, with too little to offer. All his life he had prided himself on his Persian poetry and verse; but at a time when Urdu had definitively replaced Persian as the language of literary usage, he found that, for most people, his devotion to the latter was more a matter of curiosity than appreciation. Persian scholarship was something on which he was prepared to risk his reputation; but even in this field he could not avoid being dragged into repeated and vituperative controversies. His Urdu *Diwan* and his Persian collection had gone into several editions; but he had hardly made any money in the process. For all his adroit panegyrics, the British had never given him a paisa more than his original inherited pension—and for all the appreciation the Mughal king had had, he had hardly anything else to give. In spite of his fame as a poet he had lived his life in penury and indebtedness. This was all the more galling because for him—it must be remembered—the reference point for gauging success was the past, when lesser poets were routinely rewarded with incomparably greater munificence. It is not surprising, therefore, that in his last years when—poor, in debt, and ill—he made a balance-sheet of achievements, his conclusion was that, in terms of something to show for all his poetic fame, he had hardly anything. In the final analysis, however, his regret stemmed from a larger sadness, the sadness of a man who preferred to live in the past, but was forced to live in a time when the harsh tide of change had set adrift the known moorings and anchorages even of the present.

By 1867 Ghalib's health was in very obvious decline. On his return journey from Rampur, in January 1866, he had met with an accident and was lucky to have escaped with his life. A bridge collapsed just as the palanquin in which he was seated got across. The cart with the baggage and the servants was stranded on the other side. With the baggage was the bedding, and it was a freezing winter night. With difficulty Ghalib managed to locate an inn and passed the night in considerable discomfort. The tribulations of the

journey took a heavy toll on his already frail physical
condition; it was an exceptionally cold winter, made
worse by rain and strong winds. The food available at
serais and halting places was not to his taste, and often
he would go without a meal altogether. Back home
his health improved slightly, but the reprieve was
brief. Chronic complaints, which were earlier
controlled or sporadic, now flared up. Colic which
had always troubled him became permanent. His liver
was giving trouble and he complained that he felt the
need to drink a lot of water. He also needed to pass
urine very frequently; these were probably symptoms
of an undiagnosed condition of diabetes. His diet, as
he recorded with almost a dietician's precision, was
progressively shrinking. 'My diet is the juice of seven
almonds in the morning, mixed with water sweetened
with crystallized sugar, the thick broth of two pounds
of meat at mid day, occasionally three fried *kababs*
towards evening, and five *tolas* of home-made wine
about two-and-a-half hours after sunset.'[31] Although
it is significant that, in spite of his ailments, he still
continued to take a little bit of wine, his physical
deterioration was now relentless. By the beginning of
1867 his memory was almost completely gone and
his hearing had failed totally. Interestingly, he continued
to be mentally alert, keenly observant of each stage
of his physical disintegration. He had been a victim of
palsy for some time now, and in a letter of 1866 he
noted that the trembling was so strong his hands
could not grip anything properly. In 1867 he
complained that he could not even make his own
pens. His weakness was such that he had come to

accept that he must remain prostrate most of the time. But soon he could not even walk. 'I sleep in the courtyard,' he wrote in 1867. 'Two men carry me onto the verandah and dump me in a small, dark, side room. I spend the day lying in its dingy corner. In the evening I am again carried out and dumped on a cot . . .'[32] Even in this condition, so long as it was possible, he continued to do his best to attend to the verses sent to him for correction. But by June 1867 he could not even write, and this deprived him of the joy of one of his oldest pastimes—writing letters. He now took to dictating letters whenever a friend would have the time to take them down; but his failing eyesight and trembling hands would make it impossible for him to hold a pen. Verses still continued to come to him in great numbers. He had always been conscientious about giving them his due attention, and his inability to do so now greatly pained him. In August 1867 in desperation he had a plea printed in the papers—but apparently this had little effect. 'Poems for correction and letters continue to pour in and I feel ashamed and miserable. I am old, an invalid, completely deaf, half-blind, and bed-ridden.'[33]

It is unfortunate that in these last years, when the end was so close, he was jolted by the most virulent controversy of his life. In 1859, as we've seen, Ghalib had written a critical commentary on the Deccani scholar Maulvi Mohammed Hussain Tabrizi's well-known Persian dictionary *Burhan-i-Qate,* which was published in Calcutta. His commentary, *Qate-i-Burhan*, (and a second enlarged edition called *Dirafsh-i-Kawiani,* brought out in 1865) was in line with Ghalib's consistent criticism of those who relied on the authority of the 'Indian' school of Persian writers as against the Persian classicists. But Maulvi Mohammed Hussain was a scholar with a large following in India. Ghalib's criticism aroused deep resentment. This was partly fuelled by the occasionally derisive and contemptuous tone of Ghalib's commentary. There were also some obvious factual lacunae in his criticism. Even Hali, one of his staunchest admirers, acknowledges that Ghalib was guilty of a few 'lapses', adding that this was perhaps because he wrote mostly from memory and had no reference material to cross-check with. Apparently, at the time when he was jotting down his comments, Ghalib had no intention of ever publishing them. The commentary was published later, at the intercession of his friends. It is possible that if Ghalib had written the commentary with the idea of publishing it, he would have been less harsh and more circumspect in his remarks. On the other hand, he had never been very tactful about his opinions where literary matters were concerned— and would have been happy to have a larger audience read his trenchant critique. However, it is almost certain that he underestimated the outcry that followed. Several pamphlets criticizing the book surfaced and it seemed as though the whole town was ready to do battle with Ghalib.

Hali felt that the entire outrage took place because Ghalib had rocked the boat of established literary opinion. But there were other factors too. This was not the first time that Ghalib had provoked the literary establishment or become the focus of literary controversy. In Calcutta in 1828 he had, perhaps even more dramatically, raised a hornet's nest. But between then and now there was a qualitative difference. Debate on the finer points of Urdu and Persian literature was then largely confined to a smaller group, drawn mostly from the feudal elite. The middle classes and the literate among those lower on the social scale were interested but peripheral observers. They enjoyed poetry, many were well read, but none of them were generally expected—or given much opportunity—to articulate their views on such matters. Literary controversies, differences of opinion and the legitimacy of standpoints were then debated and battled out with greater restraint and decorum. By 1865, the tide of literary involvement—facilitated by the expansion of the publishing industry and the improvement in communications—had swept past the confines of decorous *mushairahs*. The breakdown of the old socio-political order, with its attendant shifts in economic power and changes in social perceptions and behaviour, had given the middle and lower classes greater sanction and opportunity to be heard. The framework of literary debate had been irrevocably enlarged; and it could not be controlled or confined at will.

It is interesting that at the height of the controversy Ghalib sought to do just that—by invoking his social standing against the brashness of some detractors. Replying to one of his critics he wrote: 'He has used all the choicest epithets of abuse to describe me, not stopping to think that even if Ghalib is no scholar and no poet, yet he has a certain standing as one of noble birth and noble degree . . . a man of distinguished family, a man known to the nobility and gentry and maharajahs of India and numbered by the British among the nobly born.'[34] But such attempts were futile. In 1866, Aminuddin Khan of Patiala wrote a particularly filthy and obscene pamphlet. Ghalib's initial reaction was to ignore it. 'If you are kicked by a donkey, do you kick it back?' he is supposed to have asked. He had not much stamina or energy left for battle, and was perhaps inclined to follow the advice of one of his own couplets:

Listen not if someone speaks ill,
Speak not if someone does ill;
Stop him if he is going astray,
Forgive him if he to fault is prey.[35]

But the contents of the pamphlet were so intolerably insulting that in December 1867 he filed a case for defamation before the British Assistant Commissioner's court.

Men of importance appeared as witnesses on behalf of both parties. On Ghalib's side were ranged Lala Pyare Lal Ashob, Hakim Latif Hussain, Maulvi Nasiruddin and Lala Hukum Chand. Maulvi Ziyauddin, Professor of Arabic at Delhi College, Maulvi Sadiuddin and a few other scholars appeared for the defendant. The legal point at issue was whether the insinuations made by Aminuddin could be unequivocally characterized as obscene; the aim of the defence was to prove that the sentences in the pamphlets could be given interpretations at variance with what Ghalib said they meant. This was not difficult to do since

Aminuddin had succeeded in getting important scholars to testify in his support and the arguments were put before a British judge who knew little on the subject. Ghalib soon realized that the parameters of existing law would not bring him justice; on the contrary, each day of testimony was only making matters worse. According to Hali, it was extremely painful for Ghalib to listen to people like Maulvi Ziyauddin, who not only prostituted their scholarship to whitewash Aminuddin's transparently culpable language, but also made the most derogatory remarks—accusing Ghalib of being a drunkard and a man without any fear of God. Therefore, on 23 March 1868, Ghalib decided to put an end to the continuing humiliation and dropped proceedings.

Hali's account brings out an important element of the episode: the dispute was literary, but the attack on Ghalib was increasingly personal. This cannot merely be explained away by the lack of conventions and norms in the conduct of such disputes, or by the prevalent *style* of expressing differences in opinion. One gets a distinct impression that the conservative Muslim lobby used the occasion to attack Ghalib for his lifelong, and publicly avowed, irreverence towards organized religion and the orthodox establishment. It must be assumed that this kind of opposition had existed before. But in the early part of the nineteenth century the Sufi *tariqah* had a hold and a following that helped Ghalib keep the proponents of Islamic orthodoxy at bay—and even hope for understanding and indulgence from some of its votaries. It is possible that after 1857, when the Muslim community was singled out for persecution—and its leading members bore the brunt of British wrath—for some of its members there was a 'recoiling' or a returning to the security of established religion and ritual. This is not to assert that there was any organized fundamentalist movement, but to merely acknowledge that in moments of trauma communities sometimes seek refuge in the unquestioning acceptance of religious dogma. And, to note further, that the orthodox Islamic establishment had never really been emasculated by public support for religious eclecticism in the previous decades. It is plausible that in the 1860s the *mullahs* were getting more responsive audiences than they had before; and if this was so it is understandable why, in the case of Ghalib—one of nineteenth-century India's most flamboyant and provocative critics of the religious establishment—a literary controversy became so virulent an occasion for personal attack. Hali lends credence to such a hypothesis when he notes that at this time Ghalib was receiving a great number of anonymous letters which attacked his *way of life* in the most vicious and abusive language. Moreover, by 1866, Ghalib's personal base of power and influence was almost non-existent: the king who, despite of being an orthodox Muslim, had indulged him, was dead in exile; the old Muslim feudal aristocracy— whose influential members respected him and could be counted among his personal friends—was in shambles; the British had new partners for their rule in the city; he was old, ill, and in debt, with access only to Rampur for royal patronage, and there too the new Nawab was not as warmly disposed to him as his father had been. For several reasons, therefore, the controversy over *Qate-i-Burhan* was more than a literary matter; in a great part, it gave conservative Muslim opinion the weapon with which to attack Ghalib at a time when he was obviously vulnerable, and when—because of the widened ambit of involvement in literary debate—more people could be brought into the battle. All his life Ghalib had baited the religious preacher, the *vayiz,* proclaiming his love for wine and flaunting his indifference to the demands of formal religion. Now, the *mullahs* were getting their own back. In a sense it is not surprising that a literary controversy should have reduced itself to such a situation. What Ghalib believed in he highlighted in his writings. Where he was concerned, criticism at a literary level could very easily spill over into a criticism of his views as a whole. The *Qate-i-Burhan* controversy, perversely enough, provides proof of Ghalib the integral literary person; the poet indistinguishable from what he believed in, and the man undifferentiated from what he wrote about. What must have been especially galling to his critics was that in spite of the severity of their attack, he remained unrepentant. Perhaps he was too tired, and too weak physically, to fight back as spiritedly as he would have liked to; but he was still strong enough to defeat his detractors, by remaining adamant about not compromising his commitment to his spiritual vision. At this time some of his closest friends were prone to inadvertently hurt him. Hali recalls with regret and remorse how he himself, carried away by his spiritual punctiliousness, lectured Ghalib—around this time—

on the importance of saying the five prayers. Ghalib's embittered but unyielding reply was that, yes, he had never kept a fast, or said a prayer, thus, he was a 'sinner' who deserved to be 'hung' with his face blackened and his body thrown to the dogs and crows—if they would deign to eat such a damnable thing. But, even so, without doubt he had always believed in the oneness of God, and the words 'Nothing exists but God' had always been on his lips.

In his last year, Ghalib was racked with anxiety about the repayment of his debts which stood at a little over Rs 1,000. Since the end was obviously close, his creditors had become aggressively insistent. To die without paying one's debt was also not the way of a good Muslim. For Ghalib, this was an instance where religious injunction and honourable practice coincided. It is ironical that a man who all his life had been so cavalier about money—knowingly living beyond his means and borrowing recklessly—should, in his final moments, be so concerned about the squaring of accounts. He knew that after his death there was no way the debt could be paid. In fact one of his greatest worries was how his wife, with no source of income, would manage without him. The elder grand-nephew, Baqir Ali, had obtained remunerative employment at Alwar but he had his own family to look after. Hussain Ali, the younger one, was still with him and unemployed. To complicate matters further, Hussain Ali's marriage had been fixed. The marriage was repeatedly deferred because of shortage of money, a circumstance deeply humiliating for Ghalib. Obviously, creditors were not the answer.

Credit was given to a person who had the time to repay. The only other source was Rampur. In July 1868 Ghalib wrote to the Nawab with three requests: first, that his outstanding debts be paid off; second, that a special grant be made to enable him to perform the marriage of Hussain Ali; and, third, that the stipend of Rs 100 which he received be given after him to Hussain Ali. Ghalib had never hesitated to ask for favours from his royal or powerful patrons. He considered that by doing so he was not only fulfilling his own role—as per prevailing norms—of an honourable courtier, but, also giving his patrons the *opportunity* to indulge a poet of his worth and calibre. But now there was a totally uncharacteristic abjectness and desperation in his asking. He knew he had very little time left and a repeated refrain, in his increasingly desperate letters, was that the Nawab take a quick decision. For a while there seemed some hope when Nawab Mirza Khan (Dagh) interceded at Rampur on his behalf. But the Nawab remained non-committal. When Ghalib died, neither money nor assurances had come from Rampur.

A few days before his death, Ghalib was prone to lapse into unconsciousness. But almost until the very end his mind remained alert. Khwaja Azizuddin Aziz of Lucknow visited him a little before his death. He noted that 'he (Ghalib) had a book (probably the *Diwan* of *Qa'ani*) on his breast which he was reading—his eyes probing into it . . .'[36] While Aziz was there Ghalib's food was brought in. Aziz got up to leave but Ghalib beckoned him to stay. 'You took the trouble perhaps to see me. That is very kind of you,' Ghalib said in a feeble voice. 'Did you notice my weakness, it is difficult for me to move about; did you see the condition of my sight, I do not recognize a man; did you mark my hearing capacity, although one may shout as loudly as possible, I cannot hear; you have noticed my mode of reciting a *ghazal*—you have listened to my *kalam*. There is one thing left—what I eat and how much I eat; please note before going away.'[37] The sharpness of mind and inimitable sense of humour remained till the very end.

Hali went to see him the day before he died. Ghalib had just then regained consciousness after several hours in a coma, and was dictating a reply to Nawab Allauddin Khan of Loharu who had enquired about his condition. 'Why enquire how I am?' Ghalib replied. 'Ask my neighbours after a day or two.' In his final moments the following verse was often on his lips.

My dying breath is ready to depart
And now, my friends, God, only God, exists.[38]

The end came on 15 February 1869. He was buried at noon in Sultanji, the family graveyard of the Loharu house, near the mausoleum of Nizamuddin Auliya. Nawab Ziauddin Khan of Loharu, Hakim Ahsanullah Khan and Nawab Mustafa Khan Shefta, were among the eminent people present. The funeral expenses were defrayed by Nawab Ziauddin Khan. In a final tribute to the man's religious transcendence, there was some confusion as to whether the funeral rites should follow Shia or Sunni ritual. On Nawab Ziauddin's insistence he was interred according to Sunni ritual. His wife died exactly a year later.

> What work has stopped
> Without Ghalib the distressful?
> No need to cry so much
> Or raise voices lamentful.[39]

Glossary

abdar—servant-in-waiting

akhada—wrestling pit

angarkha—long, loose coat/robe buttoned on the side

angrez—foreigner/ Englishman

arzi—petition

attar—fragrant oil made primarily from the damask rose

badshah—king

bahuroopias—quick change artists

Bakr-i-Id—Muslim festival

bazaar—marketplace

begum—Muslim princess/lady of rank

bhai—brother

bhands—folk artists

Bostan—famous Persian epic

burka—a loose garment like a caftan with veiled eye-holes

burra kooshee—very glad

chabootra—courtyard

chamar—person from the lowest caste in traditional Hindu society

chana jor garam—spicy/ savoury gram eaten as a snack

chandni—awning/white cloth used as a carpet

chausar—backgammon

chobdar—usher

chooridar—close fitting pyjamas with gathers at the ankles *chowk*—market square

chowkidar—watchman/ guard

dad—justice, beast

dak—mail, post, letter, parcel

dam—net

daman—skirt

dargah—a particular place for a burial or cremation

darwesh—saintly man

dastangos—storytellers

dewan—financial/prime minister

deewani—revenue of an area

Diwan-i-Am—Hall of Public Audience

Diwan-i-Khas—Hall of Private Audience

diwankhana—men's apartment

domni—singing and dancing girl

durbar—audience chamber; reception; body of officials in an Indian court

gali—alley, lane

ganjfa—old Indian card game

gayaki—mode of classical music recital

ghazal—Persian/Arabic verse form of not more than eighteen couplets, the first two lines and even numbered lines thereafter rhyming together

ghee—clarified butter

Ghusal-i-Sehat—function of ceremonial ablutions

hamam-ghars—bathrooms

hookah—water tobacco-pipe

hurkaras —attendants who announce visitors/town cries

huqqabardars—attendants who fill the tobacco-pipe

Idgah—Islamic place of worship

jageer—government revenues of a tract of land assigned with power to administer

jamadar—Indian officer of police

jharna—fountain

jubbah—toga-like garment

kabutarbazi—pigeon-flying

kahr—palanquin bearer

kalam—poetic verse, poetry

kathak—north Indian dance form

katra—marketplace

khansama—cook

khayal—form of light north Indian classical music

khillat—robe of honour

khus khus—fragrant grass

kos—measure of distance

kotha—courtesan's house

kothi—residence

kotwal—chief constable/magistrate

kucha—self-contained area within the city

kurta—knee-length loose shirt

lalqand—red cloth/napkin in which *paans* are traditionally wrapped

lurhiya—cart

madrasa—traditional Muslim school

mahajan—trader

mansabdar—feudal order of rank

mardanah—men's apartment

maulvi—Muslim priest/learned man

mazaar—place where a holy person is buried

mehfil—literary congregation

mian/miyan—friend

mohalla—neighbourhood

mohur—former Persian/Indian gold coin

mukarrar—Encore!

mukhtarnama—power of attorney

mukhiya—village chief

mullah—Muslim learned in law or theology

mushairah—congregation of poets

namak-halali—loyalty

namak-harami—disloyalty

nashist nishast—seating arrangement at a *mushairah*

nazrana—presentation of gift

nazr—gift to a superior

neem—margosa

paan—betel leaf

pakora—fried savoury made of gram flour and vegetables

patangbazi—kite-flying

perwanah—petition

peshkash—presentation of request/gift

Pir-o-Murshid—spiritual guide

punkah—wide, rectangular frame of cloth, edged with thick frills, suspended from the ceiling and pulled to and fro with an attached rope/fan

purdah—veil/curtain for women's apartment

qasida—panegyric

qata—couplet

qazi—Muslim magistrate/judge or religious personage

rakhi—sacred thread tied on a brother's wrist

rath—chariot

ratna—jewel

rubai—four-lined stanza

Sadr-us-Sadr—Chief Interpreter of Muslim law

sahukar—trader

sair—stroll

saki—one who serves drinks

salaams—salutations

salatin—distant minor relations of the royal family

sarkar—government

satta—gambling

sati—Indian widow who burns herself on the pyre of her husband

serai—caravanserai

shagird—pupil/protégé

shairi—poetry

shisha—crystal

shauq—desire

shuqa—royal command

sikka—inscription/coin

sunnad—royal direction

taikhana—basement

takhallus—*nom de plume*

tamasha—show/fuss

tariqah—manner, etiquette

tarz-i-ada—manner of speech/style

tattis—bamboo/rush curtains/sun blinds

tehzib—etiquette

tehzibat—culture

thanedar—watchman/police

thumri—form of light north Indian classical music

umara—nobility

Urdu Diwan—collection of Urdu verse

ustad—teacher

vayiz—sermonizer

vazir—prime minister

wara—locality

yunani—school of traditional medicine

zamindar—landed gentry

zenana—women's apartment

Appendix

Note by the Chief Secretary (G. Swinton) on the
Case of Assud Oollah.

19th August 1830.

Assud Oolla states himself to be the Nephew of the
late Nawab Nussur Oolla Beg Khan, who held the
district of Agra under General Perron, and who came
over to Lord Lake in the Marhatta War, when, for his
good services he had certain lands bestowed on him
in the District of Agra, on an Istumraree tenure at a
Jumma of Rupees 15,000. These were the Pergunnas
of Sonk and Sirsa, the revenue of which, Assud Oolla
in his petition represents, amounted to more than a
lack of Rupees.

Nussur Oolla Khan was the Son-in-Law of the late
Nawab Ahmed Buksh Khan, Chief of Ferozepore Etc.

When Nussur Oolla Khan died, he left a Mother,
a widow, three Sisters and two Sons, Viz: the Petitioner
and his Younger Brother Yoosuf Alla Khan (or Mirza
Yoosuf).

The Petitioner further states that there was another Person named Khajeh Hajee, who was no relation of Nussur Oolla Khan, but was connected by marriage, he being the son of a Niece of Nussur Oolla Khan's Father's wife. This Person however seems to have assumed the management of Nussur Oolla Khan's Affairs, and on his death, is stated to have conspired with Ahmed Buksh Khan to defraud the Family of the deceased. Ahmed Buksh Khan as the Father-in-Law of Nussur Oolla Khan and the natural Guardian of his Family, obtained from Lord Lake a remission of the quit rent payable by him for Ferozepore on the condition of providing for Nussur Oolla Khan's Family; and the Petitioner asserts, that the Nawab unjustly set up Khajeh Hajee as the principal Person of Nussur Oolla Khan's Family, and allotting 5,000 Rupees per annum for the general support of the Family distributed it as follows:

To Khajeh Hajee	2,000
To Nussur Oolla Khan's Mother	1,500
To the Petitioner	1,500

On Khajeh Hajee's death, Ahmed Buksh Khan continued the portion of 2,000 to his Children.

When the Mother died, her portion went to her eldest Daughter (Sister of Nussur Oollah Khan) who, out of it, supported her two Younger Sisters.

The Petitioner States that out of his portion, he has supported his younger Brother, who, he complains was left unprovided for by Ahmed Buksh Khan. It is probably, however, that the Sum of 1,500 settled on

Assud Oollah was intended for the joint support of the two Brothers as the other 1,500 Rupees seem to have been intended for the Females, the three Aunts of the Petitioner.

It may be useless to enquire now whether Khajeh Hajee was entitled to share with the Heirs of Nussur Oollah Khan, since he has been acknowledged as a Member of the Family in the Perwanna of the 4th May 1806, which Ahmed Buksh Khan obtained under the Seal and Signature of the Governor General in Council. But it may be useful to enquire, whether Ahmed Buksh Khan acted up to the condition of his Sunnud, when he allotted 5,000 per annum only for the maintenance of Nussur Oolla Khan's Family, including Khajeh Hajee, and whether his heir and successor Shumsoodeen Khan is bound to make a larger provision for them.

It will be useful to enquire also whether, as asserted by the Petitioner the Sunnud by Lord Lake dated 6th June 1806 is a forgery, and whether the case has been fully investigated.

Without going therefore into all the particulars stated by the Petitioner in his several Memorials, to which, however, I beg reference as containing much information which I shall take for granted is known to Government, I propose to submit merely an account of what has lately taken place.

Assud Oolla came to Calcutta in 1828, and presented a memorial to the Persian Secretary Vide Memorial received 28th April 1828; and recorded 2nd May, no. 46.

The order passed on that Memorial was 'ordered

that the Petitioner be informed that the above Petition ought to be addressed to the Resident at Delhi.'

On the 24th of February 1829, the Resident at Delhi, Sir E. Colebrooke reported to Government, that Assud Oolla had presented a Petition to him, the purport of which was 'that on the death of Nussur Oolla Khan, who held in Makurreeree for his life the Pergunnas Saunk and Sirsa at a quit rent of 15,000, the quit rent between 20,000 and 30,000 at which the late Ahmed Buksh Khan held the lands of Ferozepore Etc. had been relinquished in consideration of Ahmed Buksh Khan making himself responsible for the support of Nussur Oolla Beg Khan's Family, and that for such support Ahmed Buksh has never paid more than 5,000 Rupees annually, out of which he has paid 2,000 to one Khajeh Hajee, an alien to the Family, 1,500 Rupees to one of the Petitioner's Sisters, leaving a Brother and Aunts wholly unprovided for.'

Sir Edward Colebrooke proceeds to state 'The Sunnud of Ferozepore from Government, to Ahmed Buksh Khan under date 4th May 1806, contains the following clause which is all I can trace relative to the subject: 'The support and maintenance of Khajeh Hajee and the other dependents (Mootaulliquan) of Mirza Nussur Oolla Beg Khan deceased, are upon you, and you will on requisition in case of necessity, have in readiness for the Sirkar fifty Horsemen.'

In concluding his report Sir Edward Colebrooke requested to be furnished with Copies of any Documents on the records of Government, which might appertain to the case.

In reply an Extract from Lieutenant Colonel

Malcolm's Dispatch of the 4th May 1806, regarding the settlement made with the Nawab Ahmed Buksh Khan was sent to the Resident at Delhi on the 13th March 1829, and he was called to investigate and report on the complaint preferred by the Petitioner.

On the 5th December 1829, Mr. Hawkins, the officiating Resident at Delhi, solicited the attention of Government to Sir Edward Colebrooke's letter of 24th February, to which he stated no answer had been returned. He was informed in reply, that an answer had been sent on the 13th March, since which time no report on the case had been received, and he was furnished with a Copy lest the Original had been mislaid.

On the 5th May last, Mr. Hawkins submitted his report on Assud Oolla's case. It would appear that he had referred Assud Oolla's Petition to the Nawab Shumsoodeen Khan (son and successor of the late Ahmed Buksh Khan) for his answer to the complaint. A translation of Shumsoodeen's reply, and what is called 'Lord Lake's letter dated 7th June 1806', specifying the persons who were to receive the 5,000 Rupees a year, accompanied Mr. Hawkins' report, and he states as his opinion, that the complainant had no right to more than what was expressly provided by Lord Lake for him, and his brother Mirza Yoosuf viz: 1,500 per annum, which the Nabob Shumsoodeen he observed, has all along been willing to pay.

In reply, Government stated on the 28th May last, that it concurred in Mr. Hawkins' decision.

Assud Oolla on the 7th July forwarded an English Petition complaining against Mr. Hawkin's decision on the basis of a Sunnad, which he asserts is a forgery, and requests that the records of Government may be searched in proof of this.

On the 28th July, he again complained against Mr. Hawkin's proceedings as evincing a partiality for the Nabob Shumsoodeen, and requests to be favoured with a Copy of the Orders of Government. He also enclosed a Letter to my address, a translation of which accompanies—and this repeated and direct appeal to myself has induced me to look into all the papers, and to trouble Government with the foregoing narrative, more especially, as it appears to me that there are grounds to believe that Assud Oolla's complaint is not without some foundation.

No letter from Lord Lake dated 7th June 1806, is forthcoming on the records of Government.

It does not appear that the Original has been submitted to Mr. Hawkins.

It appears to be desirable that the Letter of the 7th June, should be produced and examined, and if doubts as to its real nature be entertained at Delhi, it should be sent to the Presidency.

If Shumsoodeen Khan should endeavour to evade this demand by saying the Original is lost, there will be strong presumption against him.

Shumsoodeen Khan's reply as submitted in Hawkins' Dispatch of the 5th May last is written in a very flippant style—and it meets Assud Oolla's assertions by remarking that he is a poet, and avails himself of a poet's privilege to deal in romance.

But let the case be looked into seriously:—

Let us examine the Sunnad to Ahmed Buksh Khan

of the 4th May 1806, which is genuine, and was ratified by the Governor General in Council. A Copy of it will be found as an enclosure to Sir John Malcolm's Dispatch of the same date. That grant *virtually* assigns ten thousand per annum for Nussur Oolla Beg Khan's Family, though unfortunately from the loose manner in which the Sunnad of the 4th May 1806, is worded, the precise sum is not mentioned. It grants a reduction of quit rent from 25,000 to 15,000, for a specific purpose and that was the support and maintenance of Nussur Oolla Beg's Family. It alludes to *'deductions and conditions above specified',* but the deductions and conditions are only expressed above in general terms. But Lord Lake having granted this Perwana on the 4th May, and having received an answer from Government on the 16th of the same month approving what had been done, it is likely that His Lordship, then at Cawnpore, would again write to Ahmed Buksh Khan on the 7th June, regarding what was settled by the orders of the 16 of the preceding Month?

If, however, at the request of the Nabob Ahmed Buksh Khan (then in attendance on Lord Lake at Cawnpore), His Lordship had written the letter of the 7th June, would not Colonel Malcolm when acknowledging a few days afterwards (the 10th June) the receipt of the orders of Government of the 16th of May, have reported that a Letter had been addressed to Ahmed Buksh Khan, fixing a specific sum of 5,000 Rupees as the amount of provision to be granted to Nusur Oolla's Family, and explaining the grounds on which the remaining 5,000 Rupees of the remitted quit rent had not been reannexed to the sum payable by the Nabob on account of his Jagger. But no such report is forthcoming. If the Document be genuine, Ahmed Buksh Khan, it is not improbable, obtained it through some fraud; but even granting it to be an Order wittingly issued by Lord Lake, was His Lordship competent to disturb the previous arrangement sanctioned by the Governor General in Council, and is it binding on Government? I should imagine not, and whether it be genuine or fabricated, the Family of Nussur Oolla Khan, appears to be entitled to the larger allowance.

All the papers referred to in this Note, accompany for reference.

19 August 1830.   Signed G. Swinton
                    Chief Secretary to the Government

***

To:
    C. Norris, Esq.
    Chief Secretary to the Government of Bombay Pol. Dept.

Sir,
I am directed by the Honourable the Vice President in Council to transmit to you the enclosed documents . . . and to request that the Honourable the Governor, after examining the original Persian Document said to be a letter from Lord Lake by one party and pronounced to be a forgery by the other, will be pleased to state his opinion on the merits of Assud Oolla's claim, and on the assertion of that individual

that the Document is either a forgery or was fraudulently obtained.

2. The Honourable the Governor will observe that the Persian Letter does not bear any English counter Signature on the back such as is usual when Persian Letters are issued from the Persian Secretary's Office.

3. I am directed to request that the Original Papers may be returned to me, and that special care be taken of the alleged original Letter from Lord Lake that it may be returned to Nuwwab Shumsoodeen.

Fort William
22nd October 1830.

Signed George Swinton
Chief Secretary to Government

***

To:
    George Swinton
Chief Secretary to the Supreme Government at Fort William
Pol. Dept.

Sir,
I am directed to acknowledge the receipt of your letter dated the 22nd of October with its several enclosures regarding the claims of Assud Oolla Khan and requesting the sentiments of the Honourable the Governor thereon.

In reply I am directed to transmit for the purpose of being laid before the Honourable the Vice President in Council the accompanying copy of a Minute by the Honourable the Governor dated the 30th November expressing his sentiments on the question.

Bombay Castle
9th December 1830

Signed C. Norris
Chief Secretary to Government

***

Minute by the Honourable the Governor General
30th November 1830

According to my belief the Sunnud bears Lord Lake's Signature. The period at which it was obtained was one at which much business, that active operation had led to being in arrears was settled. That superior nature nobleman Ahmed Buksh Khan received and merited so much confidence from Lord Lake and all who were acquainted with him, and that was combined with such respect from the natives and liberality of sentiments, that his character may be pleaded in refutation of his having acted in the dishonourable manner supposed. If he had been guilty of such acts there must I think have been complaints from some of the parties engaged in it.

Signed J. Malcolm

Notes

Ghalib's letters are basic source material for any study of his life and times. His friends had published a compilation of his letters, *Ood-i-Hind*, in 1868, during his lifetime. Another extensive collection, *Urdu-i-Mualla*, was published just after his death. In more recent times, the most comprehensive collation of his letters has been made by Ghulam Rasul Mihr in *Khutut-i-Ghalib*, published in 1957. Other collections have been made on the basis of Ghalib's correspondence with individuals, such as Afaq Hussain Afaq's *Nadirat-i-Ghalib*, published in 1949, which is a collection of Ghalib's letters to his close friend Nabi Baksh Haqir. Imtiyaz Ali Arshi's *Makatib-i-Ghalib*, published in 1937, is a collection of Ghalib's Persian letters to the Nawab of Rampur. A collection of Ghalib's Persian letters is also a part of his *Kulliyat-i-Nasr-i-Farsi*. The relevant selections from the above works, and others have been translated in English by Ralph Russell and Khurshidul Islam in their interesting and comprehensive book, *Ghalib, Life and Letters* (London,

1969) (referred to in the Notes as L&L; RR, KI;). Russell and Islam have not only translated and edited the original material, but have also cross-checked references to establish precise dates and chronological accuracy.

Qurratulain Hyder has also made a commendable translation of a selection of Ghalib's letters, in the book *Ghalib and His Poetry* (Bombay, 1970), jointly authored by Sardar Jafri. Altaf Hussain Hali's *Yaadgar-i-Ghalib* is a wealth-house of information. Material in the National Archives of India has been very helpful for Ghalib's correspondence with the British, referred to at length in chapter entitled *The Empire in Decline*. In the chapter *The Trauma of 1857* references to Ghalib's purported diary of 1857—the *Dastanbuy*—have been taken from Professor K.A. Faruqi's English translation, (Delhi, 1970).

Verses quoted in the book from the *Diwan-i-Ghalib* have been translated by the author; the edition of the *Diwan* has been prepared by Noor Nabi Abbasi and was brought out by the Ghalib Institute in 1985. The first line of the translated verses is in Urdu in the footnotes, to help readers familiar with Urdu. For Ghalib's Persian *ghazals* the English translation by Professor Yusuf Hussain (Ghalib Institute 1980) has been used.

An Empire in Decline

1. Akhtar Qamber, *The Last Mushairah of Delhi* (a translation of Farhatullah Baig's *Delhi ki Akhri Shama*) (New Delhi, 1979), pp. 43–44.

2. Captain Mundy, *The Journal of a Tour in India,* Vol. I (London, 1832), pp. 81–84.

3. William Knighton, *Tropical Sketches or Reminiscences of an Indian Journalist,* Vol. I (London, 1855), p. 301.

4. W.H. Sleeman, *Rambles and Recollections of an Indian Official,* Vol. II (London, 1844), p. 280.

5. National Archives of India (NAI), Foreign Department Miscellaneous, No. 208, p. 21.

6. Ibid., Vol. of 1830, No. 636, p. 421.

7. Ibid., Foreign Department Miscellaneous, Vol. 208, pp. 89–90.

8. Ibid., Vol. 208, pp. 6–7.

9. Ibid., Foreign Political Consultations, 23 April 1833, Nos. 80–81.

10. Ibid., Oriental Records 420 of 1833, Foreign Political Consultations, 4 January 1836, No. 51.

11. Ibid., 537 of 1846.

12. Ibid., Foreign Political Consultations, 5 December 1836, Nos. 157–161. The legalistic framework should not lead us into believing that the petition was entirely a lawyer's draft. Obviously Ghalib did have an attorney (Pandit Hira Lal) to advise him on legal aspects. But the *style* of the drafting is inimitably Ghalibian and of a piece with his other letters to the British. Ghalib prided himself on the drafting and it is inconceivable that he would have left it solely to his attorney.

13. Ibid.

14. Ibid., 17 April 1837, Nos. 66–67.

15. Ibid., 6 July 1842, Nos. 142–144.

16. Ibid., 28 December 1842, Nos. 280–283.
17. Ibid.
18. Ibid.
19. Ibid., India and Bengal Despatches, Vol. 45 for 4 June–27 August 1845 (Despatch No. 80, p. 21).
20. S.A.I. Tirmizi, *Persian Letters of Ghalib* (New Delhi, 1969), Introduction, pp. 1–2.
21. P. Hardy, 'Ghalib and the British', in Ralph Russell (ed.) *Ghalib—The Poet and His Age* (London, 1972), p. 57.
22. P. Spear, *Twilight of the Mughals* (London, 1951), p. 57.
23. Quoted in M.A. Laird (ed.), *Bishop Heber in North India* (Cambridge, 1971), pp. 234–235.
24. Yusuf Hussain, *Persian Ghazals of Ghalib* (Ghalib Institute, 1980), p. 55.
25. *Diwan-i-Ghalib,* trans. author, *Na lut ta din ko to kab raat ke yun bekhabar sota.*
26. Ibid., *Falak se hamko aish-i-rafta ka kya kya taqaza hai.*
27. Ibid., *Aai agar bala to jigar se tali nahin.*
28. Yusuf Hussain, op. cit., p. 66.
29. *Diwan-i-Ghalib,* trans. author, *Ghalib kuch apni sa'i se lena nahin mujhe.*
30. Ibid., *Misal yeh meri koshish ki hai ki jaise murgh-i-asir.*
31. Yusuf Hussain, op. cit., p. 56.
32. *Diwan-i-Ghalib,* trans. author, *Is saadgi pe kaun na mar jaye, ai Khuda.*
33. Ibid., *Kahan tak rooon uske kheme ke peeche qayamat hai.*

34. Yusuf Hussain, op. cit., p. 78.
35. Ibid., op. cit., p. 131.
36. W.H. Sleeman, op. cit., Vol. II, p. 284.
37. A.A. Beg, *Life and Odes of Ghalib* (Lahore, 1940), p. 5.
38. Ibid., p. 6.
39. Yusuf Hussain, op. cit., pp. 78–79.
40. L&L; RR, KI; p. 27.
41. P. Spear, 'Ghalib's Delhi', in R. Russell (ed.), *The Poet and His Age*, op. cit., p. 51.
42. Q. Hyder and S. Jafri, *Ghalib and His Poetry* (Bombay 1970), p. 28.
43. *Diwan-i-Ghalib,* trans. author, *Ghurra-i-auj-i-bina-i-aalam-i-imkan na pooch.*

The City of Good Living

1. Emily Bayley, *Memoirs,* quoted in M.M. Kaye, *The Golden Calm* (New York, 1980), p. 122.
2. M. Dayal, *Rediscovering Delhi* (New Delhi, 1982), p. 205. See also Farhatullah Baig's *Phool Walon Ki Sair.*
3. L&L; RR, KI; p. 302.
4. Ibid., p. 123.
5. Bipan Chandra, *Communalism in Modern India* (Delhi, 1984), pp. 175–176.
6. C.F. Andrews, *Zakaullah of Delhi* (London, 1929), pp. 15–17.
7. L&L; RR, KI; p. 217.
8. *Diwan-i-Ghalib,* trans. author, *Kahan maikhane ka darwaza Ghalib aur kahan vayiz.*

9. Yusuf Hussain, *Persian Ghazals of Ghalib* (Ghalib Academy, 1980), p. 114.

10. *Diwan-i-Ghalib,* trans. author, *Kya zohad ko manoo ki na ho garche rihayee.*

11. Yusuf Hussain, op. cit., p. 39.

12. Ibid., p.36.

13. Ibid., p. 37.

14. *Diwan-i-Ghalib,* trans. author, *Main ahal-i-khirad kis ravish-i-khas pe nazan.*

15. Ibid., *Janta hum sawab-i-ta'at-o-zohad.*

16. Ibid., quoted in translation in M. Mujeeb, *The Indian Muslims* (London, 1966), p. 473, *Ham muvahid hain hamara kesh hai tark-i-rasoom.*

17. Ibid., trans., Yusuf Hussain, *Urdu Ghazals of Ghalib* (Ghalib Academy, 1977), p. 158, *Vafadari ba shart-i-ustvari asl-i-iman hai.*

18. Ibid., author, *Nahin kuch subh-o-zunnar ke phande mein girai.*

19. Q. Hyder and S. Jafri, *Ghalib and His Poetry* (Bombay, 1970), pp. 70–71.

20. S.A.I. Tirmizi, *Persian Letters of Ghalib* (New Delhi, 1969), Introduction, p. 31.

21. *Diwan-i-Ghalib,* trans. author, *Kaabe mein ja bajayenge naqoos.*

22. Ibid., *Jo ye kahen ki rekhta.*

23. Akhtar Qamber, *The Last Mushairah of Delhi* (a translation of Farhatullah Baig's *Delhi ki Akhri Shama*) (New Delhi, 1979).

24. Ibid., op. cit., pp. 60–61.

25. L&L; RR, KI; p. 60.

26. C.F. Andrews, op. cit., p. 57.

27. Ibid., *Zakaullah of Delhi* (London, 1929), p. 42.

28. Emily Bayley, op. cit., p. 213.
29. C.F. Andrews, op. cit., pp. 39–40.
30. *Diwan-i-Ghalib,* trans. author, *Iman mujhe roke hai to khiche hai mujhe kufr.*
31. W.H. Sleeman, *Rambles and Recollections of an Indian Official,* Vol. II (London, 1844), pp. 310–311.
32. Q. Hyder and S. Jafri, op. cit., p. 30.
33. Emily Bayley, op. cit., p. 166.
34. Ibid., p. 142.
35. Ibid., p. 143.
36. P. Spear, in R. Russell (ed.), *The Poet and His Age,* p. 45.
37. Philip Woodruffe, *Men Who Ruled India,* Vol. I (London, 1953), p. 237.
38. Pat Barr, *Memsahibs* (London, 1976, New Delhi reprint), p. 79.
39. W.H. Sleeman, op. cit., Vol. II, p. 284.
40. Philip Woodruffe, op. cit., Vol. I, p. 272.
41. M. Sadiq, *A History of Urdu Literature* (Oxford, Second edition), p. 228.
42. Thomas Bacon, quoted in J.L. Kaul, *Travellers India* (Oxford, 1982), pp. 69–70.
43. Lord Macaulay's *Minute on Education.*
44. L&L; RR, KI; p. 113.
45. Ibid., pp. 113–114.
46. Q. Hyder and S. Jafri, *Ghalib and His Poetry* (Bombay, 1970), p. 26.
47. Ibid.
48. Emily Bayley, op. cit., p. 212.
49. C.A. Bayly, *Rulers, Townsmen and Bazars* (Oxford), p. 336.

50. M. Mujeeb, *Ghalib* (Sahitya Akademi, 1970), p. 10.

51. Bishop Heber, quoted in H.A. Laurd (ed.), *Bishop Heber in North India* (Cambridge, 1971), p. 236.

52. H. Trevelyan, *The India We Left* (London, 1974). p. 42.

53. C.F. Andrews, op. cit., pp. 3–4.

54. N. Gupta, *Delhi Between Two Empires* (Oxford, 1981), p. 20.

55. Bishop Heber, op. cit., p. 235.

56. Emily Bayley, op. cit., p. 162.

57. Veena Talwar Oldenberg, *The Making of Colonial Lucknow* (Princeton, 1984), p. 11.

58. C.F. Andrews, op. cit., p. 7.

59. W.H. Sleeman, op. cit.

60. Emily Bayley, op. cit., p. 161.

61. Quoted in Pat Barr, op. cit., p. 13.

62. *Diwan-i-Ghalib,* trans. author, *Saaman-i-khur-o-khwab kahan se laoon.*

63. L&L; RR, KI; p. 148.

64. Quoted in N. Gupta, op. cit., p. 52.

65. M. Dayal, op. cit., p. 135.

66. L&L; RR, KI; pp. 111–112.

67. C.A. Bayly, op. cit., p. 307.

68. Bishop Heber, op. cit., p. 228.

69. Emily Bayley, op. cit., p. 210.

70. C.F. Andrews, op. cit., p. 7.

71. Bishop Heber, op. cit., p. 230.

72. Major Cunningham, I.O. Home, Misc., Vol. 708, p. 28; P. Spear, *Twilight of the Mughals,* p. 62.

73. W.H. Sleeman, op. cit.

74. Quoted in R. Russell and K. Islam, *Three Mughal Poets,* op. cit.

75. P. Spear, in R. Russell (ed.), *Ghalib, The Poet and His Age,* p. 49.

76. C.F. Andrews, op. cit., p. 9.

77. Emily Bayley, op. cit., p. 209.

78. M. Mujeeb, *Indian Muslims,* op. cit., p. 507.

79. Bipan Chandra, op. cit., p. 176.

80. N. Gupta, op. cit., p. 51.

81. L&L; RR, KI; p. 41.

82. Ibid., p. 102.

83. Akhtar Qamber, op. cit., pp. 52–53.

84. M. Mujeeb, *Ghalib,* p. 14.

85. Meenakshi Mukherjee, 'Reality and Realism: Indian Women as Protagonists in Four Novels', *Economic and Political Weekly*, 14 January 1984, Vol. XIX, No. 2.

86. P. Spear, in R. Russell (ed.), *Ghalib, The Poet and His Age,* pp. 50–51.

87. Akhtar Qamber, op. cit., pp. 67–68.

A Turbulent Genius

1. L&L; RR, KI; p. 179.

2. Ibid., p. 29.

3. Samad's original name was Hurmazd. He was born a Zoroastrian, but later converted to Islam.

4. Ghalib has praised him as being 'without exaggeration, the Jamasp of his time and Buzurg-mihr of the contemporary world'. A.A. Beg, *Life and Letters of Ghalib* (Lahore, 1940), p. 13.

Other Persian masters Ghalib acknowledged include Hazin, Talib Amuli, Shirazi, Zuhuri and Naziri. (See preface in Ghalib's *Kulliyat-i-Nasr-i-Farsi).*

5. This is significant in explaining the felicity with which Ghalib could later switch from Persian to Urdu. It is also important in gauging the extent to which Urdu had already begun to replace Persian as the *lingua franca.* The fact that Ghalib openly expressed contempt for Urdu, but was nevertheless writing in it at a young age, is proof of this.

6. Perhaps the greatest poet of the eighteenth century, belonging to Delhi but forced to live in exile, in Lucknow, to escape the political tumult and upheaval of Delhi. He died in Lucknow in 1810. Ghalib's verses must have therefore been taken to him before this date, i.e., before Ghalib was twelve. One more corroborative evidence to prove that he had begun to write when still very young.

7. *Shabban Khan Ki Haveli,* near *Habbash Khan Ka Phatak.*

8. For an analysis of Bedil's influence on Ghalib and an assessment of his 'difficult style', see chapter 'Ghalib, the Difficult Poet', in S.R. Faruqi, *The Secret Mirror: Essays on Urdu Poetry* (Delhi, 1981).

9. Quoted in L&L; RR, KI; p. 40.

10. *Diwan-i-Ghalib,* trans. author, *Na sata'ish ki tamanna, na sile ki parvah.*

11. Ibid., *Mushkil hai ze has kalaam mera ai dil.*

12. Yusuf Hussain, trans., *Persian Ghazals of Ghalib* (Delhi, 1980), p. 160.

13. *Diwan-i-Ghalib,* trans. author, *Ganjina-i-mani ka tilism usko samajhiye.*

14. Ibid., *Likhta hoon, Asad, sozish-i-dil se sukhan-i-garm.*

15. See Annemarie Schimmel, *A Dance of Sparks* (Vikas, 1979), p. 36.

16. Yusuf Hussain, op. cit., p. 15.

17. *Diwan-i-Ghalib,* trans. author, *Kahoon kya khoobi-i-auza-i-ibna-i-zamana Ghalib.*

18. Yusuf Hussain, op. cit., p. 63.

19. *Diwan-i-Ghalib,* trans. author, *Jab maikada chuta to phir kya jagah ki qaid.*

20. Ibid., *Vo cheez jiske liye hamko ho bihisht aziz.*

21. Ibid., *Vayiz na tum piyo na kisiko pila sako.*

22. Yusuf Hussain, op. cit., p. 90.

23. *Diwan-i-Ghalib,* trans. author, *Zam Zam hi pe chhoro, mujhe kya tauf-i-haram se.*

24. Ibid., *Raat pi Zam-Zam pe mai aur subahdam.*

25. Ibid., *Sohbat-i-rindan se vajib hai hazar.*

26. Yusuf Hussain, op. cit., p. 96.

27. *Diwan-i-Ghalib,* trans. author, *Mai se gharaz nishat hai kis roosiyah ko.*

28. Yusuf Hussain, op. cit., p. 59.

29. *Diwan-i-Ghalib,* trans. author, *Kal ke liye na aaj kar khissat sharab mein.*

30. Ibid., *Sarf-i-baha-i-mai hue aalat-i-maikashi.*

31. Ibid., *Saaf durdikash-i-paimana-i-jam hain, hum log.*

32. Ibid., *Phir dekhiye andaaz-i-gulafshani-i-guftaar.*

33. Ibid., *Ghalib chuti sharab par ab bhi kabhi kabhi.*

34. Ibid., *Deedar bada hausla saki nigaah mast.*

35. Ibid., *Khayal-i-jalwa-i-gul se kharab hai maikash.*
36. Yusuf Hussain, *Urdu Ghazals of Ghalib* (Delhi, 1977), p. 318.
37. L&L; RI, KI; p. 203.
38. By 'women' is meant courtesans who were then largely the only avenue for dalliance and romance.
39. L&L; RR, KI; p. 29.
40. Q. Hyder S. Jafri, *Ghalib and His Poetry* (Bombay, 1970), p. 32.
41. L&L; RR, KI; p. 43.
42. Malik Ram, basing his hypothesis on a couplet in Ghalib's moving elegy written after her death, has argued that, 'it would appear that she belonged to a respectable set . . . (and) had probably committed suicide fearing their affair had become a scandal in the eyes of her people and public at large. If she were a common public woman, there should have been no question of a scandal or dishonour to drive her to take her own life.' Malik Ram, *Mirza Ghalib* (National Book Trust, Second edition, 1980), p. 19. If this be the case, the affair would have been an event of considerable discussion and controversy during its occurrence and it is indeed surprising that it is mentioned *et passim* in the contemporary material available on Ghalib's life.
43. L&L; RR, KI; p. 43.
44. Ibid.
45. *Diwan-i-Ghalib,* trans. author, *Sad jalwa roobaroo hai jo miz gan uthaiye.*
46. L&L; RR, KI; p. 249.

47. M. Mujeeb, *Mirza Ghalib* (NCERT, 1970), p. 28.

48. *Diwan-i-Ghalib*, trans. author, *Tere dil mein gar na tha aashob-i-gham ka hausla*.

49. NAI, Petition to the British, April 1828, Foreign Department, Political Proceedings, Vol. 589 of 1828.

50. Ibid.

51. Ibid.

52. Ibid.

53. Ibid.

54. Ibid.

55. The exact date is uncertain. A.C.S. Gilani, *Ghalib, His Life and Persian Poetry* (Karachi, 1962), places it in August 1826; R. Russell and K. Islam in the spring of 1827.

56. NAI, Foreign Department, Political Proceedings, Vol. 589 of 1828.

57. Q. Hyder and S. Jafri, *Ghalib and His Poetry* (Bombay, 1970), p. 15.

58. A.C.S. Gilani, op. cit., p. 40.

59. L&L; RR, KI; p. 279.

60. Rarely found now but its preface is included in the Kulbat-i-Farsi.

61. He reached Delhi in November 1829.

62. A.A. Beg, *The Life and Odes of Ghalib* (Lahore, 1940), p. 38.

63. *Diwan-i-Ghalib*, trans. M. Mujeeb in *Mirza Ghalib*, op. cit., p. 28, *Karz ki peete the mai aur samajhte the ki haan*.

64. Quoted in M. Mujeeb, op. cit., p. 17.

65. Q. Hyder and S. Jafri, *Ghalib and His Poetry* (Bombay, 1970), op. cit., p. 35.

66. M. Mujeeb, *Ghalib* (Sahitya Akademi 1970), p. 23. Annemarie Schimmel makes the same point, op. cit., p. 4.
67. L&L; RR, KI; p. 105.
68. *Diwan-i-Ghalib*, trans. author, *Man, ai falak-i-pir jawan tha abhi Arif.*
69. Q. Hyder and S. Jafri, op. cit., p. 9.
70. Ibid.
71. *Diwan-i-Ghalib*, trans. author, *Ranj ze khoogar hua to insaan.*
72. Ibid., *Naghma hai gham ko bhi ai dil ghanimat janiye.*
73. Ibid., *Gila hai shauq ko bhi dil mein tangi-i-ja ka.*
74. Ibid., *Nashha-i-rang se hai vashude gul.*
75. Ibid., *Hoon mai bhi tamashai-i-rang-i-tamanna.*
76. Ibid., *Nahin nigar ko ulfat, na ho nigar to hai.*
77. Ibid., *Go hath mein jumbish nahin ankhon mein to dam hai.*
78. Ibid., *Khanjar se cheer seena agar dil na ho dunim.*
79. Ibid., *Hai nang-i-seena dil agar aatashkada na ho.*
80. Ibid., *Dil hi to hai na sang-o-khisht.*
81. Ibid., *Kyon gardish-i-mudam se ghabra na jaye dil.*
82. Yusuf Hussain trans., *Persian Ghazals of Ghalib*, op. cit., p. 91.
83. *Diwan-i-Ghalib*, trans. author, *Chalta hoon thodi door har ek tez rau ke saath.*
84. Ibid., *Jabki tujh bin nahin koi maujood.*
85. Ibid., trans. Yusuf Hussain, *Urdu Ghazals of Ghalib* (New Delhi, 1977), p. 137. *Asl-i shuhavad-o-shahid-o-mashood ek hai.*
86. Ibid., trans. author, *Kah sake kaun ki ye jalwagiri kiski hai.*

87. Yusuf Hussain trans., *Persian Ghazals of Ghalib,* op. cit., p. 143.

88. *Diwan-i-Ghalib,* trans. author, *Hasti ke mat fareb mein aajaiyo Asad.*

89. Ibid., *Tha khwab mein khayal ko tujhse muamla.*

90. Ibid., *Han khaiyo mat fareb-i-hasti.*

91. Ibid., *Hai gaib-i-gaib jisko samajhte hain ham shuhood.*

92. Ibid., *Hai vahi badmasti-i-har zarre ka khud uzrkhwah.*

93. Yusuf Hussain trans., *Persian Ghazals of Ghalib,* op. cit., p. 180.

94. *Diwan-i-Ghalib,* trans. author, *Hai paratwe khur se shabnam ko fana ki taalim.*

95. Ibid., *Hai tajalli tera samaan-i-vajood.*

96. Ibid., *Ruhmut agar qabool kare kya ha'id hai.*

97. Ibid., *Dariya-i-ma'asi tunuk aabi se hua khushk.*

98. Ibid., *Nakarda gunahon ki bhi hasrat ki mile daad.*

99. Ibid., *Dekhiyo Ghalib se gar uljha koi.*

100. Juan Mascaro trans., *The Upanishads* (London, 1965), p. 119.

101. *Diwan-i-Ghalib,* trans. author, *Nashwo numa hai asl se Ghalib farogh ka.*

102. Yusuf Hussain trans., *Persian Ghazals of Ghalib,* op. cit., p. 57.

103. *Diwan-i-Ghalib,* trans. author, *Na tha kuch to khuda tha.*

104. Ibid., trans. Yusuf Hussain, *Urdu Ghazals of Ghalib,* op. cit., p. 305.

105. Ibid., trans. author, *Ishrat-i-qatra hai dariya mein fana ho jana.*

106. Yusuf Hussain trans., *Persian Ghazals of Ghalib,*

op. cit., pp. 132–133. See also Annemarie Schimmel, op. cit., who has an entire chapter devoted to an analysis of this beautiful *ghazal*.

107. The first compilation was transcribed under the title of *Nuskha-i-Hamidia*.

108. L&L; RR, KI; p. 92.

109. Q. Hyder and S. Jafri, *Ghalib and His Poetry* (Bombay, 1970), p. 23.

110. Ibid., p. 89.

111. M. Mujeeb, *Ghalib,* op. cit., p. 28.

112. The prison poem has eighty-four verses and was first published in 1867 as part of a larger Persian collection entitled *Sabad-i-Chin*.

113. *Diwan-i-Ghalib,* trans. author, *Rahiye ab aisi jagah chal kar jahan koi na ho.*

114. Quoted by A.H. Hali, *Yaadgar-i-Ghalib*, in L&L., RR, KI; p. 70.

115. P. Spear, in R. Russell (ed.), *Ghalib, The Poet and His Age,* p. 39.

116. *Diwan-i-Ghalib,* trans. author, *Meri tankhwah jo mukarrar hai.*

117. He had been appointed the king's *ustad* in 1837.

118. *Diwan-i-Ghalib,* trans. author, *Har ek baat pe kahte ho tum ke tu kya hai.*

119. Ibid., *Manzoor hai guzarish-e-ahwal-e-vaqaee.*

120. L&L; RR, KI; p. 128.

121. *Diwan-i-Ghalib,* trans. author, *Ghalib vazifa khwar ho do Shah ko dua.*

122. A.H. Hali, op. cit., p. 100.

123. *Diwan-i-Ghalib,* trans. author, *Iftaar-i-som ki kuch agar dastgah ho.*

124. L&L; RR, KI; p. 86.

125. Ibid., p. 119.

The Trauma of 1857

1. P. Spear, *Twilight of the Mughals* (London, 1951) (Oriental Books Reprint Corporation, 1969), p. 201.

2. Asadullah Khan Ghalib, *Dastanbuy* (trans. K.A. Faruqi, Delhi, 1970), p. 31. (Extracts from *Dastanbuy* unless otherwise indicated, are from this translation).

3. It has been suggested that the title *Dastanbuy* is an allusion to a line of the great panegyrist Khaqani (d. 1199) who has used this rare word in an ode to Princess Ismatuddin; Annemarie Schimell, *A Dance of Sparks* (Vikas, 1979). This could very well be true. Ghalib's knowledge of Persian was thorough, and his love for the unusual, well known.

4. This motivation is common to two other surviving records of 1857. In both, narration of fact is transparently blended with an attempt by the authors to establish their own innocence in British eyes. See Narrations of Munshi Jiwan Lal and Mainoddin Hasan Khan (trans. C.T. Metcalfe, *Two Native Narratives of the Indian Mutiny*, London, 1898). The record of Syed Mobarak Shah, *kotwal* in 1857 under Bahadur Shah (trans. R.M. Edwards, London, 1859) is in the same mould.

5. Ghalib, *Dastanbuy*, p. 32.

6. Ibid., p. 28.

7. Ibid., pp. 40–41.
8. Ibid., p. 50.
9. Ibid., p. 40.
10. Ibid., pp. 41, 42, 44.
11. Ibid., p. 30.
12. Ibid., p. 31.
13. Mahdi Hussain, *Bahadur Shah II and the War of 1857 in Delhi* (Delhi, 1958), p. 207.
14. Ibid.
15. Ghalib, *Dastanbuy,* pp. 33–34.
16. P. Spear, op. cit., p. 207. For a more detailed account of administration, see also 'Bahadur Shah during the Revolt', in the same book.
17. Ghalib, *Dastanbuy,* p. 38.
18. L&L; RR, KI; p. 132.
19. K.A. Faruqi, Introduction to translation of *Dastanbuy,* op. cit.
20. Syed Mobarak Shah's narrative (trans. R.M. Edwards, op. cit.).
21. Ibid.
22. L&L; RR, KI; p. 150.
23. Ibid., p. 152.
24. Ibid., p. 159.
25. Ibid.
26. Ibid., p. 161.
27. Ibid.
28. Ghalib, *Dastanbuy,* p. 62.
29. Ibid., p. 69.
30. Q. Hyder and S. Jafri, *Ghalib and His Poetry* (Bombay, 1970), p. 38.
31. L&L; RR, KI; p. 177.
32. Ghalib, *Dastanbuy,* p. 59.

33. Throughout his famous trial Bahadur Shah's defence was that he was forced, on threat to his life, to acquiesce in the Revolt.

34. L&L; RR, KI; p. 154.

35. Ghalib, *Dastanbuy,* pp. 57–58.

36. Q. Hyder and S. Jafri, op. cit., pp. 34–35.

37. Ghalib, *Dastanbuy,* p. 34.

38. Ibid.

39. P. Spear, op. cit., p. 210.

40. Q. Hyder and S. Jafri, *Ghalib and His Poetry* (Bombay, 1970), p. 32.

41. K.A. Faruqi, Introduction to translation of *Dastanbuy,* p. 16.

42. Mainoddin Khan's narrative.

43. Ghalib, *Dastanbuy,* p. 51.

44. Curzon, *Speeches* (Calcutta, 1900), Vol. I, p. 223.

45. E. Hare, *Memo of the Siege of Delhi,* Kaye manuscripts, Commonwealth Office Library, Home Miscellaneous, No. 726.

46. P. Spear, op. cit., p. 226.

47. Account of a contemporary, Mrs R.M. Coopland, quoted in S. Sen, *1857* (Delhi 1957), p. 112.

48. C.J. Griffith, *Narrative of the Siege of Delhi,* ed. H.J. Yonge (London, 1910), p. 202.

49. Charles Raikes, *Notes on the Revolt in the N. Western Provinces of India* (London, 1858); S. Sen, op. cit., p. 112.

50. Capt. Richard Barton, quoted in C. Hibbert, op. cit., p. 322.

51. Ghalib, *Dastanbuy,* p. 60.

52. Q. Hyder and S. Jafri, *Ghalib and His Poetry* (Bombay 1970), p. 38.

53. In 1846 the population was 160,270; in 1863 it was only 141,709. See N. Gupta, 'Military Security and Urban Development: A Case Study of Delhi, 1857-1912', *Modern Asian Studies*, Vol. 5 No. 1 (1971).

54. Q. Hyder and S. Jafri, op. cit., p. 29.

55. L&L; RR, KI; p. 227.

56. Ghalib, *Dastanbuy, p.* 67.

57. Shefta was later released on bail.

58. Q. Hyder and S. Jafri, op. cit., p. 31.

59. Ibid., pp. 47–48.

60. L&L; RR, KI; pp. 252–253.

61. Q. Hyder and S. Jafri, op. cit., p. 39.

62. Veena Talwar Oldenberg, *The Making of Colonial Lucknow* (Princeton, 1984), p. 34.

63. N. Gupta, 'Military Security and Urban Development', op. cit.

64. Veena Talwar Oldenberg, op. cit., p. 39.

65. Ibid.

66. L&L; RR, KI; p. 213.

67. Q. Hyder and S. Jafri, op. cit., p. 41.

68. By An Old Indian, *Calcutta to the Snowy Range* (London, 1866), p. 189.

69. N. Gupta, *Delhi Between Two Empires* (Oxford, 1981), p. 29.

70. C.J. Griffith, *Narrative of the Siege of Delhi,* ed. H.J.Yonge (London, 1910); also C. Hibbert, op. cit., p. 320.

71. Q. Hyder and S. Jafri, op. cit., p. 32.

72. Ibid., p. 36.

73. Ibid., pp. 39–40.
74. Ibid., p. 39.
75. Ibid., p. 43.
76. Ibid., p. 39.
77. Ibid., p. 40.
78. L&L; RR, KI; p. 227.
79. Q. Hyder and S. Jafri, op. cit., pp. 42–43.
80. *Diwan-i- Ghalib,* trans. author, *Hai maujzan ik kulzum-i-khoon kaash yahi ho.*

Last Years

1. Q. Hyder and S. Jafri, *Ghalib and His Poetry* (Bombay, 1970), p. 45.
2. *Diwan-i-Ghalib,* trans. author, *Ug raha hai dar-o-diwaar se sabza Ghalib.*
3. Q. Hyder and S. Jafri, op. cit., p. 47.
4. N. Gupta, *Delhi Between Two Empires* (Oxford, 1981), p. 72.
5. Q. Hyder and S. Jafri, op. cit., p. 47.
6. Ibid., p. 33.
7. L&L; RR, KI; p. 291.
8. M. Sadiq, *A History of Urdu Literature* (Oxford, Second edition), p. 246.
9. L&L; RR, KI; p. 246.
10. Q. Hyder and S. Jafri, op. cit., p. 45.
11. L&L; RR, KI; p. 245.
12. A.A. Beg, *Life and Odes of Ghalib* (Lahore, 1940), p. 76.
13. *Diwan-i-Ghalib,* trans. author, *Sukhan mein khama-e-Ghalib ki aatash afshani.*
14. L&L; RR, KI; pp. 300–301.

15. Q. Hyder and S. Jafri, op. cit., p. 48.
16. *Diwan-i-Ghalib,* trans. author, *Maut ka ek din muayyan hai.*
17. Ibid., *Muddat hui hai yaar ko mehman kiye huye.*
18. Ibid., *Phir vaz'a-e-ahtiyaat se rukne laga hai dam.*
19. Ibid., *Vo baada-i-shabana ki sarmastiyan kahan?*
20. Ibid., *Mara zamane ne Asadullah Khan tumhe.*
21. Q. Hyder and S. Jafri, op. cit., p. 46.
22. *Diwan-i-Ghalib,* trans. author, *Na teer kaman pe hai na saiyaad kameen pe.*
23. Ibid., *Safina jabki kinare pe aa laga, Ghalib.*
24. Ibid., B.N. Raina, *Raina's Ghalib* (A transcreation of Mirza Ghalib's selected verse) (Calcutta, 1984). *Yaad thi, hamko bhi, rangarang bazm araiyan.*
25. L&L; RR, KI; p. 271.
26. Q. Hyder and S. Jafri, op. cit., p. 51.
27. Ibid., pp. 51–52.
28. Yusuf Hussain, *Persian Ghazals of Ghalib* (Delhi, 1980), p. 171.
29. Q. Hyder and S. Jafri, op. cit., p. 51.
30. Yusuf Hussain, op. cit., p. 37.
31. L&L; RR, KI; p. 346.
32. Q. Hyder and S. Jafri, op. cit., p. 54.
33. Ibid., p. 55.
34. L&L; RR, KI; p. 361.
35. *Diwan-i-Ghalib,* trans. author, *Na suno gar bura kahe koi.*
36. Quoted in A.A. Beg, op. cit., p. 77.
37. Ibid., p. 78.
38. Ibid., p. 369.
39. *Diwan-i-Ghalib,* trans. author, *Ghalib-e-khasta ke baghair kaun se kaam band hain.*

Index